UNDERSTANDING COMMON LAW LEGISLATION

UNDERSTANDING
COMMON LAW
LEGISLATION

Drafting and Interpretation

F. A. R. BENNION

OXFORD
UNIVERSITY PRESS

OXFORD
UNIVERSITY PRESS

Great Clarendon Street, Oxford OX2 6DP

Oxford University Press is a department of the University of Oxford.
It furthers the University's objective of excellence in research, scholarship,
and education by publishing worldwide in

Oxford New York

Athens Auckland Bangkok Bogotá Buenos Aires
Cape Town Chennai Dar es Salaam Delhi Florence Hong Kong Istanbul
Karachi Kolkata Kuala Lumpur Madrid Melbourne Mexico City Mumbai
Nairobi Paris São Paulo Shanghai Singapore Taipei Tokyo Toronto Warsaw
with associated companies in Berlin Ibadan

Oxford is a registered trade mark of Oxford University Press
in the UK and in certain other countries

Published in the United States
by Oxford University Press Inc., New York

© F. A. R. Bennion 2001

The moral rights of the author have been asserted
Database right Oxford University Press (maker)

First published 2001

British Library Cataloguing in Publication Data

Data available

Library of Congress Cataloging in Publication Data
Bennion, Francis Alan Roscoe.
Understanding common law legislation: drafting and interpretation/F.A.R. Bennion.
p. cm.
Includes bibliographical references and index.
1. Statutes. 2. Law—Interpretation and construction. 3. Legislation. I. Title.
K284.B46 2001   328.3'73—dc21   2001045167
ISBN 0-19-924777-3

1 3 5 7 9 10 8 6 4 2

Typeset in Sabon by
Cambrian Typesetters, Frimley, Surrey

Printed in Great Britain
on acid-free paper by
T.J. International Ltd, Padstow, Cornwall

Dedicated to the memory
of the late

Sir Rupert Cross QC DCL FBA

*Quondam Vinerian Professor in the
University of Oxford*

*An academic lawyer who believed in
the vital importance of statutory
interpretation, and acted
on his belief*

Contents

Note: Detailed indications of the contents of each chapter will be
found in Chapter Summaries at pages 201–22.

Author's Note

This book distils and updates within a brief compass published writings on statute law and statutory interpretation which span a period of nearly forty years, being contained in half a dozen books and many more articles. The chief books are *Statute Law* (3rd edn, Longman, 1990), *Halsbury's Laws of England*, title *Statutes* (4th edn. reissue, Butterworths, 1995), and *Statutory Interpretation* (3rd edn., Butterworths, 1997, supplement 1999). Since its first publication in 1984, the last named work has also been updated each year in an article, under the title 'Statute Law', included in the *All England Law Reports Annual Review* (Butterworths). It is intended to continue this annual updating. The list of articles is too lengthy to set out here, but may be found on my website <www.francisbennion.com.>

I began the distillation process with a set of articles that appeared in 1998 and 1999 in *Justice of the Peace*.[1] They form the basis of Chapters 1 to 12 of the present book. Chapter 1 is also partly derived from an article which appeared in *Public Law*.[2] Chapters 13 and 14 largely derive from a series of three articles published in *Justice of the Peace* in 2000.[3] Chapters 15 and 16 are mainly based on an article which appeared in *Public Law*.[4] Chapter 17 was written for this book. Chapter 18 is based on my article 'Teaching law management', which was included in the book *Reviewing Legal Education*.[5]

As this is a work of originality rather than research, I hesitated about equipping it with a bibliography. I settled instead for a list of books, articles, etc. referred to. The names of authors mentioned in the list are also included in the index.

FRANCIS BENNION

---

[1] The articles appeared in volume 162 (1998) at pages 356, 436, 516, 696, 856, and 995 and in volume 163 (1999) at pages 264, 364, 484, 624, and 683.

[2] 'Consequences of an overrule' [2001] PL 450.

[3] The articles appeared in volume 164 (2000) at pages 316, 336, and 361. They were also published as a single article in 31 UWLA [Los Angeles] Law Review (2000) 1. A shortened version ('Distinguishing judgment and discretion') appeared in [2000] PL 368.

[4] 'What interpretation is "possible" under section 3(1) of the Human Rights Act 1998?' [2000] PL 77.

[5] Edited by Professor P. B. H. Birks (Oxford University Press, 1994).

Abbreviations

All ER = *All England Law Reports*.

Bennion Code = F. A. R. Bennion, *Statutory Interpretation* (3rd edn., Butterworths, 1997 as updated by 1999 Supplement).

Blackstone = Sir William Blackstone, *The Commentaries on the Laws of England* Adapted to the present state of the law by Robert Malcolm Kerr (4th edn., London: John Murray, 1876).

NLJ = *New Law Journal*.

PL = *Public Law*

Table of Cases

United States

Table of Statutes

Ireland

United Kingdom

Introductory

For many years a legal periodical flourished which called itself the *Anglo-American Law Review*. In 2001 it changed its name to the *Common Law World Review*. This change belatedly recognized that there are not just two but many countries that use and apply the system known as the common law; and that collectively these may indeed be described as the common law world. A feature of this world is that nowadays it largely operates through statutes enacted by a country's democratic legislature, and that these mainly fall to be construed according to a uniform system of rules, presumptions, principles, and canons evolved over centuries by common law judges. The statutes subject to this interpretative regime may justifiably be called common law statutes. They are the main subject of this book, along with the said uniform system.[1]

Construing common law statutes has often been found difficult as an analytical concept. There are many reasons for this. One I concentrate on in this book is that those in charge of legal education have paid an attention to the subject which is insufficient, considering its importance. Often they have paid the subject no attention whatever. When they have paid it any attention they have often done so in a mistaken way, as I shall endeavour to show. This is a serious matter for democratic societies wishing to live under the rule of law.

In the life of the law as we know it lawyers who have not been taught statutory interpretation appear in court, day in and day out, before judges who labour under the same handicap of ignorance. From the viewpoint of legal coherence, the result is chaos. Even though the collection of legal skills known as statutory interpretation was over centuries mostly produced by judges, their successors are largely unaware of it. So they flounder, and our society suffers. Often they do not realize they are floundering, but

---

[1] It has to be admitted that a common law country may take a blinkered course, and refer only to books on statutory interpretation designed for that country. This is particularly true of the United States (see for a recent example *An Introduction to Statutory Interpretation and the Legislative Process* by Abner J. Mikva and Eric Lane (1997) Aspen Law & Business New York, N.Y.). That does not affect the truth of the proposition here advanced.

that lack of judicial awareness obviously does not improve the situation. So what can be done?

Over centuries the common law rules, presumptions, principles, and canons, which I call the 'interpretative criteria', were produced by the judges case by case, ad hoc and higgledy-piggledy. They needed for modern use to be reduced to order. I did reduce them to order in my lengthy textbook *Statutory Interpretation*, the first edition of which appeared in 1984, but little notice was taken. The book explained that there are a great many interpretative criteria, and that where these conflict in a particular case there must be a judicial process of weighing and balancing. I demonstrated that it is wrong to teach law students, as had been almost universally done, that the interpretative criteria solely consist of the literal rule, the mischief rule and the golden rule, and that courts simply choose between them. This reformist teaching of mine has been continued through successive editions of my larger book, but continues to be ignored. Consult even the latest edition of almost any other book on statutory interpretation and you will find the same old parrot cry trotted out: 'the interpretative criteria consist of the literal rule, the mischief rule and the golden rule, and the court chooses between them.' It amounts to a serious breakdown in communication, which the present book aims to address by presenting the issues briefly.

Because of the difficulties people find in statutory interpretation, I first thought of calling this book *Threading the Legislative Maze*. That title occurred to me when reading a memoir by the excellent Hitchin solicitor Reginald Hine, *Confessions of an Un-Common Attorney*.[2] Hine told us that one Arthur Warwick had observed in 1637 that there be many turnings and winding meanders in the law, and that we should daily endeavour to learn from those who threaded the labyrinth before us.[3] Hine reported Edward Gibbon as having observed that few men, without the spur of necessity, have resolution to force their way through the thorns and thickets of that gloomy labyrinth the law. But law should not be a labyrinth; and why should it be gloomy? It reflects all of life, and much of that is cheerful.

That previous title focused on three things: a verb, *to thread*, an

[2] 1st edn., London: Dent, 1946.
[3] pp. 110–11.

adjective, *legislative*, and a noun, *maze*. The adjective suggests that the type of legal intricacy we are here concerned with is that spun by legislators (although usually it is spun by legislative drafters). The legalistic wordsmiths written about here began to spin their toils at Westminster in the twelfth century. Over later centuries their methods and ways have spread to other common law countries, such as the United States, Canada, India, Pakistan, Sri Lanka, Hong Kong, Australia, New Zealand, many African countries, and many more elsewhere. This book is written for all who suffer from legislative confusion in any of these countries. It concentrates on the present day, being necessarily too short to embrace very much history.

I pass to the noun. Milton spoke of poor mankind 'in wandering mazes lost'.[4] Alexander Pope suggested the clue:

> . . . all this scene of man;
> A mighty maze! but not without a plan.[5]

Discern the plan, and you are on the way to finding a path through the maze. The *Oxford English Dictionary* (2nd edn.) thus defines the verb *thread*:

To make one's way through (a narrow place, a passage presenting difficulties or obstacles, a forest, a crowd, or the like); to pass skilfully through the intricacies or difficulties of.

Skilfully is the word here, but in the field of legislation not many seek to possess that skill. Some even doubt such a skill exists. But it does, and it is a necessary skill. The *OED* goes on to cite the 1809 example of *Gil Blas*: 'I threaded all the windings of this new labyrinth.'

So there we have it. That is what this book is mainly about. How to thread the windings of the legislative labyrinth which is spun in many common law countries honestly wishing to observe and preserve the rule of law. We cannot cover every detail; but never mind. Many think that in this field details do not matter. Some are not even sure the essentials matter. But they do.

The common law system of statutory interpretation presented here may be called the Global method both because it is worldwide

---

[4] John Milton, *Paradise Lost*, book ii, line 555.
[5] Alexander Pope, *An Essay on Man*: Epistle i, line 1.

and because it requires the interpreter to take every relevant consideration into account, including (under the doctrine of precedent) previous court decisions. Here a great many things can be relevant. In discerning the legal meaning of any enactment one needs to be aware of and respect innumerable circumambient strands of law, values, and culture.

In the case of British law there has recently been added a further level of complication, which this book also needs to address (and does, to a limited extent). Under the influence of Europe, we in Britain must now also consider what may be called the Developmental method of statutory interpretation, which as we shall see in some respects differs from the Global or common law method. Furthermore the (British) Human Rights Act 1998 introduces, in relation to the 1950 European Convention on Human Rights, what may be called the compatible construction rule. All three systems now bear upon legislation applying in the United Kingdom, though other common law countries are thankfully spared that complication.

The main chapters of this book treat discursively of these matters, references being to the prevailing Global or common law method except where the contrary appears. The strands are pulled together in a collection of chapter summaries in the final chapter, to which reference should be made for brief details of the contents of the book. Additional help is provided by the detailed Index.

The book is intended to state the law as at 31 March 2001.

1

Basic concepts I: common law statutes; the enactment; legal meaning; factual outline and legal thrust; implied ancillary rules

Common law statutes

The laws that govern the common law countries are now mostly in statutory form. Usually these laws are enactments of a democratic parliament, mediated by common law principles of interpretation—but that may in certain cases be an over-simplified description. Some common law countries have federal constitutions, while others retain a unitary legislature. A further complication, mentioned in more detail below, now exists in the case of the United Kingdom, birthplace of the common law. Yet the courts in all these countries still mostly observe the principles of the common law when it comes to statutory interpretation. It is therefore important that the uniform principles should be spelt out and generally known. This book aims to help in that object.

In the case of the United Kingdom the position is now complicated by European involvement. This book aims to set out guidance applicable to statutory interpretation in all jurisdictions of the common law, which still tends to run on uniform lines. At the same time there is a need to cater also for the way the United Kingdom itself is being influenced by European considerations. What is said in this book is intended to apply to common law statutes (by which I mean all legislation enacted in common law countries) except where the context otherwise indicates.

British interminglings

As respects Britain today the laws comprise not only Acts of the Westminster Parliament, and orders and regulations made under them, but the growing mass of European Union directives and other such outside laws. Since 2 October 2000 Britain has furthermore been governed (through treaty obligations and the Human Rights Act 1998) by the 1950 European Convention on Human Rights. All this varied legislation is accompanied by corresponding case law, that is the decisions of the courts which expound the legal meaning of the multifarious statutes. In addition the common law, mainly created over the centuries by judicial decisions in cases not ruled by statute, remains important. So at the turn of the second millennium it is not possible to look on British law as one system. It is a variegated pattern, with overlapping and conflicting rules that are often difficult to construe and reconcile. This does not of course affect other common law countries which are beyond the influence of European law.

Usually a system of law has corresponded to a political system. Each sovereign state has had its own law, which might or might not resemble the law of a given other sovereign state. Today the United Kingdom is still an independent nation, but much less so than it was a century ago. Now it has various interminglings. It is part of the European Union, and this brings contact with the system known as civil law (directly derived from Roman law). By the Human Rights Act 1998 Britain has explicitly connected domestic law to the requirements of the European Convention on Human Rights, which perhaps gives the common law a stronger human rights flavour and also impinges on United Kingdom statute law. Britain has more powerful and extensive treaty links than in the past, and these require it to take more notice of other countries' systems of law. The cult word for all this is globalization. Slowly and gradually the planet is moving towards the inevitable scenario of world government, but that is still a long way off.

In the other direction, tending to the interior of the British state, the Westminster Parliament has conferred, under the process known as devolution, limited legislative powers on countries inside the United Kingdom. This too produces consequences for the homogeneity of British law. Scotland now has its Parliament, which in the laws it makes may hark back to civilian roots and continental connections. One acute observer commented:

So here we are, facing all sorts of new and peculiarly legal challenges. A new Europe has to be made. The common law has to keep on equal terms with the civilian legal systems. The institutions on which we have so long relied are to be reformed. The Act of Union is to be loosened. Human rights are moving into the foreground.[1]

In our courts and elsewhere there is increasing osmosis between common law and civil law.[2] This can only increase the complexity of British enacted law. How can the non-specialist lawyer, never mind the uninstructed citizen, routinely comprehend, as duty requires, this mass of official verbiage? Nowadays it is proclaimed that legislation should be drafted in plain English, and worthy efforts are made to this end. Plain English is all very well, indeed highly desirable. Yet the truth is that, no matter how hard drafters may strive to be plain, modern legislation is necessarily very difficult even for experts to comprehend. This is partly because there is a mass of existing statute law, some dating back many years, which was drafted on lines very different from those advocated by plain English reformers. Also, amongst the press of subjects which the law student feels, or is told, he or she must learn, the science of legislation takes a back seat. Statute law is not fully taught, if it is taught at all. Where it is taught, it is often taught badly.

The nature of statute law

We are concerned with certain aspects of statute law, a term with two meanings. One meaning is law in statutory form, that is the body of enacted law sometimes referred to (inaccurately) as the statute book. I shall refer to statute law in this sense as 'legislation'. The other meaning is the area of knowledge and skill concerned with the nature, functioning, and interpretation of legislation. It is in the latter sense that I shall use the term 'statute law'. In this latter sense statute law possesses a quality which renders it unique among types of law. You can be a criminal lawyer without also being a tax lawyer; you can be a company lawyer without also being a conveyancer; you can be an expert in public law while

---

[1] Peter Birks, 'The academic and the practitioner' 18 *Legal Studies* (1998) 397 at 405.

[2] For example in *R v Oxfordshire County Council*, ex p Sunningwell Parish Council [1999] 3 All ER 385 Lord Hoffmann readily cited systems based on Roman law as a basis for his construction of the phrase 'as of right' in the Commons Registration Act 1965 s. 22(1)(c).

knowing little of private law, and so on. But nowadays you cannot be any sort of competent lawyer without being a statute lawyer, since legislation provides the framework for almost everything lawyers do.

The statutes this book is mainly concerned with I will call common law statutes, even though in one sense statutes override common law. What I mean by common law statutes is those drafted, and intended to be interpreted, on common law lines.

Nowadays however British legislation cannot simply be described as 'common law statutes'. It mainly consists of:

(*a*) Acts passed by the Westminster Parliament, subordinate legislation made under those Acts, and other United Kingdom subordinate legislation such as prerogative orders (together referred to as 'United Kingdom legislation');

(*b*) legislation of the Scottish Parliament, the Welsh Assembly or the Northern Ireland Assembly ('British devolved legislation');

(*c*) treaties, directives etc. of the European Union ('Community legislation'), so far as they affect the legal meaning of United Kingdom legislation or have direct effect in the United Kingdom; and

(*d*) the European Convention on Human Rights so far as, by virtue of the Human Rights Act 1998, it affects the legal meaning of United Kingdom legislation or British devolved legislation.

Only the first of these four categories can truly be described as 'common law statutes'. When intending to refer to all four of the categories I will use the term 'British legislation'.

Who needs to know?

Who needs to know about the interpretation of British legislation? One answer is: every citizen, but let us be practical. The intended readership of this book is either law orientated or fact-and-party orientated. By law orientated I mean concerned with British legislation in a general way. By fact-and-party orientated I mean concerned with such legislation as it applies to particular facts and parties.

There are many varieties of people who need to study legislation, or some aspect of it, generally—that is without having a particular case in mind. We may begin with politicians. These operate internationally, centrally or locally and may at any time be in power or opposition. Nowadays the political function is closely connected with legislation, since legislating is considered (often mistakenly) as a prime form of political action. At general elections the promises of future legislation which are set out in political party manifestos constitute the main bait for attracting voters. Before draft legislation can be worked out however, policy must be decided. It is little use taking decisions on legislative policy if you have no idea how statute law operates.

Next we may take legislators, who are politicians in another guise. We think of them as politicians when they are devising legislative policy, either in government, prospective government, or opposition. We think of them as legislators when they are engaged in the function of debating, amending and passing the parliamentary bills which convert policy into law.

The people who have the major part to play (behind the scenes) in the detail or small print of policy and legislation are the administrators and drafters, usually civil servants. Other administrative staff, whether in the civil service, local government, or any other operational organization (such as the police or revenue services), execute or supervise the actual working of legislation after it has been drafted and passed.[3]

An important section of the prospective readership of this book consists of people who teach statute law and their students. Then there are those concerned with legal reform, which should really include all those I have already mentioned. Everyone who works in the law has an interest in its reform, but we think first of those whose actual duty is law reform, such as the staffs of Law Commissions and similar bodies. Mention of law reform here includes both statute law and legislation. A person may be concerned either in the reform of the substantive law (legislation) or of the techniques of handling it (statute law).

The other type of reader this book is intended for has a particular case in mind, and the book is designed to help in handling the

---

[3] For details of administrative and executive enforcement agencies in Britain see *Bennion Code*, pp. 62–71.

law applicable to that case. We may start with the parties to a dispute or other matter. They are probably lay people who are not skilled in the law, but this does not of course mean they will not be interested in trying to understand the law as it affects their case. Then comes the solicitor who will handle the case for a party, and any other person (such as a Citizens' Advice Bureau helper or McKenzie friend) who may assist the person actually embroiled with the law. If the case gets to court we then have the barrister or solicitor who as an advocate will plead the client's case before the court. Finally, we have the judge or magistrate who will try the case, or consider it on review or appeal.

I have indicated a wide readership for this book, but that is not surprising. Legislation closely concerns every citizen. However I would utter a word of warning to lay readers. Although they should find it helpful to read this book, I would not encourage them to rely on their perception of a legal matter without expert assistance. Law, like medicine or engineering, is necessarily an expertise.

The design of this book

I should now briefly explain the ways in which this book is designed to help its readers handle statute law and legislation, and to thread the maze constituted by the body of law I have indicated. We are here concerned with threading the maze only in certain ways and to a limited extent. The book does not go as wide as it might have done. This is to ensure that what it does treat it treats to the necessary depth. The core of its treatment is indicated by a dictum of Justice Oliver Wendell Holmes Junior, founder of the American realist school of jurisprudence: 'The prophecies of what the courts will do in fact, and nothing more pretentious, are what I mean by the law.'[4] This needs to be qualified by an acute remark of Roscoe Pound's:

It is the adviser not the law that does the predicting. As Mr Justice Cardozo pointed out, a law or legal precept is a *basis* for prediction.[5]

---

[4] 'The Path of the Law', 10 *Harvard Law Review* (1897), 457 at 460–1.
[5] *II Jurisprudence* (1959) 131 (emphasis added). On this aspect see further the Index to this book.

Predicting the legal meaning of an enactment that a court would adopt is only a part of the legal practitioner's work, but it is the part to which this book is mainly devoted. Guidance on other parts concerned with legislation, such as giving advice on how far prosecutors are likely to enforce a particular criminal enactment, or what sentence is likely to be handed down for a particular offence, or how a prospective company would be best structured having regard to the Companies Acts, or how a tax avoidance scheme might most cunningly be drafted having regard to the Income Tax Acts, and so on, must be sought elsewhere. What we are concerned with here is discerning the legal meaning of a common law enactment, and not much beyond that.

Of course this book, like any book, can give only its author's view of the matter, though I have tried to reflect many opinions. At this point I would like to bring in some views on my approach which were expressed by Twining and Miers in their excellent book *How To Do Things With Rules.*[6] They say that for law students 'we consider the rules of statutory interpretation and the doctrine of precedent to be relatively minor dimensions of the problems and processes of legal interpretation'.[7] I would reply that this is true in the context of how such matters have been traditionally taught. It is not true where the rules of statutory interpretation and the doctrine of precedent are taught with full emphasis on the underlying principles. Such teaching is the intention of this book as it is the intention of my larger book *Statutory Interpretation,* where I wrote in the introduction:

That the present work, confined as it is to the common law system of statutory interpretation, should find it necessary to devote more than a thousand pages to the subject is a measure of its expansion and present complexity. However the clue that should not be missed is that statutory interpretation keys into the whole system of law; indeed that whole system is subject to the scheme of interpretation and in turn feeds into it. This means that statutory interpretation, when treated comprehensively as it is here, forms perhaps the best modern introduction to a country's entire legal system.[8]

Twining and Miers criticize the following passage in that book:

---

[6] W. Twining and David Miers, *How To Do Things With Rules,* (4th edn., London: Butterworths, 1999).
[7] Ibid. 114.   [8] *Bennion Code,* p. 2.

The natural and reasonable desire that statutes should be easily understood is doomed to disappointment. Thwarted, it shifts to an equally
natural and reasonable desire for efficient tools of interpretation. If
statutes must be obscure, let us at least have simple devices to elucidate
them. A golden rule would be best, to unlock all mysteries. Alas, as this
book demonstrates, there is no golden rule. Nor is there a mischief rule,
or a literal rule, or any other cure-all rule of thumb. Instead there are a
thousand and one interpretative *criteria*.[9]

Twining and Miers say that, for the purposes of the reader who
wishes to obtain some foothold on the way in which judges
approach interpretation, the above concise summary 'perhaps
overstates the case'.[10] However my book sets out in great detail
just what these myriad rules, presumptions, principles and linguistic canons consist of. The enquirer who desires a foothold must
surely be prepared to do some work to find where to place his
feet. I hope the present book, which aims to distil into a much
smaller space what is contained in the larger work, will help in
this.

Twining and Myers then make some more fundamental criti-
cisms of my approach. They say it is wrong to concentrate on how
a judge would decide a question of statutory interpretation
because this brings in controversies over whether or not judges
make law and whether they can be truly neutral. They add that all
too often doubts about the proper role of judges have been
misleadingly conflated with puzzles about interpretation.[11] My
answer is that puzzles about how judges construe legislation are
inextricably bound up with questions on the judicial role, and
should not be treated in isolation. This book pays attention to
both aspects.[12]

A further objection made by Twining and Miers is that in the
course of conducting their affairs people concerned with legislation inevitably take many factors into account other than how the
court would decide a point of interpretation, some of which are
intimately tied up with their respective standpoints and roles. For
example an advocate requiring to make the most of his case to the
court may take a different line to that of an adviser in a non-liti-
gious situation; and rival lawyers engaged in negotiation may each

---

[9]   *Bennion Code*, p. 3.   [10] Op. cit., 281.
[11]   Ibid. 171–2.   [12] See Index.

press an opposite view of the legal meaning of a relevant enactment.[13]

My answer here is that the question, extended to the entirety of common law legislation, of how a court would be likely to (or should) decide a point of statutory interpretation is in itself large and complex. Dealing with it adequately is a task big enough for a single book. My object in the present book is to give a satisfactory account of common law statutory interpretation in a reasonably brief compass. However the book allows for the fact that slightly different techniques may be needed by, for example, a judge, an adviser, an advocate or a negotiator. It also allows for the fact that most disputes are settled out of court, often without mentioning or even hinting that court proceedings might be brought. The likely result if court proceedings *were* brought is however always likely to be in the back of the minds of the parties and their negotiators. If it is not it ought to be.

The role of the judge

I would add this about the judiciary, whose function it is to pronounce on the legal meaning of an enactment. We are concentrating in this book on how a court might be expected to arrive at the legal meaning. In doing so we confidently assume that the judge concerned will *play the game*. This cricketing metaphor refers first to the basic requirement that the judge will not be influenced by extraneous considerations, such as having received a bribe from one of the parties. In common law countries at the opening of the third millennium we feel confident in the honesty and impartiality of all judges, which is not the case in some other countries (and was not the case in common law countries at some past times). We also feel confident that our judge will observe Dworkin's principle of integrity:

Law as integrity asks judges to assume, so far as this is possible, that the law is structured by a coherent set of principles about justice and fairness and procedural due process, and it asks them to enforce these in the fresh cases that come before them, so that each person's situation is fair and just according to the same standards. That style of adjudication respects

[13] Op. cit., 172–5.

the ambition integrity assumes, the ambition to be a community of principle.[14]

This is a way of saying that judges are expected to apply to each and every case before them the entire set of rules, principles, expectations and other guidelines that prevail within their jurisdiction and are regarded as governing the exercise of their judicial function. As Sir Carleton Allen remarked, the duty of judicial 'loyalty' is now beyond question.[15] We will not overlook the complexities of this; for example the conduct of judges in 'massaging' the literal meaning where they think it produces an unjust result or does not fit changed circumstances. However we do assume, what has always been considered to be the case, that judges will not deliberately set out to assume the role of legislators. As Sir Carleton Allen said of the English judge: 'His whole effort is to find the law, not to manufacture it . . . he cannot, however much he may wish to do so, sweep away what he believes to be the prevailing rule of law and substitute something else in its place.'[16]

There is a more subtle aspect to this question of the viewpoint a judge may be expected to bring to the task of statutory interpretation. In the past this was assumed to be uniform, as indeed it ought to be. However it tended to be the uniform viewpoint of a white upper-middle class male with an Oxbridge education, which some may nowadays think is *not* what it ought to be (others may continue to differ). One of the grounds on which the eighteenth-century jurist Blackstone praised the old system of travelling assize judges was the resulting consistency in the law:

These justices, though . . . varied and shifted at every assizes, are all sworn to the same laws, have had the same education, have pursued the same studies, converse and consult together, communicate their decisions and resolutions . . . And hence their administration of justice and conduct of trials are consonant and uniform; whereby . . . confusion and contrariety are avoided.[17]

[14] R. Dworkin, *Law's Empire* (Oxford: Hart Publishing, 1986), 243. See further Ch. 16.
[15] Sir Carleton Kemp Allen, *Law in the Making*, (4th edn., Oxford: Clarendon Press, 1946), 223.
[16] Op. cit., 262. For indications that some of our present senior judges do not subscribe to this view see pp. 144–6 below.
[17] Blackstone iii 354.

In our own day, with the increasing appointment as judges of lawyers who are men not from an Oxbridge upper-middle class background, or are women, or are persons of non-indigenous ethnic background, the likelihood of variation is greater. Here are two recent views.

In terms of judging, the argument is made that as women have such different characteristics, more women judges will lead to a radically different law and legal system, as women use their skills and perspectives to interpret the law in a different manner to men.[18]

Legal rules have evolved and developed to deal with specific disputes and problems arising within an *English* context, and are applied by *English* judges, whose experience is of things *English*. There have been few instances where the courts have given allowances for cultural difference . . .[19]

We now have in common law countries an equal-opportunities, multicultural society, and this needs to be recognized throughout the legal system. In Britain the (white English) man on the Clapham omnibus, that old touchstone of what is 'reasonable', must now be joined by other types of passenger. However it would not be right for judges' readings of enactments to differ according to their social background, gender, or ethnic origin; and it is obviously necessary for the judiciary to strive for uniformity of approach. Such uniformity is to be presumed by practitioner, teacher, and student. That is as far as we can go here. Those who wish to investigate further this fascinating topic of social variations in judges and their approach to their work must go to some other book.[20]

Are there really any rules?

Before leaving Twining and Miers I should mention, because it is relevant to this book, another point they make in relation to my larger work *Statutory Interpretation*. They say it is 'both descriptive

---

[18] Clare McGlynn, 'Will women judges make a difference?' 148 NLJ (1998) 813.

[19] Susan Edwards, 'Beyond belief—the case of Zoora Shah' 148 NLJ (1998) 667 at 668 (emphasis in original).

[20] For example, J. A. G. Griffith, *The Politics of the Judiciary* (5th edn., London: Fontana, 1997).

and prescriptive'.[21] In other words it not only describes the present rules but says they ought to be complied with. I have no quarrel with this description, which could be applied equally to the present book. However it may be helpful to expand it a little. I am saying that the system ought to be complied not because it cannot be improved but because it *is* the system. Those operating within it ought to comply with it because otherwise they will be failing in their duty: they will not be doing what people have a right to expect.

Both books aim not only to present the law and rules etc. governing common law statutory interpretation as they exist, but also to explain how they form a consistent whole and what the underlying theory is. Furthermore, both books are concerned to explain the processes of interpretation, and the various techniques, which are or ought to be used currently in relation to legislation in common law countries. If it seems complacent thus to accept the existing regime, rather than advance suggestions for its improvement, I can only say again that describing the existing system adequately is a very large task in itself. I have nothing against reform, but it needs another book.[22]

Legislation is what the legislator says it is. The *meaning* of legislation is what the court says it is. So those whose task is to find out and apply that meaning need to know how judges are supposed to arrive at it, and what their conclusions are likely to be in the case that is currently of concern to the practitioner. A technique of what might be called law handling or law management is required, but this is often lacking. We will take it step by step.

The nature of an enactment

I start with a basic concept, the *legal* meaning of an enactment. But first I should explain what an *enactment* is, for this is a term of art we shall often need to use. Bentham said that a law is either a single proposition or an assemblage of propositions. An enactment is a single proposition contained in an assemblage of propositions

---

[21] Op. cit., 371 n.
[22] Many suggestions for reform of techniques of statute law and interpretation are given in my book *Statute Law* (3rd edn., London: Longman, 1990).

such as an Act of Parliament or statutory instrument. Its usual effect is this. When the facts of a case fall within an indicated area called the factual outline, specified consequences called the legal thrust ensue.

There are many types of enactment. I take as an example a British enactment, the Criminal Damage Act 1971 s. 1(1). This specifies several offences. By omitting irrelevant words we can express one of these as follows:

A person who without lawful excuse damages any property belonging to another, being reckless as to whether any such property would be damaged, shall be guilty of an offence.[23]

This is a typical 'enactment'. The interpreter's duty is to arrive at the *legal* meaning of a relevant enactment, that is the meaning it has in law. Chief Baron Pollock said 'it is our duty to ascertain the true legal meaning of the words used by the legislature'.[24] Many factors bear on this meaning, and it may not turn out to be the same as the grammatical or literal meaning. Finding it must be done in accordance with the rules, principles, presumptions and canons governing statutory interpretation. These are referred to as the interpretative criteria, or guides to legislative intention. We will examine them later.

The legal meaning

It is the function of the court alone authoritatively to *declare* the legal meaning of an enactment. If anyone else, such as its drafter or the politician promoting it, purports to lay down what the legal meaning is the court may react adversely, regarding this as an encroachment on its constitutional sphere. Lord Wilberforce stated the classic position:

Legislation in England is passed by Parliament, and put in the form of written words. This legislation is given legal effect on subjects by virtue of judicial decision, and it is the function of the courts to say what the application of words to particular cases or particular individuals is to be. This power, which has been devolved on the judges from the earliest times, is

---

[23] This enactment is further discussed at pp. 26–7 below.
[24] *A.-G. v Sillem* (1864) 2 H. & C. 431 at 513.

an essential part of the constitutional process by which subjects are brought under the rule of law—as distinct from the rule of the King or the rule of Parliament; and it would be a degradation of that process if the courts were to be merely a reflecting mirror of what some other interpretation agency might say . . .[25]

The legislation in force at any one time consists of a large number of enactments. Some will bear the impress of judicial decisions promulgated before that time; some will not. As with other forms of law, such as the common law, those bound by statutes are expected to know of them, or at least are not excused by lack of knowledge. Blackstone said: 'if ignorance of what he *might* know were admitted as a legitimate excuse, the laws would be of no effect, but might always be eluded with impunity.'[26] This presumed knowledge of law is required to be accurate. Blackstone said of mistakes as to the purport of a law: 'if a man thinks he has a right to kill a person excommunicated or outlawed, wherever he meets him, and does so, this is wilful murder.'[27]

A person is not excepted from the principle that ignorance of law affords no excuse by the fact that the operative ignorance is that of a professional adviser.[28] Forbes J. suggested that 'having regard to the multiplicity of statutes which exist' counsel and solicitors could be excused for not recalling the existence of a relevant enactment.[29] This may save a practitioner from an action for professional negligence, but it will not excuse the client.

So we have the position that ignorance or mistake regarding it is not accepted as an excuse for failing to comply with an enactment. That translates as ignorance or mistake as to the legal meaning of the enactment, which as I have said may differ from the literal meaning. Obeying this rule is a tall order. So let us look more closely at what, at any given moment, the legal meaning of an enactment really is.

Put shortly, the legal meaning is the one that corresponds to the legislator's intention in framing the enactment. Lord Radcliffe said

---

[25] *Black-Clawson International Ltd v Papierwerke Waldhof-Aschaffenberg A.G.* [1975] AC 591. This 'degradation' was effected by the decision in *Pepper v Hart*: see pp.118–19 below.
[26] Blackstone i 28 (emphasis in original).   [27] Ibid. iv 21.
[28] *Turner & Goudy v McConnell* [1985] 1 WLR 898 at 901.
[29] *Murphy v Duke* [1985] QB 905 at 918–19; overruled in part *Cooper v Coles* [1986] 3 WLR 888.

that 'the paramount rule remains that every statute is to be expounded according to its manifest and expressed intention'.[30] This rule has been criticized as artificial. It sits uncomfortably with modern developments such as the requirement under the European Communities Act 1972 ss. 2 and 3 to construe United Kingdom enactments so as to fit Community law where possible and the requirement, under the Human Rights Act 1998 s. 3(1), to do the same in relation to the European Convention on Human Rights.[31] Yet the original legislator's intention is still the touchstone, and must remain so.

So what do you do when you need to find out the legal meaning of an enactment? First, read it through. Secondly, search out what if anything the courts have said about it. Thirdly, consider its legislative history and overall context. All this enables you to give what is necessary, namely an *informed* construction.[32] If on an informed construction you feel real doubt as to the legal meaning then you have a problem. You must go through the process of applying what I refer to above as the interpretative criteria.

Before deciding whether this is necessary you need to bear in mind that 'no form of words has ever yet been framed . . . with regard to which some ingenious counsel could not suggest a difficulty'.[33] The law recognizes a doubt over the legal meaning of an enactment as 'real' only where it is substantial, and not merely conjectural or fanciful. Even then, there is still the problem of differential readings. This is the name given to the phenomenon where different minds conscientiously arrive at different conclusions on the legal meaning. In 2001 Lord Nicholls of Birkenhead said that sometimes different minds can reach different conclusions on what fairness requires: 'Then fairness, like beauty, lies in the eye of the beholder'.[34] Or as Alexander Pope wrote in the days

[30] *A.-G. for Canada v Hallett & Carey Ltd.* [1952] AC 427 at 449.
[31] These requirements are discussed in Ch. 15.
[32] Before starting to construe any statutory words used it is necessary 'to make an informed determination' whether there is real doubt as to their legal meaning: *R v Secretary of State for the Environment, Transport and the Regions and another, ex p Spath Holme Ltd* [2000] 1 All ER 884, *per* Stuart-Smith LJ at 894 (reversed *R v Secretary of State for the Environment, Transport and the Regions and another, ex p Spath Holme Ltd* [2001] 1 All ER 195 [HL] on a point not affecting this dictum).
[33] *Pratt v South Eastern Rly.* [1897] 1 QB 718, *per* Lord Cave LC at 721.
[34] *White v White* [2001] 1 All ER 1 at 4.

when watches were unreliable: ' 'Tis with our judgments as our watches, none Go just alike, yet each believes his own.'[35]

In a general survey like this we must contemplate the great mass of subsisting enactments, each with its legal meaning. Does this meaning remain constant? If it really corresponds to the intention of the legislator, and we assume that a later legislator does not amend it, one may expect it to do so. The original legislator has enacted it and passed on. How can its meaning thereafter change? One can imagine a notional, ideal 'legal meaning' held aloft and immune to developments. That is not the position in real life, where the kind of circumstances to which the enactment applies will change over time.[36]

Sooner or later the enactment may come before the courts, who will pronounce what its legal meaning is. Until that happens, there is nothing but the notional, ideal 'legal meaning' together with a collection of non-authoritative, non-judicial conjectures (usually by practising or academic lawyers) as to what that amounts to. More accurately, the conjectures relate to what, when the enactment does come before a court, the judge is most likely to make of it. Putting the matter at its most succinct, and allowing for the possibility of judicial disagreements, the legal meaning is what it is most likely the Appellate Committee of the House of Lords, or the corresponding authority in another common law country, would say it is.

Rendering this in a rather more accurate if more lengthy way, one can say (for Britain) that the legal meaning is found as follows. If the enactment has never come before a court, the legal meaning is what it is most likely the House of Lords would say it is. If it has come before a court other than the House of Lords, the legal meaning is what that court said it was, bearing in mind that the House of Lords may think differently if it ever comes before them and overrule the lower court. If the enactment has come before the House of Lords, the legal meaning is what that House said it was, bearing in mind that the House of Lords now claims power to depart from its previous decisions.

---

[35] *Essays on Criticism* (London, 1709) i. 9. Differential readings are discussed at p. 132 below.
[36] For updating construction see Ch. 5.

Errors in legal meaning

There are further elaborations. Suppose an enactment comes into force in year E, and it is then generally agreed by the profession that its legal meaning is W. Then in year $E+5$ the enactment comes before its first court, court A, which holds that the legal meaning is not W but X. In year $E+10$ the enactment comes before court B, which does not follow the ruling of court A but decides that the legal meaning is Y. What then is the legal meaning? If court B is superior to court A, its decision blots out meaning X and substitutes meaning Y. But suppose the two courts are of equal jurisdiction? What then is the legal meaning of the enactment? Suppose further that in year $E+15$ the enactment comes before court C, a court higher than A and B, and court C decides on meaning Z. One can say that thereafter meaning Z prevails, but what was the legal meaning (i) between years E and $E+5$, (ii) between years $E+5$ and $E+10$, and (iii) between years $E+10$ and $E+15$?

These are not academic questions. In year $E+2$ a lawyer's client may have quite properly been advised that the legal meaning was W, and acted accordingly. In year $E+7$ a client may have quite properly been advised that the legal meaning was X, and acted accordingly. In year $E+12$ a client may have quite properly been advised that the legal meaning was Y, and acted accordingly. How do these clients stand after court C has pronounced its decision? Surprisingly, the law is in some disarray over these questions and no short answer is possible.

In the absence of an answer specifically given by legislation, the courts have to deal with such questions, as the course of litigation requires of them, by reference to fundamental principles dictated by legal policy, such as the need for courts to do justice.

In *R. v. Governor of H.M. Prison Brockhill, ex p. Evans (No. 2)* [37] the House of Lords considered a claim for damages for false imprisonment brought by a convicted prisoner against the governor of Brockhill Prison. Under a line of judicial authority as to the legal meaning of the Criminal Justice Act 1967 s. 67(1), known as the *Gaffney* approach, the release date of the prisoner had been calculated by the governor as 18 November 1996. However the

[37] [2000] 4 All ER 15.

Gaffney approach was in effect overruled by *R. v. Secretary of State for the Home Department, ex p. Naughton*[38]. On the normal declaratory principle of judicial precedent *Naughton* operated retrospectively (see below), so the respondent should with hindsight have been released on 17 September 1996. Was she entitled to damages from the governor, even though at the relevant time he had correctly applied the law as laid down by the *Gaffney* approach? *Held* False imprisonment is a tort of strict liability, and the governor as representing the state was not absolved by the fact that he acted correctly.

Lord Slynn said[39] that the governor could not be criticized even though the court in *Naughton* doubted the soundness of the earlier decisions on which the *Gaffney* approach was based. Lord Steyn, applying the basic rule of statutory interpretation,[40] said the relevant principles of law pulled in opposite directions and he would therefore carry out a balancing exercise.[41] He said it was 'a matter of judgment how the weight of the competing principles in the present case should be assessed'.

Evans shows that no general answer can be given to the question what is the effect on previous transactions when a ruling on the law changes: it depends on the nature of the law in question. It should also be borne in mind, whenever it becomes necessary for anyone, whether a practitioner advising a client, a court disposing of a case, or a person such as the prison governor in *Evans*, to decide what the legal meaning of an enactment is, that it is requisite, where there is real doubt on the point, to apply all relevant interpretative criteria.[42] The existing court decision will only be one of these, and the overall weight of argument may fall the other way. The interpreter does not discharge his or her duty if this investigative process is not undertaken when necessary, especially where a serious issue, perhaps affecting the liberty of the subject, depends on it.

Even where there is no real doubt as to the correctness of the earlier decision, it may still be overturned in a later case. In other words the legal meaning of an enactment may, as stated above, be X at one moment in time and Y at a later date. The later decision

---

[38] [1997] 1 All ER 426.   [39] p. 18.
[40] See *Bennion Code* s. 193.   [41] p. 20.
[42] For 'real doubt' see *Bennion Code*, pp. 15–16.

will on normal principles operate retrospectively,[43] so that Y is taken to have been the legal meaning all along. The case of the governor of Brockhill Prison needs to be distinguished from the by-law case of *Percy v. Hall*[44] where it was held that the acts of police enforcing a by-law would not be rendered unlawful by a later court ruling that the by-law was void.[45]

Legal policy

The difficult case where, without fault, a person relied on meaning X before a later court substituted meaning Y should be decided according to principles of legal policy.[46] As Schiemann LJ said in *Percy v. Hall*:[47] 'The policy questions which the law must address in this type of case are whether any and if so what remedy should be given to whom against whom in cases where persons have acted in reliance on what appears to be valid legislation.'[48] One obvious principle of legal policy that should be applied is that law should be just and court decisions should further the ends of justice.[49]

Another aspect of legal policy is the principle that law should not operate retrospectively.[50] However, because procedural changes are assumed to be beneficial and not punitive, the principle against retrospectivity does not apply to them.[51] Put more broadly, the principle against retrospectivity applies only where retrospectivity would inflict hardship. Treating the decision abrogating the *Gaffney* approach as retrospective in the case of the plaintiff in *Evans* on balance conferred a benefit.

In *Evans* the House of Lords discussed the question whether the declaratory-retrospective principle applied by the common law to decisions overruling earlier cases should be relaxed. Lord Slynn said:[52]

---

[43] See, e.g., *Miliangos v George Frank (Textiles) Ltd* [1976] AC 443; *R. v Preddy* [1996] AC 815. See also *Evans, passim*.

[44] [1996] 4 All ER 523. See *Bennion Code*, pp. 195–6.

[45] See also *Boddington v British Transport Police* [1998] 2 All ER 203.

[46] For this see *Bennion Code*, s. 263.   [47] [1997] 4 All ER 523 at 545.

[48] For the *Evans* type of case one would substitute 'have acted in reliance on what appears to be a valid court ruling'.

[49] See *Bennion Code*, pp. 614–16.   [50] See ibid., 623.

[51] See ibid., 237–40, 623.   [52] p. 19.

I consider that there may be situations in which it would be desirable, and in no way unjust, that the effect of judicial rulings should be prospective or limited to certain claimants. The European Court of Justice, though cautiously and infrequently, has restricted the effect of its ruling to the particular claimants in the case before it and to those who had begun proceedings before the date of its judgment. Those who had not sought to challenge the legality of acts done years before could only rely on the ruling prospectively. Such a course avoided unscrambling transactions perhaps long since over and doing injustice to defendants.[53]

Lord Slynn was here referring to the so-called *Barber* principle This is named after *Barber v. Guardian Royal Exchange Assurance Group*,[54] in which the Court of Justice of the European Communities (CJEC) unexpectedly held that certain occupational pensions constituted 'pay' within the meaning of the equal pay provisions of art. 119 of the EC Treaty (now art. 141).[55] The principle is largely based on the legal policy principle requiring legal certainty.[56] The declaratory nature of the CJEC's jurisdiction means that under normal principles, that is apart from the *Barber* principle, a long-held view as to the meaning and effect of a particular Community law could by virtue of a CJEC decision be overthrown retrospectively. In such cases, but only where the difficulty is extreme, the CJEC has asserted the power to modify the usual declaratory effect of its judgment by denying it retrospective effect or modifying that effect.[57]

In another case the CJEC was prepared to limit the temporal effect of one of its judgments on account of the catastrophic

---

[53] See *Amministrazione delle Finanze v Srl Meridionale Industria Salumi* (Joined cases 66, 127, and 128/79) [1980] ECR 1237 at 1260–1 (para. 10); *Coloroll Pension Trustees Ltd v Russell* (Case C-200/91) [1995] All ER (EC) 23. For an analysis of these cases see *Bennion Code*, p. 1013.

[54] Case C-262/88 [1990] ECR I-1889.

[55] The first case in which the principle which later became known as the *Barber* principle was applied was *Gabrielle Defrenne v Sabena (No 2)* (Case 43/75) [1976] ECR 455.

[56] See [1990] ECR I-1889 at 1956 (para 44). For the principle of legal certainty see *Bennion Code* s. 403.

[57] For example the CJEC held that, except where a claim had been made before that date, the direct effect of Art 119 of the EC Treaty could be relied on in order to claim equal treatment in the matter of occupational pensions only in relation to benefits payable in respect of periods of service subsequent to 17 May 1990, the effective date of the decision in *Barber*: *Neath v Hugh Steeper Ltd* (Case C-152/91) [1994] 1 All ER 929; *Coloroll Pension Trustees Ltd v Russell* (Case C-200/91) [1995] All ER (EC) 23 at 79 (para 48).

financial repercussions which the French overseas territories would face if charges later held not to be due became repayable. The test applied, as in *Barber*, was whether the parties or member states in question were reasonably entitled to consider that their conduct was in accordance with Community law.[58]

The *Barber* principle, so far as it applies to art. 119 (now art. 141), was codified by a protocol to the Treaty of Rome (added by the Maastricht Treaty) which came into force on 1 November 1993. This states: 'For the purposes of Article 119 of this Treaty, benefits under occupational security schemes shall not be considered as remuneration if and so far as they are attributable to periods of employment prior to 17 May 1990 [the date of the *Barber* decision], except in the case of workers or those claiming under them who have before that date initiated legal proceedings or introduced an equivalent claim under the applicable national law.'[59]

Lord Slynn's colleagues in *Evans* did not share his view. Lord Hobhouse said:[60]

It is a denial of the constitutional role of the courts for courts to say that the party challenging the *status quo* is right, that the previous decision is overruled, but that the decision will not affect the parties and only apply subsequently.

Factual outline and legal thrust

I said above that the usual legal effect of an enactment is that, when the facts of a case fall within an indicated area called the

[58] *Administration des douanes et droits indirects v Legros* (Case C-163/90) [1992] ECR I-4625 (para 34). Cf *Worringham v Lloyds Bank Ltd* (Case 69/80) [1981] 1 WLR 950 at 971 (para 33) where the court, after weighing and balancing the factors concerned, decided that the number of the cases which would be affected was not sufficient to require it to limit the temporal effect of its judgment. For other examples of cases where the temporal effect of a judgment of the CJEC was limited in this way see *Belbouab v Bundesknappschaft* (Case 10/78) [1978] ECR 1915 (nationality requirement affecting mineworker's pension); *Pinna v Caisse d'allocations familiales de la Savoie* (Case 41/84) [1986] ECR 1 (family allowances under provision held invalid); *Vincent Blaizot v University of Liège* (Case 24/86) [1988] ECR 379 (registration fees wrongly exacted from non-nationals).
[59] See *Bestuur van het Algemeen Burgerlijk Pensioenfonds v Beune* (Case C-7/93) [1995] All ER (EC) 97 at 104 (para 13) and 130 (para 61).
[60] p. 39.

factual outline, specified consequences called the legal thrust ensue. In other words an enactment lays down a legal rule in terms which show that the rule is triggered by the existence of certain facts. The enactment indicates these facts in outline form, omitting immaterial features. This is referred to as the *statutory factual outline*. I gave above the example of the offence of reckless criminal damage, as laid down in the following words by the Criminal Damage Act 1971 s. 1(1): 'A person who without lawful excuse damages any property belonging to another, being reckless as to whether any such property would be damaged, shall be guilty of an offence.' Here the statutory factual outline can be set out as follows.

1. The subject is any person with criminal capacity, the last three words being implied.

2. The *actus reus* (required guilty act) is without lawful excuse damaging any property belonging to another.

3. The *mens rea* (required guilty mind) is being reckless as to whether any such property would be damaged.

It is the function of a court deciding on the legal meaning of an enactment accurately to identify this area of factual relevance.

Sometimes a court will hold that the literal meaning of the outline stated in the enactment needs to be narrowed or widened in order to give effect to the legislator's true intention. The literal outline as so modified is referred to as the *judicial factual outline*. The basis of the doctrine of precedent is that to achieve fairness like cases must be decided alike. The ratio decidendi of a case involves postulating (whether expressly or by implication) the factual outline held to be laid down by the enactment, so far as relevant. If the facts of a later case fit within this judicial factual outline but demand amendment of the legal thrust of the rule, the outline is too broadly stated. If on the other hand the facts of a later case do not fit into the outline, but do elicit the same legal thrust, the outline as stated by the court is too narrow.

The legal thrust of an enactment is the legal effect arising where the material facts of the instant case fall within the statutory or judicial factual outline. In criminal law the legal thrust is often expressed, as in the above example, by saying that where the factual outline is satisfied the person in question is 'guilty of an offence'. The legal consequences of this by way of trial procedure, punishment and so forth may be spelt out by the legislator laying down the offence or left to the general law. Similarly in non-criminal law, the legal thrust gives the claimant who has succeeded in establishing that the proved or admitted facts constitute a *cause of action* a remedy in damages or otherwise.

Implied ancillary rules

I end this opening chapter by pointing out that elements in the legal thrust of an enactment may be left unexpressed by the drafter. Often they are to be treated as imported because of a general presumption based on the nature of legislation. This is that, unless the contrary intention appears, an enactment by implication imports any principle or rule of law (whether statutory or non-statutory) which prevails in the territory to which the enactment extends and is relevant to its operation in that territory. This may be referred to as an 'implied ancillary rule'.

An Act of Parliament is not a statement in a vacuum. Parliament intends its Act to be read and applied within the context of the existing corpus juris, or body of law. Any Act relies for its effectiveness on this implied importation of surrounding legal principles and rules. Thus for example Phillips LJ said that the common law requirement of fairness in decision making falls to be applied in statutory interpretation 'because of the common law principle'.[61] It is impossible for the drafter to restate in express terms all those ancillary legal considerations which are, or may become, necessary for the Act's working.

Lord Diplock said that criminal enactments 'fall to be construed in the light of general principles of English law so well established that it is the practice of parliamentary draftsmen to leave them unexpressed in criminal statutes, on the confident assumption that a court of law will treat those principles as intended by Parliament to be applicable to the particular offence unless expressly modified or excluded'.[62] Upon this principle, unless the Act creating the offence indicates to the contrary, proof

---

[61] *R. v Secretary of State for the Home Department, ex p Fayed* [1997] 1 All ER 228 at 252.
[62] *R. v Miller* [1983] 2 AC 161 at 174.

by the prosecution of a guilty mind or *mens rea* is needed to establish the commission of a statutory offence: 'even where the words used to describe the prohibited conduct would not in any context connote the necessity for any particular [mental] element, they are nevertheless to be read as subject to the implication that a necessary element in the offence is the absence of a belief held honestly *and upon reasonable grounds* in the existence of facts which if true would make the act innocent.'[63] Like everything else in the law, implied ancillary rules do not stand still. 'There has been a general shift from objectivism to subjectivism in this branch of the law',[64] so the italicized words in the preceding citation should now be treated as omitted.[65]

[63] *Sweet v Parsley* [1970] AC 132, *per* Lord Diplock at 163 (emphasis added).
[64] *B. (a minor) v Director of Public Prosecutions* [2000] 1 All ER 833, *per* Lord Steyn at 851.
[65] See the case cited in the preceding note. For a summary of this chapter see pp. 201–2 below.

2

Basic concepts II: opposing constructions; literal, purposive and developmental interpretations

Early law

The labyrinthine nature of common law legislation follows the historic British pattern. This exists because, through nearly two millennia, a number of different systems of law have in the British Isles been imposed, juxtaposed, and mingled. As one would expect, the first type of British law was custom, and we hear of British customs from before the days of the Roman occupation. Julius Caesar described the native priest-judges, called druids, who preserved and enforced the ancient Celtic customs.[1] Legislation, overriding custom, was introduced to Britain by the Roman emperor Claudius. Under his reign statutes were enacted to set up in the conquered territory the usual provincial law imposed by the conquering Roman Empire, known as *lex provinciae*.[2] No trace of these early statutes remains though custom, again as one would expect, never entirely died out.

Even today that primitive idea of custom (from the Latin *consuetudo*) retains a vestigial place in British law. It was defined as 'a law or right not written which, being established by long use and consent of our ancestors, has been and daily is put in practice'.[3] This description refers to general customs, or customs of the realm, which in early times were regarded (and still strictly are, where they prevail) as part of the common law. They are distinguished from *particular* customs, such as the law merchant, and *local* customs, such as the law of a particular manor or parish. Sir Carleton Allen pointed out that the term 'customs of the realm' is

---

[1] J. H. Baker, *An Introduction to English Legal History* (3rd edn., London: Butterworths, 1990), 2.

[2] Peter Salway, *Roman Britain* (Oxford: Clarendon Press, 1981), 87.

[3] W. Rastall, *Les Termes de la Ley* (London: Stationers' Company, 1624).

misleading, since most rules early regarded as general customs did not derive from the people but either originated in royal charters or statutes or were developed by judges. He added in a passage which conveys the gist of what early law still means today:

> The cardinal fact in the settlement of our medieval law is the gradual domination of a permanent central tribunal over the jurisdiction of local Courts. This process, beginning under Henry I, may be said to have become irresistible under Henry III; royal justice establishes approximate uniformity in essentials as against the bewildering diversity of local custom, and the supreme custom becomes the custom of the King's Court. There is still a great variety of usages in manors, boroughs and localities; but in what may be called the working basis of a general system of justice, the royal Courts carry on, and have ever since continued, a perpetual process of reconciliation and harmonisation, so that local divergences, though always respected and often jealously safeguarded, do not impair the symmetry of the main fabric. Beyond doubt, the greater part of this process of consolidation was the conscious task of the king's expert advisers.[4]

This conveys much that is still relevant. Early isolated communities in a land where, although a few people often travelled long distances, the majority stayed put and lacked communication even with neighbouring villages, tended to acquire and hold to their own individual customs. These acquired the force of law simply because things changed little from generation to generation and the local authorities of the day naturally felt it was safest to continue doing and enforcing what their forbears had always done and enforced.

Our generation thinks differently. It constantly tinkers with the law, and seeks thereby to create and re-create a 'new' society. This is vain endeavour, for human nature does not change. Our medieval ancestors did not fantasize about continually changing their society for the better, even though change was sometimes forced on them from outside. Except in the case of invasions of the realm such as those by the Danes, and setting aside the incursions of outlaws, the main outside force on local communities emanated from the king's court, and in particular the king's justices. We see a modern touch in the final sentence of the above

---

[4] Sir Carleton Kemp Allen, *Law in the Making* (4th edn., Oxford: Clarendon Press, 1946), 120.

quoted passage, acknowledging the contribution of what we would today call the higher civil service.

The common law still contains elements derived from the distant past. One of these is the old corpus of ecclesiastical law 'which was, and still is, part of the general law of England'.[5] The Victorian judge Lord Blackburn said:

The ecclesiastical law of England is not a foreign law. It is a part of the general law of England—of the common law—in that wider sense which embraces all the ancient and approved customs of England which form law, including not only that law administered in the Courts of Queen's Bench, Common Pleas, and Exchequer, to which the term Common Law is sometimes in a narrower sense confined, but also that law administered in Chancery and commonly called Equity, and also that law administered in the Courts Ecclesiastical, that last law consisting of such canons and constitutions ecclesiastical as have been allowed by general consent and custom within the realm—and form, as is laid down in *Caudrey's Case* (1591) 5 Co. Rep. 1, the King's ecclesiastical law.[6]

The early medieval practice, when faced with the need for change in the law, was to alter it by a royal charter which, though silently introducing reforms, purported merely to *declare* long-standing custom. This was in the days before open parliamentary legislation was established. The most prominent example is Magna Carta, reluctantly granted by King John (along with the Charter of the Forest) in 1215. Soon afterwards the institution of Parliament emerged from the king's court and council (*curia regis*). The term 'Parliament' derives from the French *parlement*. This in turn looked back to the Latin *parliamentum*, a colloquy. The earliest use of 'Parliament' in the sense we are discussing was in the *curia regis* roll of November 1236. Matthew Paris, writing in Latin, describes a later meeting of Parliament in 1246.[7] Loosely translated, his account reads: 'Summoned by regal edict, the nobles of the English Parliament assembled in London at a universal Parliament consisting of prelates (including bishops, abbots and priors), together with the earls and barons, to discuss the state of the realm.' When this body's decrees became formal they were called

---

[5] Lord Denning in *Hyde v Tameside Area Health Authority* [1981] CA Transcript 130.

[6] *Mackonochie v Lord Penzance* (1881) 6 App Cas 424 at 446.

[7] His Latin text is set out in William Stubbs, *Select Charters* (9th edn., Oxford: Clarendon Press, 1913), 328.

statutes, from the late Latin *statutum* a decree, decision or law. In this way we got the earliest statutes, from which we get the current term *statute law*. Shortly afterwards it became the custom to call a piece of such legislation by the name *Act* of Parliament from the medieval Latin *actus*.

In the previous chapter I described some basic concepts in statute law, mainly concerned with the importance of the enactment as the unit of inquiry. It was shown that the *legal* meaning of an enactment is what matters, since this is taken to correspond to the original legislator's intention. The legal practitioner, so far as necessary for his or her case, must try to work out precisely what the legal meaning of a relevant enactment is. As I said in Chapter 1, where there is an existing judicial decision on the point, it is usually assumed that the law is as indicated by that decision. This is not necessarily true however. Doubts may exist about the correctness of the decision. It may have been decided mistakenly (*per incuriam*), or without full argument. The profession may expect it to be overruled if it comes before a higher court. Even where the profession does not expect this, it may still be overruled.[8]

More on the legal meaning

Whenever it becomes necessary to decide what the legal meaning of a doubtful enactment is, whether by a practitioner advising a client, a court disposing of a case, or in any other way, all relevant interpretative factors must be found out and applied if the job is to be done properly. An existing precedent (unless by a court superior to the one in question) is only one of these factors, and the weight of argument may on balance fall the other way. The interpreter's duty is not accomplished if this investigative process is not fully carried out, especially where a grave issue, perhaps affecting the liberty of the subject, depends upon it.

A temporal element may enter the process. As indicated in Chapter 1, even where the legislature has not intervened the legal

---

[8] As happened when in *Bacchiocchi v Academic Agency Ltd* [1998] 2 All ER 241 the Court of Appeal surprisingly overruled *Department of the Environment v Royal Insurance plc* [1987] 1 EGLR 83: see F. A. R. Bennion, 'Last orders at *La Pentola*' 148 NLJ (1998) 953, 986.

meaning of an enactment may appear to be X at one moment in time and Y at a later date. If this is due to the overruling of an earlier decision, the later authority will on normal principles operate retrospectively. This is because a court is deemed to *declare* the law, not alter it.[9] It can present problems for those who in the meantime quite properly acted on the basis that meaning X was correct.

The importance of the enactment as the unit of inquiry is that it is usually the estimated operation of an individual enactment that gives rise to relevant issues of fact or law. The point in a particular case can usually be reduced to a small compass, though care and effort may be needed to define it. This is worth while, for it avoids unnecessary argument and consequent lengthening of court proceedings. It also avoids confusion. It may in the end avoid injustice. As Sir Edward Coke said about complaints that too many authorities were cited to the court: 'This were easily holpen, if the matter (which ever lieth in a narrow room) were first discerned, and then that everyone that argueth at the bar would either speak to the purpose or else be short.'[10] Perhaps they could do both.

An issue of fact may be whether or not a party committed a certain act. Before it can be known whether that really is a material issue, it must first be ascertained whether a fact of that kind is required by what in Chapter 1 I described, citing an example, as the factual outline laid down by the enactment. I now take another example.[11] This concerns the legal meaning of an enactment which, without departing from the official text, can be rendered as follows:

(1) Any person who in any public place
(2) uses insulting behaviour
(3) whereby a breach of the peace is likely to be occasioned
(4) shall be guilty of an offence.

Here clauses (1) to (3) constitute the factual outline, while clause (4) expresses the legal thrust. The case turned on clause (2). The

---

[9] But see pp. 23–5 above.
[10] Co. Rep: Preface to Part X.
[11] Based on the circumstances in *Parkin v Norman* [1983] QB 92.

defendant D argued that the legal meaning of this could be fully expressed as follows:

> (2) uses behaviour which is of an insulting nature, and which he intends to be insulting, and which in fact insults another person

However the prosecutor P argued for the following version:

> (2) uses behaviour which is of an insulting nature, whether or not he intends it to be insulting, and whether or not another person is in fact insulted

Before the issue of fact arose of whether or not D had committed a relevant act, that is one falling within the factual outline, it was necessary to settle an issue of law, namely which of these two versions was correct or in other words what was the exact nature of the factual outline (so far as relevant to the instant case). The court favoured P's version.

Opposing constructions

This leads us to another conclusion. In most cases where statutory interpretation is required, the argument boils down to which of two opposing constructions the court will prefer. Lord Wilberforce said of the Rent Act 1968 s. 18 'the section is certainly one which admits, almost invites, opposing constructions'.[12] This analysis applies to any enactment where there is real doubt as to its legal meaning.

It is sometimes said of the opposing constructions that one presents a wider and the other a narrower legal meaning. Here it is necessary to remember that we are speaking of a wider or narrower construction of the enactment forming the unit of inquiry, and not necessarily of the Act as a whole. For example the unit of inquiry may be a proviso cutting down the effect of a section. A wider construction of the proviso then amounts to a narrower construction of the section. Take for example a case which turned on the meaning of a phrase in the Income Tax Act 1952 s. 25(3) which concerned the legal thrust of that provision

---

[12] *Maunsell v Olins* [1974] 3 WLR 835 at 840.

where an item of the taxpayer's income had been understated and a penalty was due.[13] The argument concerned the amount of the penalty. Lord Reid said:[14]

I can now state what I understand to be the rival contentions as to the meaning of s. 25(3). The appellants [the Crown] contend that 'treble the tax which he ought to be charged under this Act' means treble his whole liability to income tax for the year in question . . .

The rival construction, put forward by the taxpayer, was treble the tax which he would have been charged for that item of income if it had been correctly declared.

In a few cases, there may be no sense in which one of two constructions is 'wider' or 'narrower' than the other. For example an enactment may determine whether a person who undoubtedly needs a licence for some activity needs one type of licence (say a category A licence) or another type (category B). If the legal meaning of the enactment is uncertain, the opposing constructions will respectively require a category A and a category B licence.

Although the rival advocates put forward two opposing constructions, the court may reject both and substitute its own. It may even hold that the case does not, after all, turn on a point of construction, which amounts to saying that there is no real doubt as to the legal meaning of the enactment. An enactment regulating taxis made it an offence for an unlicensed cab to display a notice which 'may suggest' that the vehicle is being used for hire.[15] The opposing constructions put forward in the magistrates' court for 'may suggest' were (a) 'is reasonably likely to suggest' and (b) 'might possibly suggest'. The court rejected both, holding that on the facts opposing constructions were not needed since there was no real doubt that the notice in question fell within the wording of the enactment.

One type of case where, although there may be real doubt over an enactment, opposing constructions do not arise is where the enactment confers a discretion or requires the exercise of judgment. Here more than one correct answer may be possible, though it is not right to say (as is sometimes done, even by judges) that the enactment is therefore ambiguous. Except for a judgment on a

[13] *Inland Revenue Commissioners v Hinchy* [1960] AC 748.
[14] p. 766.
[15] *Green v Turkington* [1975] Crim. LR 242.

question of fact, both these types of enactment (which must be carefully distinguished) require evaluation of a conceptual question of law, that is one related to a particular abstract concept such as justice or reasonableness, or what is 'proper'. The contrast between judgment and discretion is dealt with more fully below.[16]

Central function of the legal practitioner

The formulating and resolution of opposing constructions of an enactment, and the exercise of judgment or discretion, are aspects of the central function of a legal practitioner who is involved in a particular case. Whether the practitioner is advising a client, or acting as the client's advocate before the court, or acting as the court itself, this function can be stated as follows. In law the central function of the practitioner involved in a case is to go through the mental process of reaching a legal conclusion by applying the relevant law to the relevant facts. This is a continuous two-way operation. Without considering all the facts of the case (including possible facts currently unknown), the practitioner cannot determine which legal rules (whether laid down by statute or otherwise) are relevant. At the same time, without considering all the relevant law the practitioner cannot determine which facts are relevant.

When acting as an *adviser* in a case the practitioner conveys the legal conclusion reached to the client, along with the reasoning supporting it and a statement of the consequences. When later acting as an *advocate* in the case, the practitioner seeks to persuade the court of the correctness of the conclusion previously reached when giving advice. When acting as the *court*, the practitioner evaluates the arguments put forward on both sides and determines, as a matter of judgment, which is the correct legal conclusion.

I end this chapter with a basic question. What underlies any doubts there may be as to the legal meaning of an enactment? Before we even start trying to understand, let alone master, the technique of handling or managing statutes we need to ask what exactly the interpreter of a particular legislative text is supposed to

---

[16] See Chs. 13 and 14.

be doing. Is the interpreter's task to arrive at the literal or grammatical meaning of the text and apply that every time? Or is it, at least occasionally, to go further and apply a purposive but strained meaning? Or is the remit wider still, sometimes requiring the interpreter to depart altogether from the text, using it merely as a starting point for developing the underlying juridical idea? These may be called respectively literal construction, purposive construction, and developmental construction. Each has its place in the spectrum of law, as I explain in the next chapter.[17]

---

[17] For a summary of this chapter see pp. 203–4 below.

3

Grammatical and strained meanings

The interpreter's task

The fundamental question for the interpreter of common law legislation may be expressed as: what exactly is the nature of my task? The answer may seem obvious, but in truth it is not. On a daily basis, the practitioner needs to find out what the law has to say on a particular point, so that the client may be correctly advised or the case may be properly argued or decided. The more learned practitioners may already know the answer. The more sanguine may think they do; but find out they are mistaken. It is well to be cautious.

In our modern society, as I have said, people are constantly tinkering with the law believing they will improve on what their predecessors, wise or unwise, achieved. This easy belief often turns out to be a monstrous misjudgement. What was taught yesterday is today regarded as merely of historic interest, but that is to throw overboard hard–earned wisdom. Our society is always changing. It is difficult to keep up, but the lawyer must constantly try. The wise lawyer also bears in mind that even today past wisdom may have its uses.

The historic purpose of statutory interpretation is to arrive at the presumed intention of the legislator in promulgating the enactment in question. This may be taken to be the same as the presumed intention of the person who composed the enactment, the legislative drafter. We need now to ask this question: what basic approach did the drafter intend the statute user to adopt? There are many possibilities, but for the moment we can narrow the choice down to three. Did the drafter intend the user always to adopt a literal interpretation, or where necessary depart from this and use a purposive but strained interpretation, or even on occasion arrive at a developmental interpretation departing altogether from the text and using it merely as a starting point? I will now discuss these three methods in turn.

The literal meaning

The starting point in statutory interpretation must always be the ordinary linguistic meaning of the words used, that is their grammatical signification apart from legal considerations. The grammatical meaning of a common law enactment is the meaning it bears when, as a piece of English prose, it is construed according to the rules and usages of grammar, syntax, and punctuation, and the purely linguistic canons of construction.

It is important to remember that the grammatical meaning includes both what is expressed and what is implied. In ordinary speech or writing it is a recognized communicative method to say expressly no more than is required to make the outline clear, obvious detail remaining unexpressed. The legislative drafter, always striving for brevity, feels it necessary to adopt the same method. 'It is sometimes said that a draftsman should leave nothing to implication. This is nonsense. No communication can operate without leaving part of the total communication to implication'.[1] It has even been said, as in the following important dictum concerning the first Interpretation Act, that what is expressed *includes* what is implied:

It is not easy to conceive that the framer of [Lord Brougham's Act (1850) 13 & 14 Vict. c. 21], when he used the word 'expressly', meant to suggest that what is necessarily or properly implied by language is not expressed by such language. It is quite clear that whatever the language used necessarily and naturally implies is expressed thereby.[2]

The grammatical meaning may be clear, ambiguous or obscure. It is clear when, apart from legal considerations, there is no real doubt about it. It is ambiguous when grammatically capable of more than one meaning.[3] It is obscure when the language is disorganized, garbled or otherwise semantically confused or opaque. An enactment may be clear, ambiguous, or obscure in relation to

[1] Reed Dickerson, *Materials on Legal Drafting*, (2nd edn., Boston: Brown, 1986).
[2] *Chorlton v Lings* (1868) LR 4 CP 374, *per* Willes J. at 387.
[3] 'An ambiguity is a word or phrase fairly open to diverse meanings, the classic example being "twelve o'clock" which, save for users of the 24-hour clock, could equally mean midday or midnight': *Imperial Chemical Industries plc v Colmer (Inspector of Taxes)* [2000] 1 All ER 129, *per* Lord Nolan at 133.

all possible facts (absolute clarity, ambiguity, or obscurity), or certain facts only (relative clarity, ambiguity or obscurity). Where in either case the text is obscure, the reader first needs to determine what was the intended grammatical meaning. The version of the text adjusted to reflect that meaning, which may be called the corrected version, is thereafter to be dealt with as if it had been the actual wording.

The literal meaning of an enactment in relation to particular facts is arrived at as follows. Where the grammatical meaning is clear, that is the literal meaning. Where the enactment is ambiguous, any of the possible grammatical meanings may be called the literal meaning. Where the enactment is obscure the meaning of the corrected version, or, where the corrected version is ambiguous, any of its possible meanings, is the literal meaning.

To give an enactment a literal construction is to apply the literal meaning or, in the case of ambiguity, one of the literal meanings. The so-called literal rule of construction requires that an enactment should always be accorded its literal meaning. This supposed rule is based on judicial dicta such as the following: 'Where the language of an Act is clear and explicit, we must give effect to it, whatever may be the consequences . . .'[4] 'If the words of an Act are clear, you must follow them, even though they lead to a manifest absurdity. The court has nothing to do with the question whether the legislature has committed an absurdity.'[5] 'It seems to this court that where the literal reading of a statute . . . produces an intelligible result, clearly there is no ground for reading in words or changing words according to what may be the supposed intention of Parliament.'[6]

In the common law world, dicta like these are not followed today. The so-called literal rule of interpretation nowadays dissolves into a rule that the text is the primary indication of legislative intention, but that the enactment is to be given a literal meaning only where this is not outweighed by more powerful interpretative factors.

[4] *Warburton v Loveland* (1832) 2 D & Cl (HL) 480, *per* Tindal CJ at 489.
[5] *R v City of London Court Judge* [1892] 1 QB 273, *per* Lord Esher MR at 290.
[6] *R v Oakes* [1959] 2 QB 350, *per* Lord Parker CJ at 354.

Purposive construction

One of these more powerful factors arises where to apply a literal construction would not further the purpose of the legislator in framing the enactment. The purpose of Parliament in passing an Act, other than a purely declaratory, codifying or consolidation Act, is to provide a new remedy to serve as a cure for the mischief with which the Act deals. The purpose of a particular enactment contained in the Act is to be arrived at accordingly.

Parliament is presumed to intend that in construing an Act the court, by advancing the remedy which is indicated by the words of the Act for the mischief being dealt with, including the implications arising from those words, should aim to further every aspect of the legislative purpose. A construction which promotes the remedy Parliament has provided to cure a particular mischief is now known as a purposive construction. Where a literal construction promotes this remedy there is no point in also calling it a purposive construction, except when choosing between possible grammatical constructions of an ambiguous passage. Accordingly the term purposive construction is usually confined to cases where the literal meaning is departed from: in other words a strained construction.

A strained meaning is any meaning other than the literal meaning. 'When the purpose of an enactment is clear, it is often legitimate, because it is necessary, to put a strained interpretation upon some words which have been inadvertently used'.[7] The courts have ceased to follow judges, however eminent, who once refused to accept the legitimacy of strained construction. For example Lord Reid said:

It is a cardinal principle applicable to all kinds of statutes that you may not for any reason attach to a statutory provision a meaning which the words of that provision cannot reasonably bear. If they are capable of more than one meaning, then you can choose between those meanings, but beyond that you must not go.[8]

This confident dictum would not be followed today. There are

---

[7] *Sutherland Publishing Co v Caxton Publishing Co* [1938] Ch 174, *per* Mac-Kinnon LJ at 201.
[8] *Jones v DPP* [1962] AC 635 at 668.

very many modern cases where courts have attached meanings to enactments which by no stretch of the imagination could be called meanings the words are grammatically capable of bearing. Here is just one example, where the House of Lords approved a purposive-and-strained construction of the phrase 'information contained in a publication' in the Contempt of Court Act 1981 s. 10 (which cuts down the common law powers of the courts to deal with contempts in relation to a reporter's sources of information). The House widened the cited phrase to include information communicated and received for the purposes of a publication which had not yet come into existence and might never do so. 'This seems to be a necessary interpretation; otherwise a defendant such as Mr Goodwin [a journalist whose information had not been published] would be worse off than if he had already published . . .'[9] The truth is that sometimes the arguments against a literal construction are so compelling that even though the words are not, within the rules of language, capable of another meaning they must be given one.

Under the common law system strained construction is not to be carried too far however. Viscount Simonds, referring to the suggestion by Denning LJ in the court below that judges should 'fill up the gaps and make sense of the enactment', said in words which have become celebrated that this 'appears to me to be a naked usurpation of the legislative function under a thin disguise of interpretation'.[10] While not an effective defence of the so-called literal rule, this dictum was justified in relation to Denning's expansive version of purposive construction. This followed the extreme European model, rather than the more limited version which applies in the common law world. As we shall see, the latter method brings in every conceivable interpretative criterion that is relevant while remaining as far as possible loyal to the language chosen by the legislator. It is also loyal to earlier judicial decisions, applying the doctrine of precedent by which the common law has developed but which European jurists tend to reject.

---

[9] *X Ltd v Morgan-Grampian (Publishers) Ltd* [1991] AC 1, *per* Lord Lowry at 55. For further examples of strained construction see *Bennion Code*, s. 158.
[10] *Magor & St Mellons RDC v Newport Corpn* [1952] AC 189 at 190.

The basic approach

I return to our opening question, namely what basic approach did the drafter intend the statute user to adopt? I would answer as follows. Nowadays, a legislative drafter in the common law world never intends the literal rule to be adopted. In the case of an enactment unaffected by European considerations, or delegated legislation made thereunder, the drafter now intends the interpreter to apply the Global or common law method and where necessary adopt a purposive-and-strained construction. In the case of legislation where the European approach applies, the drafter intends the interpreter when necessary to adopt a Developmental construction using the text merely as a starting point.[11]

---

[11] Developmental construction is further discussed in Ch. 15. For a summary of this chapter see pp. 204–5 below.

4

Consequential and rectifying constructions

In the last chapter we saw that under the common law or Global system the so-called literal rule of construction of legislative texts dissolves nowadays into a somewhat different rule. The text is indeed the primary indication of legislative intention, but the literal meaning is to be applied only when not outweighed by more powerful factors. There are occasions when, as Baron Parke said, the language of the legislature must be modified to avoid inconsistency with its intentions.[1]

As we saw in the previous chapter, not to apply the literal meaning is to give the enactment a strained construction. Four main reasons may justify (and in some cases positively require) stretching the literal meaning in this way: (1) where the consequences of applying a literal construction are so obviously undesirable that Parliament cannot really have intended them, (2) an error in the text which falsifies Parliament's intention, (3) a repugnance between the words of the enactment and those of some other relevant enactment, and (4) changes in external circumstances since the enactment was originally drafted. In this chapter we look at the first two of these.

Consequential construction

We should all have regard, if possible *before* acting, to the likely consequences of what we propose to do. The consequential construction rule of interpretation echoes this truism. It is presumed to be the legislator's intention that when considering, in relation to the facts of the instant case, which of the possible readings of the enactment corresponds to its legal meaning, the court should assess the likely consequences of adopting each construction. This means

[1] *Miller v Salomons* (1852) 7 Ex 475 at 553.

the consequences not only for the parties in the instant case but also (if similar facts should arise in future) for the law generally under the doctrine of precedent.

Mustill J. said that a statute 'cannot be interpreted according to its literal meaning without testing that meaning against the practical outcome of giving effect to it'.² If on balance the consequences of a particular construction are more likely to be adverse than beneficent, this tells against that construction. The prima facie rule is that words have their ordinary meaning. 'But that is subject to the qualification that if, giving words their ordinary meaning, we are faced with extraordinary results which cannot have been intended by Parliament, we then have to move on to a second stage in which we re-examine the words . . .'³

Lord Radcliffe cynically remarked that 'it sometimes helps to assess the merits of a decision if one starts by noticing its results and only after doing that allots to it the legal principles upon which it is said to depend'.⁴ This echoes the extraordinary remark by the American Judge Posner that a judge 'rarely starts his inquiry with the words of the statute, and often if the truth be told, he does not look at the words at all'.⁵ If that were true the American people would be suffering anarchy rather than enjoying democracy, and the common law world must reject it.

Some terms have both an ordinary and a technical meaning, for example the word 'assigned'. The Housing Act 1985 s. 91(1) says a secure periodic tenancy 'is not capable of being assigned'. In one case two women were joint tenants. One moved out of the property, executing a deed of release of her interest. It was held by the House of Lords that, although in law 'assigned' has a narrow technical meaning excluding a release, as a matter of ordinary usage it is wide enough to include a release; and that to avoid an artificial result, the wide meaning must be given here.⁶

Consequences should be considered not only where a strained construction may be necessary but also where the grammatical

² *R. v Committee of Lloyd's, ex p Moran* (1983) *Times* 24 June.
³ *Re British Concrete Pipe Association* [1983] 1 All ER 203, *per* Donaldson MR at 205.
⁴ *ICI Ltd v Shatwell* [1965] AC 656 at 675.
⁵ Richard A. Posner, 'Statutory Interpretation—in the Classroom and in the Courtroom' (1983) 50 University of Chicago Law Review 800, 807–8.
⁶ *Burton v Camden London Borough Council* [2000] 1 All ER 943 (Lord Millett dissenting).

meaning is ambiguous. As Lord Reid said: 'It is always proper to construe ambiguous words in the light of the reasonableness of the consequences.'[7] Where the literal application of an enactment would yield adverse results this indicates that the court should *curtail* its application, a procedure known as strict construction. Where the application yields a beneficent result the opposite applies and the court may *widen* its application, a reading known as liberal construction. The consequences of a particular construction are 'adverse' if the court views them with disquiet, though a consequence clearly intended by Parliament is not to be treated as adverse just because the judge personally dislikes it. Any other consequences (whether neutral or positively advantageous) may be called 'beneficent'. The prospect of a strongly adverse consequence in itself raises doubt as to the legal meaning of the enactment.

The consequential test covers a wide field. A result is 'adverse' if it frustrates the purpose of the Act, or works injustice, or is contrary to public policy, or is productive of inconvenience or hardship. There are many other possibilities. If a consequence is beneficent, the court will wish it to transpire. So Peter Gibson J. said, in a case concerning the Building Societies Act 1962 s. 1(1), that he would be loath to find that 'the very sensible proposals' made by the scheme which was before the court lay outside that enactment.[8]

Rectifying construction

The court is there to put things right where it can, in other words to do justice. When it comes to statutes, it is presumed that the legislator intends the court to apply a construction, called a rectifying construction, which puts right any error in the drafting of the enactment where this is required in order to give effect to the legislator's purpose.

Drafting errors frequently occur.[9] So we find for example Nourse J. saying of the Law of Property Act 1925 s. 3(3) that the

---

[7] *Gartside v IRC* [1968] AC 553 at 612.

[8] *Nationwide Building Society v Registry of Friendly Societies* [1983] 1 WLR 1226 at 1230–1.

[9] For an account of the various types of drafting error see F. A. R. Bennion, *Statute Law* (3rd edn., London: Longman, 1990) Ch. 19.

draftsman either overlooked or misunderstood the fact that the opening words were rendered inappropriate by changes made in the 1925 property legislation itself.[10] Such human mistakes must not be allowed to frustrate Parliament's will. Occasionally Parliament itself steps in to correct them. It has even tried to provide statutory means to that end.[11] More usually, Parliament leaves rectification in the hands of the judiciary.

Sometimes it is obvious what change of wording is needed. Thus where an enactment authorized a defendant to apply to have the action transferred to 'the County Court in which he resides or carries on business' the court clearly had to read in the words 'for the area' after 'Court'. In other cases the error may not be so easy to identify. A famous example of an incomplete text is the Statute of Frauds Amendment Act 1828 (Lord Tenterden's Act) s. 6. This says 'no action shall be brought whereby to charge any person upon or by reason of any representation or assurance made or given concerning or relating to the [character etc.] of any other person, *to the intent or purpose that such other person may obtain credit, money, or goods upon,* unless such representation or assurance is made in writing [and signed].'[12] Clearly some words are missing at the end of the italicized passage, but in the leading case three judges each took a different view on what the missing words were.[13]

Instead of intended words being omitted, unintended words may be included. In a case on the Lands Clauses Consolidation Act 1845 s. 9 Brett J. said:

The word 'such' . . . is insensible. It is a canon of construction that, if it be possible, effect must be given to every word of an Act of Parliament . . . but that if there be a word or phrase therein to which no sensible meaning can be given, it must be eliminated. It seems to me therefore that the word 'such' must be eliminated . . .[14]

A further possibility is that the words are confused. In Britain the

---

[10] *In re Rowhook Mission Hall, Horsham; Channing-Pearce v Morris* [1985] Ch 62 at 80.

[11] See for example the Acts of Parliament (Mistaken References) Act 1830 (repealed) and the unsuccessful attempt made by the Government in 1977 to procure the passing of the Acts of Parliament (Correction of Mistakes) Bill.

[12] Emphasis added.

[13] *Lyde v Barnard* (1836) 1 M & W 101.

[14] *Stone v Yeovil Corpn.* (1876) 1 CPD 691 at 701.

Queen's printer will correct minor typographical errors, as with the Landlord and Tenant (Rent Control) Act 1949 s. 11(5). This referred to s. 6, instead of s. 7, of the Furnished Houses (Rent Control) Act 1946. The error was corrected in subsequent published copies of the 1949 Act. Sometimes an error is made in transcribing an enactment for inclusion in a consolidation Act. Here there is an inference that the original wording should be followed. Section 125(2) of the Law of Property Act 1922 empowered trustees to appoint agents for 'executing and perfecting assurances of property'. In the Trustee Act 1925 s. 23(2) this appears as *insurances* of property, but the intended meaning is obvious and should be given effect.

Two errors appear in the repeal Schedule to the Interpretation Act 1978 (a consolidation Act).[15] The short title of the National Health Service Reorganisation Act 1973 is given as 'The National Health Reorganisation Act 1973', while a reference is made to Sch. 5 to the Medical Act 1978 instead of Sch. 6. In neither case is there any doubt as to what was meant, and the court would read the references in their intended form.

Rectification of a more substantial kind may be required where the error is latent rather than apparent. The drafter may have misconceived the legislative project, or based the text on a mistake of fact. Alternatively an error may have been made as to the applicable law. If the drafter misconceives the factual nature of the legislative project the literal wording is likely to be ineffective. The court may be able to remedy this by applying a strained construction which accommodates the true facts without causing injustice or other disadvantage. Here is an example.

Section 8(1) of the Food and Drugs Act 1955 said that a person who sold 'any *food* intended for, but unfit for, human consumption' committed an offence.[16] This misconceived the legislative project, which was to safeguard the public from being supplied (as food) with any deleterious substance whether truly food or not. In one case brought under this provision children asked for lemonade in a shop and were given corrosive caustic soda, which they drank.[17] The defence argued that caustic soda is not food. It was held that to rectify the misconceived project, a strained construction

---

[15] Schedule 3.   [16] Emphasis added.
[17] Section 151(1) of the 1955 Act defined 'food' as including drink.

was necessary. The expression 'sells any food' must be taken to
mean 'sells anything (whether a food or not) *as* a food'.[18]

Where the literal meaning of the enactment goes narrower than
the object of the legislator (*casus omissus*), the court may need to
apply a rectifying construction widening that meaning. Nowadays
it is regarded as not in accordance with legal policy to allow a
drafter's ineptitude to prevent justice being done and the legislator's intention implemented. It was not always so, as the following
example shows.

Section 21 of the Matrimonial Causes Act 1857 empowered a
magistrate to make an order protecting the property of a deserted
wife. It allowed the husband to apply for the discharge of such an
order to 'the magistrate . . . by whom the order was made'. When
a Mr Sharpe sought to exercise this right '[h]e discovered that the
magistrate who had made the order was dead; and the question
what was now his proper course of action came before a bench
composed of Cockburn CJ, Blackburn and Shee JJ, who decided
unanimously that this was a *casus omissus*, and that it was not
competent for the husband to apply to some other metropolitan
magistrate who might present the advantage of being alive'.[19]
Here we have the classic conflict, between an unimaginative
drafter and an unyielding court. Sandwiched between, incapable
of helping himself, the innocent litigant is crushed. It is safe to say
it would not be allowed to happen today.

It is correlative to the principle that law should be coherent and
self-consistent that, where two different statutory systems do not
occupy all the required space, the court should be ready to fill the
gap. For example it was held that since magistrates were not
empowered to issue a search warrant to deal with the proceeds of
an alleged crime held in a bank account, the High Court should
fill the gap by using the power to preserve the subject matter of a
cause of action which was conferred by RSC Ord. 29 r. 2. Forbes
J. said that 'this court should be ready to fill that particular gap'.[20]
Again, where a literal construction of the phrase 'a matter relating
to trial on indictment' in the Supreme Court Act 1981 s. 29(3)
(which withdraws such a matter from the jurisdiction of higher

---

[18] *Meah v Roberts* [1977] Crim. LR 678.
[19] Amos, 'The Interpretation of Statutes' (1934) 5 CLJ 163. Although Amos did
not give the case reference, it was presumably *Ex p Sharpe* (1864) 5 B & S 322.
[20] *West Mercia Constabulary v Wagener* [1982] 1 WLR 127 at 131.

courts) would have had the result that no appeal lay from certain Crown Court decisions, the House of Lords avoided this by applying a narrow meaning to the phrase.[21]

RSC Ord. 29 r. 11(2)(a) as amended allowed an interim payment of damages in respect of a person 'whose liability will be met by . . . an insurer concerned under the Motor Insurers' Bureau agreement'. The drafting of this was defective in two ways: (1) the name of the agreement was actually the Uninsured Drivers' Agreement, and (2) the words should also have covered the case where the liability would be met by the Motor Insurers' Bureau itself, which was not an 'insurer'. It was held that this was a *casus omissus* and the court should rectify the wording.[22] Millett LJ said that 'if possible' the rule should be given the correct construction. It was only 'possible' to do this by giving a strained construction. This decision is of interest in relation to the Human Rights Act 1998 s. 3(1), which states that primary and subordinate legislation must be construed in a way which is compatible with the Convention rights '[s]o far as it is possible to do so'.[23]

Under the common law or Global system, gap-filling by the courts must not be carried too far. In the previous chapter I described how in 1952 Viscount Simonds rejected the suggestion by Denning LJ that judges should 'fill up the gaps and make sense of the enactment'. Denning returned to the attack thirty years later, when he said that the rebuff by Viscount Simonds no longer hurt and he believed the court must fill in the gaps where an updating construction was needed.[24] It has been suggested that a distinction should be drawn between 'interpretative gap-filling', which is legitimate, and 'substantive gap-filling', which is not.[25] This is probably as near as one can get to defining the boundary of legitimate judicial activism in the common law world.

Just as a case which is within the object of an enactment but outside its wording is described as a *casus omissus*, so it is appropriate to describe the reverse as a *casus male inclusus*.[26] The literal

---

[21] *Re Smalley* [1985] AC 622.   [22] *Sharp v Pereria* [1998] 4 All ER 145.
[23] This is discussed in Ch. 15 below.
[24] *R. v Barnet London Borough Council, ex p Nilish Shah* [1981]. Updating construction is described in the following chapter.
[25] Bankowski and N. MacCormick in ch. 10 of N. MacCormick and R. S. Summers, *Interpreting Statutes: A Comparative Study* (Aldershot: Dartmouth, 1991).
[26] This term was suggested by the late Professor Glanville Williams.

meaning of some enactments takes their coercive force wider than
is necessary to remedy the mischief aimed at. As Harman LJ
remarked of the Leasehold Property (Repairs) Act 1938: 'Like
most remedial Acts of that sort, it catches the virtuous in the net
which is laid for the sinner.'[27] Here is another example. Section 32
of the Sexual Offences Act 1956 makes it an offence for a man
'persistently to solicit or importune in a public place for immoral
purposes'. The courts have held that s. 32 must be treated as
limited to immoral purposes of a sexual nature.[28] At one time it
was even thought that it applied only to homosexual acts.[29]

Some form of rectification is essential where the court is faced
with conflicting texts. 'In such a situation . . . the court is affirma-
tively required to give the enactment a "rectifying construction"
. . .'[30] If the texts are within the same Act, the conflict is generally
to be resolved by construing the Act as a whole. If the texts are in
different Acts, the later Act usually prevails. I will consider
conflicting texts in more detail in the next chapter.[31]

---

[27] *Sidnell v Wilson* [1966] 2 QB 67 at 79.
[28] *R. v Kirkup* [1993] 1 WLR 774.
[29] *Crook v Edmondson* [1966] 2 QB 81.
[30] *R. v Moore* [1995] 4 All ER 843, *per* Sedley J. at 850.
[31] For a summary of this chapter see pp. 205–6 below.

5

Contradictory enactments and updating construction

A century ago, in a town in south-west Ireland, a little girl was sent by her grandmother to buy boiled crabs for supper. When the little girl returned home her grandmother found the crabs were bad, and the matter came to trial at the Cork Assizes. In the witness box the little girl turned to the judge and said of the fish-monger 'My Lord, I asked him to pick out the crabs, so as to show that I relied upon the seller's skill and judgment.' The judge: 'And where did you learn the fourteenth section of the Sale of Goods Act, my good girl?' The child became confused, and could not answer. Upon being told that she attended the nearby Black Rock convent, the judge said: 'Such is the progress of modern education that children are taught by heart sections of Acts of Parliament in convents and by Holy Nuns!'[1] I retell this old story as a reminder to the faithful of what we are about. Up and down the land, statutes are not some out of the way dusty nuisance. They are part of everyday life, and we had better understand them if we can.

In Chapter 4 I explained the nature of strained construction and suggested that under the common law or Global system of statutory interpretation there are four main reasons requiring this. I went on to discuss the first two, namely (1) where the consequences of a literal construction are so undesirable that Parliament cannot have intended them, and (2) where an error in the text would, if taken literally, falsify Parliament's intention. Now we turn to the other two reasons for departing from the literal meaning.

Repugnant texts

First comes the case where there is a repugnance between the words of the enactment and those of another relevant enactment,

---

[1] See A. M. Sullivan QC, *The Last Serjeant* (London: Macdonald, 1952), 117.

whether in the same Act or elsewhere. Attempting to obey both runs counter to the rules of logic. When two relevant texts contradict each other, both cannot be given a literal application. To do so would contravene the logical principle of contradiction or *principium contradictionis*. This was stated by Aristotle in the form that two contradictory statements cannot both at the same time be true. Thus one cannot without defect of reasoning advance both a universal affirmative proposition ('all S is P') and a particular negative proposition ('some S is not P'). Equally one cannot legitimately advance both a universal negative proposition ('no S is P') and a particular affirmative proposition ('some S is P').

A common application of the logical principle of contradiction is in relation to contradictory enactments within the same Act. In itself enactment A may be clear and unambiguous. So may enactment B, located elsewhere in the Act. But if they contradict each other they cannot both be applied literally. A undoes B, or B undoes A. The court must do the best it can to reconcile them, but this can be achieved only be giving one or both a strained construction. Judges often complain of such inconsistency within an Act. Lord Hewart CJ said of the Shops (Sunday Trading Restrictions) Act 1936 Schs. 1 and 2: 'Sir William Jowitt, appearing on one side in this case, frankly admitted that the provisions of these two Schedules, taken together, and compared and contrasted with each other, were, to his mind, unintelligible.'[2]

A solution may be found by applying the principle that an Act is to be read as a whole. This means that an enactment within it is not treated as standing alone but is to be interpreted in its context as part of the Act. As the American Justice Holmes said, 'you let whatever galvanic current may come from the rest of the instrument run through the particular sentence'. Where, on the facts of the instant case, the literal meaning of the enactment under inquiry is inconsistent with the literal meaning of one or more other enactments in the same Act, the *combined meaning* of the enactments is to be arrived at. A notional amalgamated text must be produced before the interpreter can advance towards the legal meaning. The way this is done is similar to the producing of a 'corrected version' of the text in a case of semantic obscurity.[3]

[2] *London County Council v Lees* [1939] 1 All ER 191 at 196.
[3] See Ch. 3.

The essence of 'construction as a whole' is that it enables the interpreter to perceive that a proposition in one part of the Act is by implication modified by another provision elsewhere in the Act. Coke referred to this as construction *ex visceribus actus* (from the guts of the Act).[4] It requires that, unless the contrary intention appears, three principles should be applied: (1) every word in the Act should be given a meaning, (2) the same word should be given the same meaning, and (3) different words should be given different meanings. So in one case the Court of Appeal rejected the appellant's argument that the Perjury Act 1916 s. 1(1) applies only where the witness believes his false statement to be material, because this reading would render s. 1(6) of the Act meaningless.[5]

Lord Herschell LC said that where there is a conflict between two sections in the same Act: 'You have to try and reconcile them as best you may. If you cannot, you have to determine which is the leading provision and which the subordinate provision, and which must give way to the other.'[6] Failing any other way of reconciliation the court may under an old rule, that in *Wood v Riley*, adopt the principle that the enactment nearest the end of the Act prevails.[7] This rule was supported by the practice, which in the case of private and personal Acts still prevails, of placing saving clauses at the end of a parliamentary Bill with the intent that they should override anything inconsistent in the earlier part. Nicholls LJ said in 1990 that this useful rule was obsolete: 'Such a mechanical approach . . . is altogether out of step with the modern, purposive, approach to the interpretation of statutes and documents.'[8] This confident dictum overlooks the possibility that there may be no means of deciding between conflicting provisions on purposive grounds, when a rule of thumb is obviously needed.

Where the literal meaning of a general enactment covers a situation for which specific provision is made elsewhere in the Act, it is presumed that it was intended to be dealt with by the specific provision. This is expressed in the maxim *generalibus specialia derogant* (special provisions override general ones). Acts often

---

[4] 1 Co Inst 381 1b.   [5] *R. v Millward* [1985] QB 519.

[6] *Institute of Patent Agents v Lockwood* [1894] AC 347 at 360.

[7] See *Wood v Riley* (1867) LR 3 CP 26 at 27 ('the known rule is that the last must prevail').

[8] *Re Marr and another (bankrupts)* [1990] 2 All ER 880 at 886.

contain general provisions which, when read literally, cover a situation for which specific provision is made elsewhere in the Act. The more detailed a provision is, the more likely it is to have been tailored to fit the precise circumstances of a case falling within it, so that it should prevail over a general provision. This maxim gives a useful rule of thumb for dealing with such a situation.

Under the so-called doctrine of implied repeal, if a later Act makes contrary provision to an earlier, Parliament (though it has not expressly said so) is taken to intend the earlier to be repealed. I say 'so-called' because this is not really a separate doctrine. It is an application of the general linguistic principle that the meaning of a passage is to be gathered from implications as well as express words.[9]

In an early case it was held that a statute creating a capital offence was impliedly repealed by a later Act imposing a penalty of £20 for the like offence.[10] However in the absence of outright contradiction the courts tend to presume that Parliament does not intend an implied repeal. This presumption is stronger where modern precision drafting is used. It is also stronger the more weighty the enactment. Lord Wilberforce said extra-judicially that he was reluctant to hold that an Act of such constitutional significance as the Union with Ireland Act 1800 was subject to implied repeal.[11]

A similar principle applies to amendment. Where the provisions of a later Act are repugnant to those of an earlier, the later by implication amends the earlier so far as is necessary to remove the inconsistency. By later enacting a contradictory provision Parliament (though it has not said so) is taken to intend an amendment of the earlier provision. Again this is a logical necessity. As stated above, two inconsistent texts cannot both be held valid without contravening the principle of contradiction.

Updating construction

The last of the four reasons for departing from the literal meaning and adopting a strained construction concerns what is known as

[9] See p. 40 above.
[10] *R. v Davis* (1783) 1 Leach 271.
[11] *Report by the Committee of Privileges on the Petition of the Irish Peers* (1966) HL Session Papers (53).

updating construction. Here Acts can be divided into two categories. There is the usual case of the Act that is intended to
develop in meaning with developing circumstances (called an
ongoing Act) and the comparatively rare case of the Act that is
intended to be of unchanging effect (a fixed-time Act). It is
presumed that Parliament intends the court to apply to an ongoing
Act a construction that continuously updates its wording to allow
for changes since the Act was initially framed. While it remains
law, it is to be treated as *always speaking*. This means that in its
application on any date, the language of the Act, though necessarily embedded in its own time, is nevertheless to be construed in
accordance with the need to treat it as current law.[12] Relevant
changes since the original Act was passed may occur in social
conditions or values, use of words, surrounding law, judicial
outlook, economic conditions, technology, medical science, or
other factors.

I will briefly deal first with the fixed-time Act, to get it out of
the way. A fixed-time Act has a once and for all effect. Contrary
to the usual rule, it is intended by Parliament to be applied in the
same way whatever changes might occur after its passing. It is to
such an Act, and not to an ongoing Act, that the oft-quoted words
of Lord Esher apply: 'the Act must be construed as if one were
interpreting it the day after it was passed.'[13] Thus it was held that
the statute 39 Geo. 3 (1798) s. 25, which exempted 'any hospital'
from land tax, was intended by Parliament to apply only to hospi-
tals which were in existence at the time the Act was passed.[14]

A common type of fixed-time Act is that which has the nature
of a contract, an obvious instance being a private Act. The courts
treat this as a contract between its promoters (or that portion of
the public directly interested in it) and the enacting Parliament.[15]
This is illustrated by a story which is perhaps apocryphal. When
divorce was possible only by Act of Parliament an unhappily
married town clerk was promoting a local waterworks Bill. In
clause 64, mingled with technical provisions about filter beds and
stopcocks, appeared the phrase 'and the marriage of the Town

---

[12] *Fitzpatrick v Sterling Housing Association Ltd* [1999] 4 All ER 705 at 711, 726.
[13] *The Longford* (1889) 14 PD 34, at 36.
[14] *Lord Colchester v Kewney* (1866) LR 1 Ex. 368 at 380.
[15] *Milnes v Mayor etc. of Huddersfield* (1886) 11 App. Cas. 511.

Clerk of ――― is hereby dissolved'. Nobody noticed it while the Bill was going through Parliament, but when Royal Assent was given the town clerk duly found himself divorced. Since this was evidently a fixed-time enactment, it did not apply on the entry into office of any future town clerk of the named town.[16]

It is presumed that Parliament intends the court to apply to an ongoing Act a construction that continuously updates its wording to allow for changes since the Act was initially framed. As Lord Woolf MR said of the National Assistance Act 1948: 'That Act had replaced 350 years of the Poor Law and is a prime example of an Act which is "always speaking". Accordingly it should be construed by continuously updating its wording to allow for changes since the Act was written.'[17]

Different types of change can call for an updating construction. While the enactment may continue in force, the mischief at which it was originally directed may change, or even (if Parliament's remedy works) disappear altogether. Next, there may be changes in relevant law. Later amendments of the law may mean that the legal remedy provided by the Act to deal with the original mischief has become inadequate or inappropriate if construed literally. The court must make allowances for the fact that the surrounding legal conditions have changed. It also follows that legal references in an enactment must be updated to allow for subsequent alterations. This has been recognized from very early times. Thus 'lords' in Magna Carta was taken to include later created ranks of nobility.[18] A reference to 'tax' in an old pre-income tax enactment was held to include income tax.[19]

Changes in social conditions may affect construction. Section 17 of the London Hackney Carriage Act 1853 makes it an offence for a cab driver to 'demand or take more than the proper fare'. The literal meaning clearly prohibits taking a tip, but the tipping of cab drivers became an accepted social custom. So it was held in 1981 that tipping did not contravene s. 17.[20]

---

[16] The story is told in Sir Robert Megarry, *Miscellany-at-Law* (London: Stevens, 1955), 345.

[17] *R. v Hammersmith and Fulham London Borough Council, ex p M* (1997) *Times* 19 February. This language was repeated by Sir Richard Scott V-C in *Victor Chandler International v Customs and Excise Commissioners and others* [2000] 2 All ER 315 at 322.   [18] 2 Co Inst 35.

[19] *Gissing v Liverpool Corpn.* [1935] Ch 1.

[20] *Bassam v Green* [1981] Crim. LR 626.

Here is another example. Under the enactments dealing with the legal process known as distress it was formerly assumed that if a debtor's outer door was found locked this indicated that the key had been deliberately turned so as to exclude the sheriff's officer or bailiff. Therefore the enactments meant that official could lawfully break down the door to gain entry. Social habits are different today, so by updating construction these enactments must be reinterpreted. 'It is not [nowadays] wrong for a tenant, without more, to lock the door. If the tenant does not know of the bailiff's intended re-entry at any particular time then to leave his door locked and to absent himself about his normal affairs is his right.'[21]

Precedents on the meaning of 'family' are likely to go on being departed from as public perceptions of sexual and familial morality, especially regarding homosexuality, continue to change. In 1999 Lord Clyde said:

It can be seen from the decided cases that the concept of 'family' developed over time to extend to unmarried heterosexual couples ... The judges in *Helby v Rafferty* [1979] 1 WLR 13 had difficulty in accepting that a word which had been repeated throughout the successive Rent Acts could change its meaning from time to time. But as a matter of construction I see no grounds for treating the provisions with which we are concerned as being in the relatively rare category of cases where Parliament intended the language to be fixed at the time when the original Act was passed ... The general presumption is that an updating construction is to be applied (see Bennion *Statutory Interpretation* (3rd edn., 1997) p. 686).[22]

Developments in technology may call for changed interpretation.[23] So too may changes in the meaning of words. Where an

---

[21] *Khazanchi v Faircharm Investments Ltd* [1998] 2 All ER 901, *per* Morritt LJ at 912–13.

[22] *Fitzpatrick v Sterling Housing Association Ltd* [1999] 4 All ER 705 at 725–6. In that case the House of Lords decided by a majority that 'family' included a homosexual couple.

[23] See for example *Gambart v Ball* (1863) 32 LJCP 166 (photography held to be within the Engraving Copyright Act 1734); *A.-G. v Edison Telephone Co. of London Ltd.* (1880) 6 QBD 244 (telephone held to be a 'telegraph'); *Chappell & Co Ltd v Associated Radio Co. of Australia Ltd* [1925] VLR 350 (radio broadcast a 'performance in public' under pre-broadcasting Copyright Act); *Grant v Southwestern & County Properties Ltd.* [1975] Ch. 185 (tape recording of telephone conversation a 'document'); *Hawkins v Harold A. Russett Ltd* [1983] 1 All ER 215 (clip-on container held to be part of a lorry for purpose of overhang restrictions);

expression used in an Act has changed its original meaning, the Act may have to be construed as if there were substituted for it a term with a corresponding modern meaning.[24] The old meaning of the word 'engine' was very wide. It derives from the Latin *ingenium*, and formerly meant any product of human ingenuity. Its modern meaning is much narrower, and denotes a mechanical contrivance with moving parts. Section 31 of the Offences against the Person Act 1861 makes it an offence to set or place 'any spring gun, mantrap, or other engine' calculated to endanger life. In one case the accused rigged up a trap designed to inflict an electric shock when his wife opened a french window. He was convicted of placing an engine, contrary to s. 31, but on appeal the conviction was quashed. Lord Parker CJ said:

> as a matter of common sense, it is difficult to see how today at any rate one could aptly refer to these two electric wires as amounting to a spring gun, mantrap or other engine. The court has come to the conclusion that, particularly as this is a penal statute, the meaning to be given to it is the more limited meaning of 'engine' as meaning a mechanical contrivance. It also accords with common sense, it seems to this court, as to the natural meaning today of 'engine'.[25]

This decision was clearly incorrect, since the intention of Parliament was to punish use of anything falling within the *old* meaning of 'engine', prevailing at the time the Act was drafted. The court should have applied an updating construction, as if in s. 31 Parliament had used a word such as 'contraption' rather than 'engine'.

Other examples of expressions used in legislation whose meanings have changed include 'blackmail' (once confined to the extorting of protection money), 'discover' (which used to mean uncover rather than find), 'fraudulent' (which once had a wide meaning equivalent to wrongful), 'indecent' (formerly unbecoming or indecorous), 'police' (which formerly meant the peace or good order of a place), 'sad' (sober and discreet), and 'trespass' (which formerly denoted any form of wrongdoing).[26]

Derby & Co Ltd v Weldon (No 9) [1991] 1 WLR 652 (reference in RSC Ord. 24 to a 'document' includes computer database); *Victor Chandler International v Customs and Excise Commissioners and another* [2000] 2 All ER 315 ('advertisement or other document' updated to include a teletext advertisement).

[24] *The Longford* (1889) 14 PD 34.
[25] *R. v Munks* [1964] 1 QB 304 at 307.
[26] For a summary of this chapter see pp. 207–8 below.

6

Drafting techniques and the Interpretation Act

If you would understand statutes you need to know the technique employed by the people who draft statutes. That is fairly obvious when you think about it, yet few study this technique.

The importance of drafting technique

President Clinton showed the importance of drafting technique in a television piece about the Lewinsky tapes, transmitted worldwide on 21 September 1998. As explained below, the drafting of the definition of 'sexual relationship' formed the centrepiece of the President's exculpatory testimony to the grand jury. This important event is an answer to those (and they are many) who think legislative drafting and its technique to be of less than compelling interest, scarcely worth teaching to law students. In truth that technique has a profound influence, one way or another, on the way law operates, or should operate.

We may begin with a brief mention of the fact that different types of Act are drafted in different ways. There is not space in this book to describe all the different types of Act.[1] One type we do need to notice however is the consolidation Act. This confines within one brand-new Act numerous provisions from older Acts that are *in pari materia*, that is which all deal with the same area of law. From the viewpoint of interpretation, there is one prime distinction to be drawn in relation to consolidation Acts. This is between straight consolidation and consolidation with amendments. The former is presumed not to change the law. The latter will do so only within the indicated limits.

---

[1] For a detailed description of these see *Bennion Code*, s. 28.

Statutory definitions

Another important drafting technique concerns statutory definitions. These are required for various purposes, the most obvious of which is to clarify the intended meaning of a term used in the enactment. Clinton's case in Washington turned mainly on whether the President committed perjury when he denied on oath that he had had a sexual relationship with Ms Lewinsky. In his testimony he alleged that, in common with the ordinary citizen, he would argue that a couple have a sexual relationship if, *and only if*, vaginal intercourse takes place. On that basis he did not have a sexual relationship with Ms Lewinsky because their sexual acts together did not go beyond fellatio.

An alternative definition of sexual relations was that laid down by the judge in the case Paula Jones brought against Clinton, in which the President testified on oath. This involved saying that a person has a sexual relationship with another person if, *and only if*, the two have sexual relations, this term being defined as follows:

a person engages in 'sexual relations' when the person knowingly engages in or causes . . contact with the genitalia, anus, groin, breast, inner thigh, or buttocks of any person with an intent to arouse or gratify the sexual desire of any person . . . Contact means intentional touching, either directly or through clothing.

President Clinton claimed that even on this definition he did not have a sexual relationship with Ms Lewinsky because the sexual acts were done solely by her, the gratified Commander-in-Chief taking a wholly passive role. Clinton argued implausibly, though on familiar legal lines, that while A is having sexual relations with B, B may not be having sexual relations with A. These legalistic arguments saved Clinton from impeachment. The example graphically illustrates the need for care and skill in the drafting and construction of legal definitions, which is not easy.

Another example of this need is furnished by a definition of 'resides with'. This, like the definitions which concerned President Clinton, is what is called a clarifying definition. The Housing Benefit (General) Regulations 1987 reg. 7 says that a person is to be treated as not liable to make payments in respect of a dwelling if he 'resides with' a person to whom he is liable to make such payments and that person is a close relative of his or his partner. Regulation 3(4) says: 'A person resides with another only if they share any accommodation, except a bathroom, a lavatory or a communal area.' The drafting of this is disfigured by a common error, producing ambiguity.

The type of definition just cited can be reduced to: 'Situation A exists only if condition B is satisfied.' But this has two possible meanings: (1) 'Situation A exists whenever condition B is satisfied', or (2) 'Situation A exists only if condition B is satisfied, but does not necessarily exist when it is satisfied.' In each case an additional term is impliedly added to the original statement 'Situation A exists only if condition B is satisfied.' In case (1) this additional implied term can be expressed as 'Situation A always exists if condition B is satisfied', while in case (2) the additional implied term can be expressed as 'Situation A does not necessarily exist even though condition B is satisfied.' A person called on to decide between the two meanings will need to do so by applying the basic rule of statutory interpretation, namely that 'it is taken to be the legislator's intention that the enactment shall be construed in accordance with the general guides to legislative intention laid down by law; and that where these conflict the problem shall be resolved by weighing and balancing the interpretative factors concerned'.[2] The ambiguity could have been avoided by spelling out the intended additional implied term in the original definition.[3]

The Interpretation Act 1978, which lays down many statutory definitions of general application, states that they apply 'unless the contrary intention appears'.[4] Similar statements usually appear in Acts providing *ad hoc* definitions. Whether the defining enactment says so or not, a statutory definition does not apply if the contrary intention appears from the place in which the defined term is used. The legislator is always free to disapply a definition, whether expressly or by implication.

---

[2] This basic rule is more fully explained in Ch. 9.

[3] As with the above examples concerning President Clinton, this shows the need to add the words 'and only if' where these are intended.

[4] Interpretation Act 1978 s. 5, which relates to definitions set out in Schedule 1 to the Act.

Other types of statutory definition

In addition to clarifying definitions there are at least five other types of statutory definition, which I will now briefly describe.

A *labelling definition* uses a term as a label denoting a complex concept that can then be referred to merely by use of the label, instead of the drafter having to keep repeating the full description. This technique has long been adopted to avoid the unnecessary prolixity previously displayed in our legislation, for example in the statute 16 & 17 Cha. 2 [1664] c. 7 of which the following is a brief sample:

every proprietor of books and maps and charts and cuts and pictures, and all prints whatsoever within the City of London, or in any other place, except the two Universities, shall reserve 3 printed copies on the best and largest paper of every book and map and chart and cut and picture and of all prints whatsoever now printed or reprinted by him with additions or alterations; and shall before any public vending of the said books or maps or charts or cuts or pictures or other prints bring them to the Master of the Company of Stationers . . .

This is a taste of what used to be common before the setting up in 1869 of the Parliamentary Counsel Office, where nearly all British Government Bills (not applying exclusively to Scotland) have ever since been drafted. It is what I call disorganized composition. The above passage presents several problems of construction, but an obvious amelioration would be to avoid constant repetition of the phrase 'books and maps and charts and cuts and pictures' (which also occurs elsewhere in the Act) by the use of a labelling definition such as: 'In this Act "prints" means books, maps, charts, cuts, pictures or other printed matter.'

Where an Act contains numerous amendments of another Act with a complex title it is common practice to refer to the latter (by use of a labelling definition) as 'the principal Act'. A labelling definition may be in indirect form, as in the following: 'Any reason by virtue of which a dismissal is to be regarded as unfair in consequence of subsection (1) or (3) is in this Part referred to as an inadmissible reason.'[5]

A *referential definition* attracts a meaning already established

---

[5] Employment Protection (Consolidation) Act 1978 s. 56(5).

in law, whether by statute or otherwise. For example the Charities Act 1960 s. 45(1) said that in the Act 'the term "ecclesiastical charity" has the same meaning as in the Local Government Act 1894'. This method carries a danger, since the Act referred to may later be amended or repealed. Here the principle is that unless the amending or repealing Act contains an indication to the contrary, the amendment or repeal does not affect the legal meaning of the referential definition.

An *exclusionary definition* deprives the term of a meaning it would or might otherwise be taken to have. One of the earliest exclusionary enactments is the Treason Act 1351, stated in its preamble to be enacted because 'divers opinions have been made before this time what case should be adjudged treason, and what not'. By not mentioning them, the Act excluded certain forms of violently anti-social conduct which had earlier been charged as treason, such as highway robbery and kidnapping for ransom.

It tends to mislead if a wide term is artificially cut down by an exclusionary definition. The long title of the Animal Boarding Establishments Act 1963 says it is: 'An Act to regulate the keeping of boarding establishments for animals.' All the way through, the Act refers to 'animals.' Only when they get to the definition section at the end are readers informed that in the Act 'animal' means 'any dog or cat'!

An *enlarging definition* is designed to make clear that the term includes a meaning that otherwise would or might be taken as lying outside it. Section 454(3) of the Income and Corporation Taxes Act 1970 began: 'In this Chapter, "settlement" includes any disposition, trust, covenant, agreement or arrangement . . .' Lord Morton said: 'the object of the subsection is, surely, to make it plain that . . . the word "settlement" is to be enlarged to include other transactions which would not be regarded as "settlements" within the meaning which that word ordinarily bears.'[6] The typical form of an enlarging definition is 'T includes X'. This is taken to signify 'T means a combination of the ordinary meaning of T plus the ordinary meaning of X.' In other words the mention of X does not affect the application of the enactment to T in its ordinary meaning.[7]

---

[6] *Thomas v Marshall* [1953] AC 543 at 556.
[7] *Nutter v Accrington Local Board* (1878) 4 QBD 375 at 384; *Deeble v Robinson* [1954] 1 QB 77 at 81–2; *Ex p. Ferguson* (1871) LR 6 QB 280 at 291.

Where an enlarging definition widens the defined term to include matters not normally within it, this may lead to confusion unless the drafter is careful. This happened with a definition in the Police and Criminal Evidence Act 1984 s. 23, which says that in the Act 'premises' includes 'any place and in particular . . . any vehicle'. Section 19(3) empowers a constable to seize 'anything which is on the premises'. With a vehicle, does it empower him to seize not only anything on the vehicle but the vehicle itself? This question arose in a recent case.[8] Under the ordinary meaning of 'premises' the question cannot arise for the constable 'will not be able to seize and retain premises where they are immovable property because of the physical impossibility of doing so'.[9] 'In my judgment there is no reason why the word "anything" . . . should not include "everything" where the nature of the premises makes it physically possible for the totality of the premises to be seized and retained by the police, and where practical considerations make that desirable.'[10] The Court of Appeal so held, though it has to be pointed out that reading 'anything' as 'everything' does not really do the trick because s. 19(3) then empowers the constable to seize 'everything which is on the premises' but still not the premises itself. This must go down as a bold example of rectifying construction.[11]

A *comprehensive definition* sets out to provide a full statement of everything that is to be taken as included in the term. Section 46 of the Charities Act 1960 says: 'the term "charitable purposes" means purposes which are exclusively charitable according to the law of England and Wales.' This comprehensively describes the concept in question. It is also an example of a referential definition, since it draws on the legal meaning of 'charity'.

A definition may be qualified by what is known as *the potency of the term defined*. Whatever meaning may be expressly attached to a term, it is important to realize that its ordinary dictionary meaning is likely to exercise some influence over the way the definition will be understood by the court. As has been said, it is impossible to cancel the ingrained emotion of a word merely by an announcement.[12] Thus Lord Browne-Wilkinson had regard to the

---

[8] *Cowan v Commissioner of Police of the Metropolis* [2000] 1 All ER 504.
[9] *Per* Roch LJ at 513.   [10] *Per* Roch LJ at 513.
[11] For rectifying construction see Ch. 4.
[12] R. Robinson, *Definition* (Oxford: Clarendon Press, 1950), 77.

potency of the term defined when he said of the definition of 'wages' in the Wages Act 1986 s. 7(1) 'it is important to approach such definition bearing in mind the normal meaning of that word'.[13] In a criminal case the prosecution alleged that the conduct of a salaried manager of a tied public house in selling his own beer on the premises and pocketing the proceeds fell within the statutory definition of theft as set out in the Theft Act 1968 s. 5. Rejecting this argument, Lord Lane CJ said: 'If something is so abstruse and so far from the understanding of ordinary people as to what constitutes stealing, it should not amount to stealing.'[14]

Weightless drafting

Reverting to the theme of sexual intercourse, we turn finally to a point suggested by an article by Stephen O'Doherty.[15] Mr O'Doherty says of the Sexual Offences Act 1956 that its drafts-man[16] had no doubts about the meaning of the term 'sexual intercourse' in s. 44 'because he gave no definition for it'. The conclusion does not follow from the premiss, and this uncovers an interesting aspect of drafting technique. The good drafter, who has much to do, declines to waste time on matters that carry no weight. Wherever possible he or she engages in what might be called weightless drafting. This shortens and simplifies wording where there is no weight on its exact meaning. Section 44 says: 'Where on the trial of any offence under this Act it is necessary to prove sexual intercourse (whether natural or unnatural), it shall not be necessary to prove the completion of the intercourse by the emission of seed, but the intercourse shall be deemed complete upon proof of penetration only.' Why was no definition of 'sexual intercourse' provided? It was not, as Mr O'Doherty says, because the drafter had no doubts about what it means. It was because there was no weight on its meaning and so it was unnecessary to

---

[13] *Delaney v Staples* [1992] 1 AC 687 at 692.

[14] *Attorney General's Reference (No. 1 of 1985)* [1986] QB 491 at 507.

[15] 'Rape and indecent assault—changing perceptions' 162 JP (1998) 676.

[16] I use the preferred spelling rather than Mr O'Doherty's 'draughtsman', which is usually regarded as referring to persons who draw pictures, plans, or diagrams. It is in any case now customary to use the sex-neutral 'drafter', since much legislation is today drafted by women. It is time judges caught up with this development.

waste his time, and complicate matters, by devising a definition. In effect the drafter was saying 'whatever this phrase may or may not mean, it does not require emission, just penetration'. The purpose was limited to resolving a doubt relating to the question of emission.

There is another piece of weightless drafting in s. 44. If it mattered, there would be hot dispute nowadays about what the 1956 drafter thought he (it was probably he) thought he was talking about when he referred to unnatural intercourse. Probably the drafter did not stop to think just what he meant about that term either, because again there was no weight on it. Its sole purpose was to prevent anyone arguing that s. 44 did not apply to offences such as buggery because it was by implication limited to 'natural' sexual intercourse.[17]

----

[17]   For a summary of this chapter see pp. 208–9 below.

7

Transitional provisions and the Cohen question

We continue the examination of drafting technique begun in the last chapter, beginning with the vexed question of retrospectivity.

The problem of retrospectivity

In response to the 1998 Omagh bomb outrage in Northern Ireland, thought to have been committed by the so-called Real IRA, the Parliament of the Irish Republic (the Dail) passed an emergency Act in one day, under which the Irish police, the Garda Siochana, were expected to be able to arrest the leaders of the Real IRA on the following day. This did not happen. It was alleged that the drafter of the emergency Act had overlooked the need to give the Act some retrospective effect, so that the police could take account of evidence gathered before it was passed.[1]

There are two aspects to this story. The first is that it shows that a legislative drafter needs to possess and use imagination. The second concerns the general question of retrospectivity in legislation, a thorny subject. On the first aspect I will quote from the first of my books dealing with the technique of legislative drafting, written in the early 1960s.

The draftsman ought not to be concerned with policy as such, but he is concerned, and has a duty, to see that the policy decision is effected in a way that will be workable. He should therefore be alert to observe flaws in the policy scheme which may interfere with its smooth working when transformed into law. For this he also needs some degree of imagination. By visualising what a scheme will mean in terms of real life when it comes to be put into operation, the draftsman may be able to suggest improvements and point out defects . . . As Sir Courtenay Ilbert said in *Legislative Methods and Forms*, page 240: 'If a parliamentary draftsman is to do his

---

[1] *Sunday Times*, 6 Sept. 1998.

work well, he must be something more than a mere draftsman. He must have constructive imagination, the power to visualise things in the concrete, and to foresee whether and how a paper scheme will work out in practice'.[2]

The question of retrospectivity in legislation requires more detailed examination. Unless the contrary intention appears, most enactments are presumed not to be intended to have a retrospective operation. This rule recognizes the nature of law. The essential idea of a legal system is that current law should govern current activities. If we do something today, we feel that the law applying to it should be the law in force today, not tomorrow's backward adjustment of it. Such, we believe, is the nature of law. Those who have arranged their affairs in reliance on the law as it currently stands should not later find that their plans have been retrospectively upset.[3]

Dislike of *ex post facto* law is enshrined in the United States Constitution[4] and in the constitutions of many American states, which forbid it. The principle is that *lex prospicit non respicit* (law looks forward not back).[5] Retrospectivity is 'contrary to the general principle that legislation by which the conduct of mankind is to be regulated ought, when introduced for the first time, to deal with future acts, and ought not to change the character of past transactions carried on upon the faith of the then existing law.'[6] The basis of the principle against retrospectivity 'is no more than simple fairness, which ought to be the basis of every legal rule'.[7]

This is all very well, but in real life it is often necessary, as our Irish story above shows, to give a statute some retrospective effect. The drafter needs to think very carefully about this, visualizing just how the legislative scheme will work out in practice. It is all part of the story of *transitional provisions*, perhaps the most neglected area in statute law (which has many neglected areas).

---

[2] F. A. R. Bennion, *Constitutional Law of Ghana* (London: Butterworths, 1962), 344.
[3] See *EWP Ltd v Moore* [1992] QB 460 at 474.
[4] Art. I, s. 9(3).
[5] D. Jenkins, *Eight Centuries of Reports* (London: In the Savoy, 1734), 284.
[6] *Phillips v Eyre* (1870) LR 6 QB 1, *per* Willes J. at 23.
[7] *L'Office Cherifien des Phosphates v Yamashita-Shinnihon Steamship Co Ltd* [1994] 1 AC 486, *per* Lord Mustill at 525.

Transitional provisions

Where an Act contains substantive, amending or repealing enactments, it should also include transitional provisions which regulate the coming into operation of those enactments and where necessary modify their effect during the period of transition. If the drafter has forgotten to include such provisions expressly, the court is required to draw such inferences as to the transitional arrangements as, in the light of the applicable interpretative criteria, it considers that Parliament should be taken to have intended.

Express transitional provisions spell out precisely when and how the operative parts of the Act are to take effect. They serve an essential purpose, since merely to say that an enactment comes into force on a specified date is often insufficient to produce a clear legal meaning in all possible circumstances. Lord Bridge said that the purpose of a transitional provision is 'to facilitate the change from one statutory regime to another', citing Thornton's statement that 'The function of a transitional provision is to make special provision for the application of legislation to the circumstances which exist at the time when that legislation comes into force.'[8] Failure by the drafter to include adequate transitional provisions is a frequent cause of avoidable difficulty to statute users. Faced with the task of working out the intended transitional operation of the Local Government, Planning and Land Act 1980 s. 47, Waller LJ said: 'The absence of any transitional provisions has made the construction of this section difficult because it is possible to argue in favour of more than one date.'[9]

It is important for the interpreter to realize, and bear constantly in mind, that what appears to be the plain meaning of a substantive enactment is often modified by transitional provisions located elsewhere in the Act. Often these are tucked away in an obscure place, where they are easily overlooked. Consequences of overlooking them can be severe. The transitional provisions in the Magistrates' Courts Act 1980 (a consolidation Act) were overlooked by numerous prosecutors and others concerned with the working of magistrates' courts. In several cases this required the

---

[8] *Britnell v Secretary of State for Social Security* [1991] 2 All ER 726 at 729–30.

[9] *Cardshops Ltd v John Lewis Properties Ltd* [1983] QB 161 at 165.

discharging of juries and the obtaining of bills of indictment in the High Court. One commentator said:

> The confusion has arisen because many magistrates' courts have been committing all cases for trial under provisions of the Magistrates' Courts Act 1980, which came into force on July 6 [1981]. Yet tucked away in a schedule to the Act[10] is a transitional provision unnoticed by many courts, to the effect that where proceedings began before July 6, committals should be made under the old enactments.[11]

The Cohen question

Old hands know they must be on the alert for transitional provisions in Acts, but not all readers of legislation are old hands. This raises a vexed question concerning the drafting of legislation. For what type of reader is the text intended? Is it for lawyers only, or anyone who rides the famous Clapham omnibus? No authors can word a text correctly if they have not first decided who the intended reader is. There has been much confusion on this point. As we saw in Chapter 1, ignorance or mistake as to the legal meaning of an enactment is not accepted as an excuse for failure to comply with it, yet most people who are bound by the law are non-lawyers. Many of those who make the law are non-lawyers. Even some people who have to apply the law, such as lay magistrates, are non-lawyers. Does all that mean legislation must be drafted so as to be understood by the lay person?

Certainly there are judicial dicta favouring that. In a 1949 case[12] Lord Justice Cohen formulated what has since been called the Cohen question.[13] It had to be decided whether a Mrs Wollams was a 'member of the family' within the meaning of the Rent Acts.[14] On appeal Cohen LJ said that the question the county court judge should have asked himself was: 'Would an ordinary man, addressing his mind to the question whether Mrs Wollams was a member of the family or not, have answered Yes

---

[10] Sch. 8, para. 2(1).

[11] Terence Shaw (Legal Correspondent), *The Daily Telegraph*, 30 Sept. 1981.

[12] *Brock v Wollams* [1949] 2 KB 388 at 395.

[13] So described by Lord Diplock in *Carega Properties SA (formerly Joram Developments Ltd) v Sharratt* [1979] 2 All ER 1084 at 1086.

[14] See p. 59 above.

or No?' Lord Evershed MR borrowed from Shakespeare's *Henry V* to amplify the description 'an ordinary man' in the Cohen question as a man 'base, common, and popular'.[15] This appears misconceived, having regard to Shakespeare's use of the latter phrase. Pistol challenges the disguised King Henry, who replies that he is a friend. Pistol goes on: 'Discuss unto me; art thou officer? Or art thou base, common, and popular?' The standard can hardly be that of the ordinary man in this sense; and it seems that the Cohen question needs reframing. The words to be construed are put together by legislative drafters, and these are not ordinary men. Like learned judges, they are highly educated men (or women). The standard must be at least that of the ordinary person of good education. When choosing their words, drafters do not consciously don the mental equipment of a Pistol, even supposing that lay within their powers.

Yet it is important that the law should be ascertainable by the citizen. Lord Justice Buckley referred to the statute user as 'a man who speaks English and understands English accurately but not pedantically'.[16] Lord Diplock said:

The acceptance of the rule of law as a constitutional principle requires that a citizen, before committing himself to any course of action, should be able to know in advance what are the legal consequences that will flow from it. Where those consequences are regulated by a statute the source of that knowledge is what the statute says. In construing it the court must give effect to what the words of the statute would be reasonably understood to mean by those whose conduct it regulates.[17]

The last sentence means that legislation should be drafted so as to be understood by a lay person, and not necessarily one who is educated to Lord Justice Buckley's standard. It carries the weighty authority of the late Lord Diplock. Many would instinctively agree with it. Yet is it right? The question is so important that we must investigate further.

[15] *Langdon v Horton* [1951] 1 KB 666 at 669. See *Henry V*, iv. i. 37.
[16] *Benson (Inspector of Taxes) v Yard Arm Club Ltd* [1979] 1 WLR 347 at 351.
[17] *Black-Clawson International Ltd v Papierwerke Waldhof-Aschaffenberg AG* [1975] AC 591 at 638.

Understanding the law

In his *Utopia* Sir Thomas More said: 'All laws are promulgated to
this end, that every man may know his duty; and, therefore, the
plainest and most obvious sense of the words is that which must
be put upon them.' This is an argument for the literal rule of
construction, which was considered in Chapter 3. It assumes that
legislative texts are indeed addressed to lay persons. Yet there are
many factors indicating the other way. One was pointed out by
the Association of First Division Civil Servants: 'What appears
clear to the layman may not be certain in meaning to the courts;
and much of the detail in legislation, which can appear obfusca-
tory, is there to make the effect of the provisions certain and resistant to legal challenge.'[18]

Another inexorable constraint on legislative wording is the
need to conform to the language of the existing law. An Act
intended to amend the law (as most Acts are) must fit into the
existing *corpus juris* or body of law as well as expressing the
reforming intention of the legislator. It must fit not only the existing language (which may well be unnecessarily complex if we
could start again) but also the existing concepts. Where the two
aims conflict, as they sometimes do, it is more important that the
text should be effective than that it should be clear.[19] Furthermore
obscurity in legislation is very often caused not by unnecessary
complication of language but by complication (whether unnecessary or not) of thought. When I started drafting the Sex Discrimination Act 1975 for example I began by writing: 'A person
discriminates against a woman if on the ground of her sex he
treats her less favourably than he treats or would treat a man.'
The intolerable complexity of that Act arose not from any wish of
mine but because those instructing me insisted on overlaying it
with innumerable refinements, exceptions, conditions, and exclu-
sions. In doing so they were genuinely seeking to conform to the
popular will as manifested in representations from trade unions,

---

[18] Cited in paragraph 219 of *Making the Law*, the report of the Hansard Society
Commission on the Legislative Process, issued on 2 Feb. 1993 (London: The
Hansard Society for Parliamentary Government).

[19] I say this remembering desperate occasions when I strove to draft a Finance
Bill clause so that it fitted effectively into the frightful mess known as the Income
Tax Acts and did not cost the country millions in lost tax revenue.

women's groups, employers' organizations and other lobbies. The price of that deferring to democratic principle was the said complication. There are other causes of legislative complexity. An obvious one is that a Bill has to run the gauntlet of parliamentary debate and amendment in both Houses. This imposes specific requirements on the drafter, who could usually produce a much better final text if free to start all over again rejigging Parliament's final product. What of the legislator who, like most, is a non-lawyer? Am I really accepting that Bills and draft statutory instruments have to be beyond the understanding of their nominal creators? This would appear paradoxical, if not perverse. There is a long history of this aspect, too long to examine here. Until recently Bills were drafted according to the four corners doctrine, under which legislators were supposed to be able to understand the gist of a Bill without going beyond its terms (that is without looking at any other document). Unfortunately this distorted the finished product, so a system of textual amendment was adopted instead.[20] Under this system an amending Act consists of verbal alterations to the wording of the original Act, so as to make it mean what is now intended. This kind of amendment is difficult to understand by MPs, but improves the finished product for the benefit of the user. When the original Act is reprinted as textually amended it states the new law as clearly the system allows.

As the result of a recommendation made by the House of Commons Select Committee on Modernisation, and adopted by both Houses, explanatory notes have since 1998 been published for all Government Bills, which makes comprehension easier.[21] As the Renton Committee said in its 1975 report on the preparation of legislation, a Bill or statutory instrument needs to be drafted in the way that is best from the point of view of its ultimate user.

Which brings us neatly back to our original question. Who is the ultimate user? Despite Lord Diplock, Sir Thomas More, and the many others who think law should be comprehensible by all, I fear the answer is plain. Whether we like it or not, law is an

---

[20] For the four corners doctrine, linked to the previous system of indirect amendment of Acts, see Bennion, *Statute Law* (3rd edn., London: Longman, 1990), 32, 228–9.

[21] See a note by the First Parliamentary Counsel in 149 NLJ (1999), 798.

expertise. A lay person would not think they could do better than a professional in assessing symptoms of illness, carrying out a diagnosis, performing a surgical operation, and issuing the prognosis. It is just the same when it comes to the products of our legislative process. That is why we have a legal profession. The duty of its members is to ensure that the lay public have the fullest and clearest explanations it is possible to provide, but unhappily only experts can understand the law.[22]

[22] For a summary of this chapter see pp. 209–10 below.

8

Words in pairs

It is a common feature in legal expression to favour use of pairs of words, whether in antithesis or apposition, in preference to a single term. The most common reason for this (often illusory) is the drafter's reluctance to rely on a solitary word, with the comforting feeling that a pair of terms somehow conveys more than the sum of its parts. A historical reason going back to the Norman Conquest was the need to supply both a French and an Anglo-Saxon version of equivalent meaning (and also possibly a Latin version). This explains conjunctions such as 'last will and testament', combining Old English *will* and Old French (from Latin) *testament*. In medieval English translations of Latin texts the translator sometimes felt a need to supply, in relation to a Latin term, *two* English words, one with a Latin root and the other with an English root. An example from a book which was translated into English around 1450 shows 'seu ratione dotis mee' translated as 'by the reson or skille of her dowre' (dowry).[1]

Even today terms of virtually identical meaning are used together, as in the Children Act 1989 s. 22(3)(a), which imposes a duty to 'safeguard and protect' a child. The two terms mean the same, so either would have sufficed on its own. Another modern example of pairing of words is the fair dealing defence in the Copyright, Designs and Patents Act 1988 s. 30(1), referring to dealing with a work 'for the purposes of criticism or review'. Another is the phrase 'fit and proper' when used to describe a person qualifying for some privilege such as the grant of a licence.[2] Here the addition of 'proper' adds little if anything to 'fit', which is no doubt why the drafter of the Consumer Credit Act 1974 was content to use the latter term only.[3] A similar example is 'harsh and unconscionable', employed in the Moneylenders

---

[1] Andrew Clark (ed.), *The English Register of Godstow Nunnery, near Oxford* (Oxford: OUP, 1905), 302.
[2] See, e.g., the Licensing Act 1964 s. 3(1).
[3] See, e.g., s. 25 of the Act.

Act 1900 s. 1 to describe what used to be called a catching bargain. The successor provision in the Consumer Credit Act 1974[4] dropped the idea of conscience and referred simply to an 'extortionate' bargain.

Yet another example is 'unsafe or unsatisfactory' as formerly applied to a criminal conviction by the Criminal Appeal Act 1968 s. 2(1). Of this Lord Devlin said that it might be that one or other of the two words was tautologous, but that a guilty verdict not reached after a proper direction and consideration of all the influential evidence would be 'unsatisfactory' whether or not it was 'unsafe'.[5] 'The new provision, in confining the test to one of safety of the conviction, may in this respect be narrower than before, depending on whether the word "unsatisfactory" signified an additional and independent ground for quashing a conviction or merely another way of saying "unsafe".'[6]

A phrase which is obviously tautologous is 'just and equitable' as used for example in the Companies Act 1985 s. 666(5)(c), where it is given as a ground for making a winding-up order. What is just must also be equitable, and vice versa. Some years ago I wrote an article referring to such a term as a 'belt and braces phrase'.[7] I gave as an example the Companies Act 1948 s. 147, requiring day-to-day books of account to be kept. It stated that such books would not be deemed proper if they did not give a 'true and fair view' of the company's affairs. When in 1976 it was proposed to replace s. 147 by more sophisticated provisions the phrase was at first retained.[8] Then an alert member of a working party set up by one of the accountancy professional bodies pointed out that the requirement in s. 147 could not be met in practice. At any one time books would not have complete entries, let alone adjustments necessary for consistency and fairness. The department yielded and the Companies Act 1976 s. 12 required

---

[4] Section 138(1).
[5] *The Judge* (Oxford: OUP, 1979), 158.
[6] *R. v Chalkley* [1998] 2 All ER 155, *per* Auld LJ at 172. The change was made by the Criminal Appeal Act 1995 s. 2(1). As shown at length in Sir Louis Blom-Cooper, *The Birmingham Six and other cases* (1997), Ch. 5, the new elliptical formula is pregnant with uncertainty because it leaves a range of complex situations undescribed (for ellipsis as a cause of doubtful meaning see Bennion, *Statute Law* (3rd edn., London: Longman, 1990), Ch. 15).
[7] 129 NLJ (1979) 748.
[8] Clause12(1) of the Companies (No 2) Bill (1976).

current accounting records to be sufficient to 'show and explain' the company's transactions. Another belt-and-braces phrase? I think not, since here the two words have somewhat different meanings.

A frequent difficulty when pairs of words are used is whether both terms need to be satisfied, or whether one will do. Words like 'and' and 'or' may be used disjunctively or conjunctively. The Court of Appeal held that in article 10 of the European Convention on the Recognition and Enforcement of Decisions Concerning Custody of Children, given the force of law by the Child Abduction and Custody Act 1985, the statement that 'recognition and enforcement' of a foreign judgment may be refused was to be construed disjunctively. This meant that a judgment might be recognized but not enforced.[9]

Here much depends on the context, and the purpose of the enactment. If an applicant is required to be 'fit and proper' then obviously he must be both fit and proper (assuming there is some difference in meaning). But if, as with the definition of 'town or village green' in the Commons Registration Act 1965 s. 22(1), the use of a green is required to be for the indulging by the inhabitants in 'lawful sports and pastimes' then it will obviously not matter if a particular green is devoted exclusively to sports (but not other pastimes) or to pastimes other than sports. The portmanteau is labelled 'sports and pastimes', and as long as the particular thing done is to be found within it all is well. This example shows that, of two broad terms linked in one phrase, one may be broader than the other: all sports are pastimes, but not all pastimes are sports.

This definition also uses another pair of terms. It refers to land allotted 'for the exercise or recreation of the inhabitants'. These terms are mutually overlapping *in part*: not all exercise involves recreation and not all recreation involves exercise. Does it make any difference that the linking word here is 'or', whereas with the other phrase it was 'and'? I would say not. Again there is a portmanteau. For the purposes of the definition it does not matter whether individual members of the public use the common

[9] *Re H (a minor) (foreign custody order: enforcement)* [1994] Fam. 105. The court had regard to the statement in A. V. Dicey and J. H. Morris, *The Conflict of Laws* (12th edn., 1993), Vol. 1, 453–4 that 'while a court must recognise every foreign judgment which it enforces, it need not enforce every foreign judgment which it recognises'.

exclusively for exercise, or exclusively for recreation, or for both. In such cases it is important that there is a multiple subject, in this case the inhabitants at large. The linking word 'or' is more likely to be disjunctive where the subject is a single entity.

The legislative drafter may employ the device known as 'hendiadys', from a Greek phrase meaning 'one by means of two'. This is defined by the *Oxford English Dictionary*[10] as a figure of speech in which a single complex idea is expressed by two words connected by a conjunction; e.g. by two substantives with 'and' instead of an adjective and substantive. An old example of its use in law is the term *law and heraldry*, meaning heraldic law. If an Act made it an offence 'to take and drive away' a motor vehicle, this would be a hendiadys. It would not be an offence merely to take a vehicle, nor merely to drive one away. Both elements would be required to be proved. Professor Pearce gives as an example of hendiadys the enactment dealt with in an Australian case which read: 'Every insurer shall promptly co-operate with the Committee and assist it to carry out its duties under this section.' It was held that one obligation only was imposed by this, and it was insufficient merely to charge failure to co-operate.[11] With hendiadys the meaning is conjoint, the signification of each term merging with, and partaking of, that of the other.

In Chapter 6 I described the technique known as weightless drafting. This arises in connection with the vague phrases 'sports and pastimes' and 'exercise or recreation', mentioned above. It is unnecessary to argue about whether when the public indulge in a particular activity, say rabbiting, it is a 'sport' or a 'pastime' because if it is not one it is the other (unless of course it is neither). With this sort of portmanteau phrase it does not make any practical difference where the dividing line is drawn between the meanings of the two terms. Indeed there are likely to be overlapping meanings. The precise meaning of each term never needs to be ascertained, because no weight rests on it. In this particular instance, some members of the public will indulge on the green or

[10] 2nd edn., 1992.
[11] *Traders Prudent Insurance Co Ltd. v Registrar of Workers' Compensation Commission* [1971] 2 NSWLR 513. See D. C. Pearce and R. S. Geddes, *Statutory Interpretation in Australia* (4th edn., Sydney: Butterworths, 1996), 112. See further on the question whether 'and' and 'or' are used conjunctively or disjunctively *Maxwell on the Interpretation of Statutes* (12th edn., 1969), 232–4.

common in sports, some in pastimes, and some in both. It would be absurd to suggest that the definition is not satisfied unless *all* members of the public who go on the green or common indulge in *both* activities.

Words used in pairs are often found to overlap in meaning. The House of Lords considered the composite expression 'repair or maintenance' in Sch. 4 (repealed) to the Finance Act 1972. Section 12 (repealed) of the Act, dealing with zero-rating for V.A.T., relieved from tax supplies of a description specified in Sch. 4. Section 12(4) empowered the Treasury to vary Sch. 4 by order. Section 46(2) said that Sch. 4 should be interpreted in accordance with the notes contained therein, and that the power to vary Sch. 4 extended to these notes. As varied by paragraph 3 of the Value Added Tax (Consolidation) Order 1976 S.I. 1976/128, Sch. 4 exempted supplies of services in the course of building or engineering work. An appended note said that this did not include 'any work of repair or maintenance'. The question was whether the latter phrase included the underpinning of foundations. *Held* It did not. Lord Roskill said:

the argument in the court below appears to have proceeded on the basis that the words 'repair or maintenance' are used in antithesis to one another . . . The two words are not used in antithesis to one another. The phrase is a single composite phrase repair or maintenance and in many cases there may well be an overlap between them.[12]

Here is another example of overlapping meaning. The Justices of the Peace Act 1997 s. 16(4)(b) allows for the removal of a magistrate for 'inability or misbehaviour'. The Sheriff Courts (Scotland) Act 1971 s. 12 provides for the removal of a sheriff for 'inability, neglect of duty or misbehaviour'. This raises the question whether a magistrate can be removed under the 1997 Act for neglect of duty. Is there an overlap in meaning in the 1971 Act phrase 'neglect of duty or misbehaviour'? In other words is neglect of duty a form of misbehaviour? On the likely supposition that it is, the phrase 'inability or misbehaviour' in the 1997 Act has the same legal meaning as the phrase 'inability, neglect of duty or misbehaviour' in the 1971 Act.

In conclusion I need to mention the *noscitur a sociis* principle,

---

[12] *ACT Construction Ltd v Customs and Excise Comrs.* [1982] 1 All ER 84 at 88.

which requires terms to be construed in the light of their surrounding words.[13] The Capital Allowances Act 1990 s. 18(1) defines the term 'industrial building or structure' as one used for 'a trade which consists in the manufacture of goods or materials or the subjection of goods or materials to any process'. Nourse LJ said 'the close proximity between the two phrases requires that the word "goods" in the second should be given the same meaning as in the first.'[14]

[13] See *Bennion Code*, s. 378.
[14] *Girobank plc v Clarke (Inspector of Taxes)* [1998] 4 All ER 312 at 315. For a summary of this chapter see pp. 210–11 below.

9

Rules of interpretation

We have looked at the main problems connected with drafting, interpreting, and applying legislation under the common law or Global system, though there are many lesser problems we do not have space to touch on. There remains the basic question. What really are the interpretative criteria, or guides to legislative intention, in this system where legislative intention is all important? There is talk of a golden rule. Does it exist? What of the so-called literal rule, and the mischief rule? I gave the short answer in a citation on p. 12 above. I wrote more about the literal rule in Chapter 3. Now I must describe how I first came to hear of these three supposed 'rules' of statutory interpretation. Many law teachers and commentators still write as if they were real. Some even seem to think they sum up the whole story. In fact they are largely illusory, and it is high time this was realized. The quotation on p. 12 goes back to 1984. The doubts expressed by Sir Rupert Cross, which I am about to discuss, date from 1976. Word should have got around by now.

A basic rule and four categories

I started to think seriously about the three supposed rules when in the 1970s I first read a little book entitled *Statutory Interpretation*. It was written by an old friend, the late Sir Rupert Cross, who had been Vinerian Professor of English Law in the University of Oxford and a close friend of my Balliol tutor Sir Theodore Tylor. The brief monograph first appeared in 1976. It was the preface to it that stimulated me to write my own much larger book with the same title. Cross wrote:

When teaching law at Oxford in the 1950s and 1960s I treated my pupils as I had been treated and told them to write essays criticising the English rules governing the subject. Each and every pupil told me that there were three rules—the literal rule, the golden rule and the mischief rule, and that the Courts invoke whichever is believed to do justice in the particular case. I had, and still have, my doubts, but what was most disconcerting was the fact that whatever question I put to pupils or examinees elicited the same reply. Even if the question was What is meant by 'the intention of Parliament'? or What are the principal extrinsic aids to interpretation? back came the answers as of yore: 'There are three rules of interpretation—the literal rule, the golden rule and the mischief rule.' I was as much in the dark as I had been in my student days about the way in which the English rules should be formulated.

Obviously Cross did not think these three so-called rules provided the answer. Having thought about the matter closely over the intervening years, I am convinced he was right. So where does the truth lie? I believe it starts with what I have worked out to be the basic rule, as follows. Under the common law or Global system it is taken to be the legislator's intention that an enactment shall be construed according to the numerous general guides laid down for that purpose by law; and that where these conflict (as they often do) the problem shall be resolved by weighing and balancing the interpretative factors concerned.

That is the basic rule, and it is simple enough. It was foreshadowed from the bench as early as 1873, when Lord Justice Cotton said judges 'are bound to have regard to any rules of construction which have been established by the Courts'.[1] There are many such rules. Also must be added certain rules of construction laid down by Parliament such as those in the Interpretation Act 1978, discussed in Chapter 6. Contrary to what is often said, the court does not 'select' any one of these many guides and then apply it to the exclusion of the rest. What the court does (or should do) is take an overall view, weigh all the relevant interpretative factors, and then arrive at a balanced conclusion.

The approach indicated by the basic rule has been described as pluralistic. This is by comparison with the simplistic so-called literal rule, formerly regarded as universal. The modern development, useful though it is, has been said to deepen the contingency or uncertainty of the law, which would of course be a bad thing. Law should be certain, so that its effect may be known. One commentator has said:

Because pluralism in statutory interpretation embraces more approaches than literalism, the contingency appears to have deepened in the sense

---

[1] *Ralph v Carrick* (1874) 11 Ch. D 873 at 878.

that it is 'grounded' in the values of plural concepts and approaches. However, another way to view this shift is to see it as a shift from the values of literalism to those of pluralism. The difficulty with accepting pluralism's values as the new basis for statutory interpretation is in identifying them.[2]

A start in identifying these plural values lies in grouping them into categories. The guides to legislative intention, otherwise known as the interpretative criteria, can be broken down into four distinct types, which may be respectively identified as rules, principles, presumptions and canons. Expanding this slightly, we may say these are: (1) common law and statutory *rules*; (2) *principles* derived from legal policy; (3) *presumptions* based on the nature of legislation; and (4) general linguistic *canons* applicable to any piece of prose.

Expanding further, we can broadly distinguish the interpretative criteria as follows. A rule of construction is of binding force, but in cases of real doubt rarely yields a conclusive answer. A principle of construction reflects the policy of the law, and is mainly persuasive. A presumption of construction arises from the essential nature of legislation, and affords a prima facie indication of the legislator's inferred or imputed intention as to the working of the Act. A linguistic canon of construction arises from the nature and use of language and reasoning, and is not especially referable to legislation.

These interpretative criteria are peculiar in that, while most general legal rules directly govern the actions of the citizen, these directly govern the actions of the court. There is however an indirect effect on the citizen. Since the court is obliged to apply an enactment in accordance with the interpretative criteria, persons governed by the enactment must read it in that light. The law in its practical application is not what an Act says but what a court says (or would say) the Act means.[3]

I will now go on to discuss these four categories in turn. The remainder of this chapter deals with the first category, rules of construction.

---

[2] Jeffrey W. Barnes, 'Statutory Interpretation, Law Reform and Sampford's Theory of the Disorder of Law' Pt II (1995) *Federal Law Review* (Australia), 77 at 127.

[3] As explained in Ch. 1, this is known as its legal meaning.

Rules of construction

A criterion is not deserving of the name *rule* unless it is compelling. The basic rule of statutory interpretation set out above is compelling, but does not take one very far. This tends to be the case with rules of statutory interpretation: where a real doubt as to meaning exists, the matter becomes one of judgment rather than predetermined response.[4]

Rules of statutory construction can be divided into those laid down at common law and those imposed by statute. Criteria laid down at common law which are worthy of the name *rule* are relatively few. They include the following among those not already described in this book.

Juridical nature of an enactment. In construing an enactment of any kind, the interpreter must treat it with due regard to its juridical nature as an enactment of that kind. There are various types of enactment. Some are comprised in primary legislation, while others are derivative or secondary. Some legal qualities are common to all types, whereas others relate only to a particular type or types (for example constitutional, European, penal or human rights aspects). The interpreter needs to be aware of the juridical nature of what is being interpreted, and construe it accordingly.

Plain meaning rule. It is a rule of law, sometimes called the plain meaning rule, that where, in relation to the facts of the instant case, the enactment under inquiry is grammatically capable of one meaning only, and on an informed interpretation[5] of that enactment the interpretative criteria raise no real doubt as to whether that meaning is the one intended by the legislator, the legal meaning of the enactment corresponds to that meaning. For this purpose (and here the plain meaning rule differs from the so-called literal rule) a meaning is 'plain' only where no relevant interpretative criterion (whether relating to material within or outside the Act or other instrument in question) points away from it. This rule determines the operation of nearly every enactment, simply

[4] For the nature of judgment see Ch. 13.
[5] For the informed interpretation rule see p. 19 above.

because nearly every enactment has a straightforward and clear meaning with no counter-indications. As Cross put it, if it were not a known fact that, in the ordinary case in which the normal user of the English language would have no doubt about the meaning of the statutory words, the courts will give those words their ordinary meaning, it would be impossible for lawyers and others to act and advise on the statute in question with confidence.[6]

It is salutary to bear this in mind. The science or art of statutory interpretation deals in the main with the pathology of law, when something has gone wrong. Usually nothing does go wrong. Lawyers, like medical practitioners, need to be on guard against losing sight of the general prevalence of healthy conditions. Sir MacKenzie Chalmers, celebrated draftsman of such enduring codes as the Sale of Goods Act 1893 and the Marine Insurance Act 1907, remarked that 'lawyers see only the pathology of commerce, and not its healthy physiological action, and their views are therefore apt to be warped and one-sided'.[7] The same can apply in relation to the pathology of law.

Commonsense construction rule. It is a rule of law (sometimes known as the commonsense construction rule) that when considering, in relation to the facts of the instant case, which of the opposing constructions of the enactment would give effect to the legislative intention, the court should presume that the legislator intended common sense to be used in construing the enactment. As Lord Goddard CJ said, 'A certain amount of common sense must be applied in construing statutes'.[8] So when a particular matter is not expressly dealt with in the enactment this may simply be because the drafter thought that as a matter of common sense it went without saying. Section 4(2) of the Courts Act 1971 provided that lay justices when sitting with a judge of the Crown Court were themselves to be treated as judges of that court. Lord Widgery CJ said that in arriving at decisions the full court must play its part.

---

[6] Sir Rupert Cross, *Statutory Interpretation* (1st edn., London: Butterworths, 1976), 1.

[7] *Sale of Goods* (12th edn., London: Butterworths, 1945), 182.

[8] *Barnes v Jarvis* [1953] 1 WLR 649 at 652.

All one need add today is really a glimpse of the obvious, so obvious that no doubt the draftsman did not think it necessary to put it in the Act, namely, that in matters of law the lay justices must take a ruling from the presiding judge in precisely the same way as the jury is required to take his ruling when it considers its verdict.[9]

It is common sense to assume that if a particular proposition is expressly laid down by an enactment, the converse, though not expressed, also applies.[10] So if A is to be treated for the purposes of an enactment as residing with B, it follows as a matter of common sense that B is to be treated for those purposes as residing with A.[11] Where an enactment refers to a thing it is assumed to mean, unless the context otherwise requires, a thing which *exists* as denoted or described by the enactment. So the reference to 'an application for planning permission' in the Town and Country Planning Act 1990 s. 78(1) (which gives a right of appeal to the Secretary of State against refusal etc. of such an application) does not cover purported applications 'which are so deficient in form and substance that no reasonable local authority or Secretary of State could reasonably treat them as "applications" within the meaning of the legislation'.[12]

Statutory rules of interpretation are principally laid down by the Interpretation Act 1978, which re-enacts propositions first placed on the statute book long ago in Lord Brougham's Act.[13] Most rules of construction laid down by statute consist of definitions, which I dealt with in Chapter 6. However some rules are in oblique form, as with the following: 'Every court in dealing with a child or young person . . . shall have regard to the welfare of the

[9] *R. v Orpin* [1975] QB 283 at 287.

[10] For a case where the President of the United States, no less, sought to dispute this commonsense truism see p. 62 above.

[11] For a case where regulations were expressly (and as it proved unnecessarily) amended to spell out this plain truth see *Bate v Chief Adjudication Officer* [1996] 2 All ER 790 at 800.

[12] *R. v Secretary of State for the Environment, Transport and the Regions, ex p Bath and North East Somerset District Council* [1999] 4 All ER 418, *per* Pill LJ at 428. The case decided that a purported application did not fail to be within s. 78(1) merely because the local planning authority considered it to be invalid on technical grounds, provided it was not deficient as mentioned.

[13] (1850) 13 & 14 Vict. c. 21. The basic idea of an Interpretation Act is indicated by the long title to Lord Brougham's Act: 'An Act for shortening the Language used in Acts of Parliament.'

child or young person'.[14] Many interpretative provisions laid down by the Interpretation Act 1978 and other Acts are not in form definitions, though they do have a defining effect. They state general propositions about the legal meaning which an enactment is to be taken to have 'unless the contrary intention appears' (to quote the exclusionary phrase used throughout the 1978 Act).

The easiest way to become acquainted with the rules laid down by the Interpretation Act 1978 is to study the Act. Lord Thring, first head of the Parliamentary Counsel Office, said of its equivalent in his day, the Interpretation Act 1889, 'it is the duty of every draftsman to know it by heart and to bear its definitions in mind in every bill which he draws'.[15] I would go further and say it is the duty of every judge, advocate and adviser, and any other person concerned with the legal meaning of legislation, to be familiar with its provisions. There are many instances in the law reports of ignorance or neglect of the current Interpretation Act giving rise to expensive problems and even miscarriages of justice.[16]

The Interpretation Act 1978

Here are just a few of the more important provisions of the present Interpretation Act, that of 1978.[17]

The term 'person'. The legal meaning of the commonly used word 'person' gives rise to a surprising amount of difficulty. To start with, it includes a body of persons, whether corporate or unincorporate.[18] As invariably, this statutory definition does not apply if, whether expressly or by implication, the context otherwise requires. So it was held that, because of the nature and attributes of a solicitor as an officer of the court, the term 'person' in the Solicitors Acts is confined to a person who could

---

[14] Children and Young Persons Act 1933 s. 44(1), which may affect the construction of any enactment to which it is applicable: see *R. v Secretary of State for the Home Department, ex p. Venables* [1997] 3 All ER 97 *per* Lord Browne-Wilkinson at 120.

[15] Lord Thring, *Practical Legislation* (London: John Murray, 1902), 14.

[16] See e.g. *R. v Adams* [1980] QB 575; *Wilson v Colchester JJ* [1985] AC 750; *R. v Pinfold* [1988] 2 WLR 635; *R. v Immigration Appeal Tribunal, ex p. Secretary of State for the Home Department* [1990] 1 WLR 1126.

[17] See also Ch. 6.   [18] Interpretation Act 1978 s. 5 and Sch. 1.

become a solicitor, thus excluding corporations.[19] In the Criminal Justice Act 1988 s. 133(1), which requires compensation to be paid where 'a person has been convicted of a criminal offence and subsequently his conviction has been reversed', the word 'person' has been held not to include a company.[20] Where the intention is to confine the statutory reference to *natural* persons, the drafting practice is to use the term 'individual'.[21] A human foetus *in utero* is not in law a person or individual, since up to the moment of birth it is regarded as not having any separate interests capable of being taken into account by the court.[22]

The Interpretation Act 1978 is silent on the question whether a reference to a 'person' is confined to persons of full age and capacity. As always it is a question of the intention of Parliament. For example it seems, although no authority can be cited, that for reasons of public safety the term 'person' in an enactment enabling a person to apply for a firearms certificate should be taken not to include a minor, or one who is otherwise not of full mental capacity. On the other hand it is possible for a term indicating an adult to be construed as including children where the legislative intention so requires. The Homicide Act 1957 s. 3, dealing with the defence of provocation, says 'the question whether the provocation was enough to make a reasonable man do as he did shall be left to be determined by the jury'. Clearly 'man' includes a woman.[23] But does it include a boy? Since boys (and girls too for that matter) are in law capable of committing murder it necessarily follows that it does.[24]

Gender. Unless the contrary intention appears, words importing the masculine gender include the feminine and vice versa.[25] In the days before sexism was frowned on, this was not always implemented. For example the Representation of the People (Scotland)

---

[19] *Law Society v United Services Bureau Ltd.* [1934] 1 KB 343.
[20] *R. v Secretary of State for the Home Department, ex p. Atlantic Commercial (UK) Ltd.* (1997) *Times*, 10 March.
[21] *Whitney v IRC* [1926] AC 37 at 43.
[22] *In re MB (an adult: medical treatment)* [1997] 2 FCR 541; *Attorney General's Reference (No. 3 of 1994)* [1997] 3 All ER 936.
[23] See below.
[24] So held in *DPP v Camplin* [1978] AC 705.
[25] Interpretation Act 1978 s. 6 (a) and (b)

Act 1868 s. 27 gave voting rights to every 'person' whose name was on the register of the general council of a Scottish university. In 1868 only males were entitled to be entered on such registers, but by virtue of the predecessor of the current provision, s. 4 of Lord Brougham's Act, all words importing the masculine gender were to be 'deemed and taken to include females . . . unless the contrary . . . is expressly provided'. In s. 27 of the 1868 Act the contrary was not expressly provided, and when the University of St. Andrews later opened its doors to women they claimed to be within s. 27, and to be therefore entitled to vote. It was held that this had not been unequivocally expressed to be Parliament's intention, and the claim could not be admitted.[26] In another case the House of Lords denied a peeress the right to sit in the House of Lords despite unequivocal words in the Sex Disqualification (Removal) Act 1919 s. 1.[27] If this Act had been applied as it ought to have been the Sex Discrimination Act 1975 would scarcely have been necessary.[28]

Number. Unless the contrary intention appears, words in the singular include the plural and vice versa.[29] This simplistic rule may cause difficulty when the drafter forgets that an enactment expressed in terms of what one person does may not work for plural cases, since the people concerned may each choose to do different things. The phrase 'words in the singular include the plural' can disguise a number of problems, and may require selective pluralizing or singularizing in complex cases. The Magistrates' Courts Act 1980 s. 20(3) says that in certain circumstances the court, after explaining specified matters to 'the accused', shall 'ask him whether he consents to be tried summarily or wishes to be tried by a jury'. This caused acute difficulty with multiple defendants in one case where the House of Lords disagreed with the Court of Appeal.[30]

The reverse rule that plural references include the singular is frequently overlooked in practice. For example a single epistle

---

[26] *Nairn v University of St Andrews* [1909] AC 147.
[27] *Viscountess Rhondda's Claim* [1922] 2 AC 339.
[28] See Bennion, 'The Sex Disqualification (Removal) Act—60 Inglorious Years' 129 NLJ (1979) 1088.
[29] Interpretation Act 1978 s. 6(c).
[30] *Nicholls v Brentwood Justices* [1991] 3 All ER 359.

was, probably erroneously, held not to be 'correspondence' within the meaning of the Law of Property Act 1925 s. 46.[31]

Time. Subject to the Summer Time Act 1972 s. 3 (references to points of time during the summer time period), whenever an expression of time occurs in an enactment this is taken to refer to Greenwich mean time, unless it is otherwise stated.[32] References to a 'month' mean a calendar month.[33]

Land. A reference to 'land' includes buildings and other structures, land covered by water, and any estate, interest, easement, servitude or right in or over land.[34] This is an important definition, often overlooked. Failing to take it into account can lead to difficulty because it is an enlarging definition of unexpectedly wide extent. An unsuspecting reader might be surprised to find, for example, that a reference to 'land' includes a right of way and a restrictive covenant.[35]

Powers and duties. Where an enactment confers a power or imposes a duty it is implied, unless the contrary intention appears, that the power may be exercised, or the duty is to be performed, from time to time as occasion requires.[36] This important rule is often overlooked in practice. It does not apply where the scheme of the legislation so indicates.[37]

---

[31] *Stearn v Twitchell* [1985] 1 All ER 631. The judgment contained no reference to the rule that plural references include the singular.

[32] Interpretation Act 1978 s. 9.

[33] Ibid., s. 5 and Sch.1.

[34] Ibid.

[35] See *R. v Hammersmith and Fulham London Borough Council, ex p. Beddowes* [1987] QB 1050.

[36] Interpretation Act 1978 s. 12(1).

[37] As in *R. v Crown Court at Stafford, ex p. Chief Constable of the Staffordshire Police* [1998] 2 All ER 812 (scheme of the Licensing Act 1964 indicated that justices could not grant a special hours certificate in respect of premises for which one was already in force). For a summary of this chapter see pp. 211–12 below.

10

Legal policy

The previous chapter explained how under the common law or Global system of statutory interpretation the various guides to legislative intention, or interpretative criteria, can be broken down into four distinct types: (1) common law and statutory rules; (2) principles derived from legal policy; (3) presumptions based on the nature of legislation; and (4) general linguistic canons applicable to any piece of English prose. That chapter dealt with the first type. This one describes the nature of the second type, namely principles derived from legal policy.

A principle of statutory interpretation embodies and reflects the inmost policy of the nation's law, which is in turn based on the nation's public policy. So far as concerns statutory interpretation by the courts, the content of public policy (and therefore of legal policy) broadly corresponds to what over the years judges from their knowledge and experience think and hold it to be. However in this the court is guided by legislation (even though not directly applicable in the instant case) as indicating Parliament's view of the content of relevant policy. For the sake of constitutional coherence, the views of judicature and legislature ought not to get out of line. For the furtherance of democracy this means that ultimately Parliament's view of policy, where it has been declared in legislation, should prevail. Subject to this overriding principle the court presumes, unless the contrary intention is shown in an Act, that the legislator intends to conform to the state's established principles of legal policy as mainly laid down by the courts.

No Act of Parliament can convey expressly the fullness of its intended legal effect. Indeed only a small proportion of this effect can be conveyed by the express words of the Act. For the rest, Parliament assumes that interpreters will draw any necessary or reasonable inference. An Act does not operate in a vacuum, but as a part of the whole *corpus juris* or body of the state's legal rules and normative substratum. General principles of law and public policy underlie and support the rules laid down by the whole body of legislation (otherwise known as the Statute Book). If it were not so the rules imposed by statute would be merely arbitrary. Even where a statutory rule does appear arbitrary (for example that one must drive on the left), there is always a non-arbitrary policy principle underlying it (road safety is socially desirable).

What we are here concerned with is the body of general legal principles which has mainly been built up, and from time to time modified, by the judiciary over centuries. It is referred to as legal policy. As we have seen, it derives from public policy; but it is the judges' long-term view of public policy as applied to law, and is confined to justiciable issues. Opposed to it is the facile recent idea that the public weal requires all ideas from the past to be jettisoned as obsolete. This is an obvious nonsense, and must be resisted.

Public policy has been described as 'a very unruly horse'.[1] It is not a concept that admits of precise definition.[2] Nevertheless it exists, and in the form of legal policy has a powerful influence on the interpretation of statutes. Legal policy consists of the collection of principles the judges consider over time that the law has a general duty to uphold. The products of these principles are sometimes referred to as constitutional rights (or in a more limited sense, discussed below, human rights). Laws J. said 'constitutional rights have effect by their recognition at common law and by the special rule of construction which the common law applies to [any] statutes by which they are sought to be overridden'.[3] Legal policy principles cannot be numbered and are being constantly developed, so an observer needs to keep up with developments. They are equivalent to what the Germans call *rechtspolitik,* directed always to the wellbeing of the community. Thus it was said in an early English case laying down legal policy very broadly that 'All such acts and attempts as tend to the prejudice of the community are indictable.'[4] Among the basic principles of common law legal policy are the following. Law should serve the public interest. Law should be fair and just. Law should be certain and predictable, self-consistent and not subject to casual change.

The constituent elements of legal policy are drawn from many

---

[1] *Richardson v Mellish* (1824) 2 Bing 229.
[2] *Egerton v Brownlow* (1853) 4 HL Cas. 1; *Besant v Wood* (1879) 12 Ch. D 605; *Davies v Davies* (1887) 36 Ch. D 369.
[3] *R. v Lord Chancellor, ex p. Lightfoot* [1998] 4 All ER 764 at 778.
[4] *R. v Higgins* (1801) 2 East 5.

sources in the common law world. These include parliamentary enactments, past judgments, ideas of natural law, and the writings of jurists. The sources are not all legal however. Religious, philosophical, and economic doctrine enters in. Political reality flavours the mixture. International obligations are not forgotten. Common sense and *savoir faire* bind the whole together. The principles may be laid down judicially in the course of statutory interpretation or in a purely common law context. In the latter event they may in a future case affect statutory interpretation. Also it must not be forgotten that the common law was born and nurtured in the context of Christianity.

As an example of the purely common law context of legal policy we may take the case of *R v Lemon*.[5] The House of Lords were called on to decide a question which Lord Scarman described as 'one of legal policy in the society of today'.[6] This was whether the common law offence of blasphemous libel requires proof only of an intention to publish the offending matter, or whether what Lord Diplock[7] called 'the mental element or mens rea' in the offence requires proof that the accused actually intended to cause offence to Christians. Their Lordships agreed that, as Lord Scarman said,[8] the point was open for their decision as a matter of principle. Lord Scarman went on: 'And in deciding the point your Lordships are not saying what the law was in the past or ought to be in the future but what is required of it in the conditions of today's society.' In reaching its decision the House took many considerations into account, including developments in the law of evidence and penal policy, the tendency of recent Acts in comparable fields, the decline in the public importance of the Church of England, the absence of convictions for blasphemy during the preceding half century, the need for consistency in various departments of the law of libel, the need for social tranquillity in a multiracial society, and Britain's international obligations under the European Convention on Human Rights. The House divided by 3 to 2 in favour of the stricter view that intention to publish is sufficient to establish the offence.

Neither principles of law nor those of wider public policy are static. In their judgments, the courts reflect developments in these principles. In the Acts they pass, legislators do likewise. There is

---

[5] [1979] AC 617.   [6] p. 664.   [7] p. 632.   [8] p. 662.

an interaction between the two. 'The fact that opinion grounded on experience has moved one way does not in law preclude the possibility of its moving on fresh experience in the other; nor does it bind succeeding generations, when conditions have again changed.'[9] On some points, legal policy may change drastically over a period. Lord Devlin referred to certain aspects of mid-nineteenth century legal policy as 'a Victorian Bill of Rights, favouring (subject to the observance of the accepted standards of morality) the liberty of the individual, the freedom of contract, and the sacredness of property, and which was highly suspicious of taxation'.[10] Such a description would not fit legal policy a century and a half later.

Legal policy changes in response to signals from all quarters, some subtle. The prevailing wind that is legal policy in a particular area backs or veers accordingly. Of its nature, said Lord Devlin, the law cannot be immediately responsive to new developments. It needs as a corrective 'the observation of the man up aloft who gauges the strength and direction of the winds of change'.[11] The more perceptive judges pick up the signals first. Others follow later.

The judicial development of the public law remedy of judicial review which began in Britain in the 1970s required among other things a broadening of the concept of *locus standi* (standing) which gave a person or body a right to sue. Slade LJ said in a 1985 case: 'The speeches of their Lordships in *R v IRC, ex p National Federation of Self-Employed and Small Businesses Ltd* [1982] AC 617 well illustrate that there has been what Lord Roskill described at p. 656G-H as a "change in legal policy", which has in recent years greatly relaxed the rules as to locus standi.'[12] The trend continued. In 2000 Richards J. referred to 'the increasingly generous approach towards standing in applications for judicial review'.[13]

The court ought not to enunciate a new head of public policy in an area where Parliament has demonstrated its willingness to

[9] *Bowman v Secular Society Ltd.* [1917] AC 406, *per* Lord Sumner at 467.
[10] *The Judge*, 15.
[11] *The Enforcement of Morals*, (Oxford: OUP, 1965), 126.
[12] *R. v HM Treasury, ex p. Smedley* [1985] QB 657 at 669.
[13] 'Public powers: preventing misuse', *JSB Journal*, Issue Nine 2000, 7. Note the abandonment of Latin here, another trend in legal policy.

intervene where it considers necessary. When Hoffman J. was asked to declare that to allow parties to determine by agreement between them that a floating charge would become crystallized if the chargor ceased trading was an innovation which was contrary to public policy he declined, saying:

The public interest requires the balancing of the advantages to the economy of facilitating the borrowing of money against the possibility of injustice to unsecured creditors. These arguments for and against the floating charge are matters for Parliament rather than the courts and have been the subject of public debate in and out of Parliament for more than a century. Parliament has responded [in various ways]. The limited and pragmatic interventions by the legislature make it in my judgment wholly inappropriate for the courts to impose additional restrictive rules on the ground of public policy. It is certainly not for a judge of first instance to proclaim a new head of public policy which no appellate court has even hinted at before.[14]

Because it takes Parliament as intending that currently accepted principles of legal policy should apply unless the contrary intention appears, the common law has developed specific principles of statutory interpretation by reference to those general principles. For example, from the general principle that it is undesirable that a person should be allowed to profit from his own wrong we have the principle of construction that if the literal meaning of an enactment would permit a person so to profit it may be correct to infer an intention by the legislator that a strained construction should be given in such cases.[15] In the context of a particular enactment a principle can usually be expressed either in general form or as restricted to statutory interpretation. Thus one can say to the citizen 'It is desirable that you should not be permitted to take advantage of your own wrong' or one can say to the court 'If the literal meaning of the Act enables a person to take advantage of his or her own wrong, it is likely that Parliament intended words of exception to be taken as implied.'

Even an interpretative criterion which appears to be limited to the construction of legislation may be found on analysis to have a wider base. The principle that a penal statute should be strictly construed is only an aspect of the principle of justice and fairness

---

[14] *Re Brightlife Ltd.* [1986] 3 All ER 673 at 680–1.
[15] See p. 172 below.

that a person ought not to suffer under a doubtful law, whether written or unwritten. If the law is doubtful as to his guilt, then maybe he is not guilty. So he should not be punished.

In a difficult case the number of relevant interpretative criteria may be high, and the task of the court in assessing their relative weight correspondingly difficult. Dworkin says of legal principle generally that 'if we tried to list all the principles in force we would fail'. He adds: 'They are controversial, their weight is all important, they are numberless, and they shift and change so fast that the start of our list would be obsolete before we reached the middle.'[16] One may accept the truth of this aphorism while regretting the shifting moralities it imports. True morality is surely unshifting.

In a particular case different elements of legal policy, for example the safeguarding of personal liberty and the need for state security, may conflict. The court then needs to weigh the conflicting elements and decide which should have predominance. However the conflict may be more apparent than real. Lord Donaldson MR, commenting on the dictum of Mann LJ that 'this court is aware of the tension which arises between considerations of liberty and the freedom to live where one wishes and considerations of national security upon the other hand', said that although they give rise to tensions at the interface, 'national security' and 'civil liberties' are on the same side. 'In accepting, as we must, that to some extent the needs of national security must displace civil liberties, albeit to the least possible extent, it is not irrelevant to remember that the maintenance of national security underpins and is the foundation of all our civil liberties.'[17]

It was said above that international obligations are not forgotten when it comes to considering what legal policy has to say on a particular matter. It is indeed a principle of legal policy that the municipal law should conform to public international law. The court, when considering, in relation to the facts of the instant case, which of the opposing constructions of the enactment would give effect to the legislative intention, should presume that the legislator intended to observe this principle. However a treaty is not law unless an Act of Parliament has made it so; otherwise the govern-

---

[16] R. Dworkin (ed.), *The Philosophy of Law* (Oxford: OUP, 1977), 64.
[17] *R. v Secretary of State for the Home Department, ex p. Cheblak* [1991] 1 WLR 890 at 906–7.

ment could, under the royal prerogative, legislate by making a treaty.[18] Again, where the words of an enactment have a wider application than the provisions of a relevant treaty, the treaty will not be held to cut down their ordinary meaning.[19] A rule of public international law which is incorporated by a decision of a competent court then becomes part of the municipal law.[20] Again, under the principle known as *adoption*, a rule of international law may be incorporated into municipal law by custom or statute.

The courts treat the need to observe treaties as a general matter of legal policy.[21] In a case on the Warsaw convention, Lord Denning MR put the point more strongly: 'The Warsaw Convention is an international convention which is binding in international law on all the countries who have ratified it: and it is the duty of these courts to construe our legislation so as to be in conformity with international law and not in conflict with it.'[22] This dictum was given statutory effect in relation to the European Convention on Human Rights by the Human Rights Act 1998 s. 3(1), which says that, so far as it is possible to do so, legislation must be read and given effect in a way which is compatible with Convention rights.[23]

Many of the principles embedded in the European Convention on Human Rights correspond to, and are indeed derived from, those previously emerging as British legal policy. This appears from the passage in the preamble to the Convention recording that the states parties agreed upon it:

Reaffirming their profound belief in those Fundamental Freedoms which are the foundation of justice and peace and are best maintained on the one hand by an effective political democracy and on the other by a common understanding and observance of the Human Rights upon which they depend; [and] Being resolved, as the Governments of European countries which are like-minded and have a common heritage of political traditions, ideals, freedom and the rule of law . . .

---

[18] *Littrell v United States of America (No 2)* [1995] 1 WLR 82, *per* Rose LJ at 88. The Human Rights Act 1998 is an example of such an Act.

[19] *The Norwhale* [1975] QB 589.

[20] *Thai-Europe Tapioca Service Ltd. v Government of Pakistan* [1975] 1 WLR 1485 at 1495.

[21] *A.-G. v British Broadcasting Corpn.* [1980] 3 WLR 109, *per* Lord Scarman at 130.

[22] *Corocraft Ltd v Pan American Airways Inc.* [1968] 3 WLR 1273 at 1281.

[23] See Ch. 15.

The passing of the Human Rights Act 1998 meant that many principles of legal policy which hitherto had been embedded in
common law were thenceforth also to be given statutory force.
They also of course continue to be directly enforceable at Strasbourg under the regime established by the Convention.[24] We
should never forget that they started life as common law principles.

[24] For the relation of Dworkin's theory of law as integrity to the effect of legal
policy as discussed in this chapter see Ch. 16 below. For a summary of this chapter
see pp. 212–13 below.

11

Interpretative presumptions

This chapter deals with the third of the four categories of guides to legislative intention or interpretative criteria under the common law or Global system, namely presumptions based on the nature of legislation. Chapter 12 will deal with the fourth category, general linguistic canons applicable to any piece of prose, and the methodology to be used in applying each of the four categories.

An interpretative presumption, which like any legal presumption is always rebuttable, is laid down at common law, that is by the judges. It affords guidance, arising out of the essential nature of legislation, as to the legislator's prima facie intention regarding the legal meaning of an enactment. The common law has laid down various presumptions about what Parliament is likely to intend regarding the operation of an Act, for example that it is not to be evaded. These presumptions are not distinct from general rules and principles of law, but are drawn from them. At the same time they recognize the essential nature of legislation, and aim in particular to further its effective working. There are many such presumptions. I shall briefly describe the most important.

It is presumed that in construing an enactment its text, in its setting within the Act or other instrument containing it, is to be regarded as the pre-eminent indication of the legislator's intention. When called upon to construe an Act, the court regards its primary duty as being to look at the text and say what, in itself, it means in law. 'The safer and more correct course of dealing with a question of construction is to take the words themselves and arrive if possible at their meaning without, in the first instance, reference to cases.'[1] So the text is the starting point, and the centre of the interpreter's attention from then on. It is the text, after all, that is being construed.

It is then presumed that the literal meaning of the text is to be followed unless other factors indicate the contrary. As explained in Chapter 3, the 'literal meaning' corresponds to the grammatical

---

[1] *Barrell v Fordree* [1932] AC 676, *per* Lord Warrington of Clyffe at 682.

meaning where this is straightforward. If however the grammatical meaning, when applied to the facts of the instant case, is ambiguous then any of the possible grammatical meanings may be described as the literal meaning. If the grammatical meaning is semantically obscure, then the clear grammatical meaning likely to have been intended (or any one of them in the case of ambiguity) is taken as the literal meaning. The point here is that the literal meaning is one arrived at from the wording of the enactment alone, without consideration of other interpretative criteria. When, for the purpose of arriving at the overall legal meaning of the enactment, account is taken of such other criteria it may be found necessary to depart from the literal meaning and adopt a strained construction.[2]

In general under the common law or Global system, the weight to be attached to the literal meaning is greater than applies to any other interpretative criterion. It may occasionally be overborne by other factors, but they must be powerful indeed to achieve this. It follows that where a form of words is laid down by statute for use in certain circumstances it is safest to adhere to this, even though to do so may not be essential. The Police and Criminal Evidence Act 1984 s. 77 requires the trial judge to instruct the jury to bear in mind the special need for caution in relation to a confession made by a mentally handicapped person. Stuart Smith LJ said that although the judge did not have to follow any specific wording, he would be wise to use the statutory phrase 'special need for caution'.[3]

The coercive, often penal, nature of a statutory power means that the court will prefer to give it a literal, rather than expansive, construction. 'A power conferred by Parliament in general terms is not to be taken to authorise the doing of acts by the donee of the power which adversely affect the legal rights of the citizen, or the basic principles on which the law of the United Kingdom is based, unless the statute conferring the power makes it clear that such is the intention of Parliament.'[4]

It will be seen that there is no literal *rule* of interpretation in the sense that the literal meaning must invariably be followed. Deter-

---

[2] Strained construction is described in Ch. 3.
[3] *R. v Campbell* (1994) *Times* 13 July.
[4] *Pierson v Secretary of State for the Home Department* [1997] 3 WLR 492, *per* Lord Browne-Wilkinson at 502.

mining when it is to be departed from is the interpreter's most difficult task.

The rule in Heydon's Case

A well-known presumption arises under the rule in *Heydon's Case*.[5] Here the sixteenth-century Barons of the Exchequer resolved:

That for the sure and true interpretation of all statutes in general (be they penal or beneficial, restrictive or enlarging of the common law), four things are to be discerned and considered:

(1) what was the common law before the making of the Act;
(2) what was the mischief and defect for which the common law did not provide;
(3) what remedy the Parliament hath resolved and appointed to cure the disease of the commonwealth; and
(4) the true reason of the remedy,
   and then the office of all the judges is always to make such construction as shall-
   (a) suppress the mischief and advance the remedy, and
   (b) suppress subtle inventions and evasions for the continuance of the mischief *pro privato commodo* (for private benefit), and
   (c) add force and life to the cure and remedy according to the true intent of the makers of the Act *pro bono publico* (for the public good).

This resolution, which is still relevant (particularly in relation to tax avoidance), gave rise to what is sometimes known as the mischief rule; and later to what is today perhaps the most important presumption of all, that a purposive construction is to be given. That presumption has already been explained.[6] So too have the presumptions regarding a consequential construction and a rectifying construction.[7]

Absurdity

It is an aspect of consequential construction, not previously dealt with, that Parliament does not intend 'absurd' consequences to flow from the application of its Act. This presumption leads to

---

[5] (1584) 3 Co. Rep. 7a.   [6] See Ch. 3.   [7] See Ch. 4.

avoidance by the interpreter of six types of undesirable consequence: (1) an unworkable or impracticable result, (2) an inconvenient result, (3) an anomalous or illogical result, (4) a futile or
pointless result, (5) an artificial result, and (6) a disproportionate
counter-mischief.

The courts thus give 'absurd' a far wider import than it has in
ordinary modern English, where it simply means foolish, ridicu-
lous or silly. Judges keep to the older meaning, which the *Oxford
English Dictionary* gives as: 'out of harmony with reason or
propriety; incongruous, unreasonable, illogical'. It was in such a
sense that Claudius told Hamlet that his excessive mourning for a
dead father was 'To reason most absurd'.[8] The derivation is from
the Latin *surdus*, deaf. We commonly speak even today of a
person being deaf to reason.

Here is an example of a judicial decision which avoided an
unworkable or impracticable result. Where an enactment refers to
a thing it is presumed that it means a thing which is capable of
existing, so the reference to 'another legal estate not in existence'
in the Law of Property Act 1925 s. 65(2) 'can only have been
intended to refer to a legal estate which was capable of existence'.[9]

The following is an example of a decision avoiding a construction that would have caused unjustifiable inconvenience to
persons who were subject to the enactment. Section 8 of the Shops
Act 1950 empowered a local authority to make orders fixing the
time at which shops, or any specified class of shops, were to be
closed for serving customers. By s. 74(1) of the Act 'shop' was
defined as including any premises where a retail trade or business
was carried on. It was held that this did not empower a local
authority to make an order by which different 'premises' within
one department store had to close at different times, since this
would cause the owner of the store unjustified inconvenience.[10]

The court seeks to avoid a construction that creates an anomaly
or otherwise produces an irrational or illogical result. If the
Vagrancy Act 1824 s. 6 (powers of arrest) had been treated by the
court as partially repealed by the Police and Criminal Evidence
Act 1984 s. 26(1) 'the absurd position would arise that a citizen

---

[8] *Hamlet*, I. ii. 103.
[9] *Ingram and another (executors of the estate of Lady Ingram (deceased)) v
Inland Revenue Commissioners* [1997] 4 All ER 395, *per* Nourse LJ at 402.
[10] *Fine Fare Ltd. v Aberdare UDC* [1965] 2 QB 39.

would be entitled to arrest a person under [s. 6] whereas a constable would not'.[11] It was therefore held that this construction would not be adopted.

The presumption against avoiding a futile or pointless result is illustrated by a case where Clauson J. based his decision on the fact that the effect of an alleged disqualification of a councillor would be that there would have to be an immediate by-election where the disqualified man would then be eligible for re-election to the vacant office. The judge said: 'I cannot think that the legislature intended such a whimsical result.'[12]

The law can deem anything to be the case, however unreal, but the law is brought into disrepute if it dignifies with legal significance a wholly artificial hypothesis. When counsel argued that the Theft Act 1968 s. 22(1) required the prosecution to prove that an alleged handling of goods was not done in the course of stealing them, the Court of Appeal rejected the argument on the ground that it would require the court to engage in artificial reasoning. Lord Lane CJ said: 'We do not believe that this tortuous process, leading in some cases to such an artificial verdict, could have been the intention of Parliament'.[13]

The last of the six categories of presumption against 'absurdity' is concerned with avoiding a disproportionate counter-mischief The court sets itself against a construction that, while it cures the mischief the enactment was designed to remedy, does so only at the cost of setting up a disproportionately worse counter-mischief. Such a result is unlikely to have been intended by Parliament in framing the enactment, so the court rejects it.

Here is an example. An enactment dealing with the licensing of river pilots was intended to remedy the mischief caused by the operations of unskilful pilots. Where one possible construction of the enactment would have prevented there being any pilots at all for a substantial period Dr Lushington looked 'at the mischief which would accrue' from this construction and adopted the other reading of the enactment.[14]

---

[11] *Gapper v Chief Constable of Avon and Somerset Constabulary* [1998] 4 All ER 248, *per* Swinton-Thomas LJ at 250.

[12] *Bishop v Deakin* [1936] Ch. 409 at 414.

[13] *R. v Cash* [1985] QB 801 at 806.

[14] *The Beta* (1865) 3 Moo PCCNS 23 at 27. For a summary of this chapter see pp. 213–14 below.

12

Linguistic canons and interpretative technique

This chapter explains the last of the four categories of guides to legislative intention or interpretative criteria under the common law or Global method, namely general linguistic canons applicable to any piece of prose. It then describes the methodology to be used in applying the four categories.

Linguistic canons of construction

A linguistic canon of construction reflects the nature or use of language generally. It does not depend on the legislative character of the enactment in question, nor indeed on its quality as a legal pronouncement: it applies in much the same way to all forms of language. So linguistic canons are not confined to statutes, or even to the field of law. They are based on the rules of logic, grammar, syntax and punctuation; and the use of language as a medium of communication generally.[1] When judges say, as they sometimes do, that the principles of statutory interpretation do not materially differ from the principles applicable to the interpretation of documents generally, one presumes it is these linguistic canons they have in mind. It follows that the linguistic canons of construction are used to arrive at the literal meaning of an enactment.

As we have seen, the first linguistic canon is that an Act or other legislative instrument is to be read as a whole, so that an enactment within it is not treated as standing alone but is interpreted in its context as part of the entire instrument.[2] Hence Sir Richard Scott V-C said of the Consumer Credit Act 1974: 'It is certainly right to try and construe the 1974 Act as a whole'.[3] The

---

[1] *Effort Shipping Co. Ltd. v Linden Management SA* [1998] 1 All ER 495, *per* Lord Cooke of Thorndon at 513.
[2] See Ch. 5 above.
[3] *Dimond v Lovell* [1999] 3 All ER 1 at 10.

essence of construction as a whole is that it enables the interpreter to perceive that a proposition in one part of the Act may by implication be modified by another provision elsewhere in the Act.[4]

Sometimes terms of virtually identical meaning are used in conjunction. This involves surplusage, since either term suffices on its own. Surplusage or tautology is to be distinguished from intentional overlap: legislation often provides two or more overlapping remedies.[5]

It may happen that no sensible meaning can be given to some word or phrase. It must then be disregarded.[6] Thus the Court of Appeal held that the Administration of Justice Act 1960 s. 13(2) (appeal in cases of contempt of court), should be read as if the words 'for committal or attachment' were, as Parker LJ put it 'not there at all'. This was because otherwise a company could not appeal under the Act which, Parker LJ said, would be 'defeating the plain legislative purpose'.[7]

It is presumed that a word or phrase is not to be taken as having different meanings within the same instrument, unless this intention is evident. Where therefore the context makes it clear that the term has a particular meaning in one place, it will normally be taken to have that same meaning elsewhere.

Sometimes words of the same spelling are capable of different meanings, whether slightly different or altogether different. The same is true of phrases. Philologists call these terms *homonyms*. A drafter needs to take care not to use homonyms with different meanings in the same Act without making the intended meaning clear in each place. The House of Lords split 3-2 on the meaning of 'issue' in relation to shares, as used in the Income and Corporation Taxes Act 1988 s. 299A.[8] As Lord Hanworth MR earlier observed, 'it is impossible to say that the word "issue" is used in all Acts of Parliament and in all circumstances with the same

---

[4] See, e.g., *Cooper v Motor Insurers' Bureau* [1985] QB 575 (meaning of 'any person' in the Road Traffic Act 1972 s. 145(3)(a) restricted by an implication arising from s. 143(1)).

[5] See, e.g., *Harrods Ltd. v Remick* [1998] 1 All ER 52 (the fact that a certain type of discrimination fell within the Race Relations Act 1976 s. 30 or s. 31 did not mean it could not also be caught by s. 7 of the Act). See also the discussion of pairs of words in Ch. 8.

[6] See *Stone v Yeovil Corpn.* (1876) 1 CPD 691.

[7] *A.-G. v Hislop* [1991] 1 All ER 911 at 917, 918.

[8] *National Westminster Bank plc v IRC* [1995] 1 AC 119.

meaning'.[9] The court said in a rent case: 'Considerable difficulty arises in the construction of the Real Property Limitation Act 1833 by reason of the word "rent" being used in two different senses throughout—*viz.* in the sense of a rent charged upon land, and of a rent reserved under a lease.'[10]

It is presumed that the drafter did not indulge in elegant variation, but kept to a particular term when wishing to convey a particular meaning. Accordingly a change in the term used is taken to denote a different meaning. Blackburn J. said: 'It has been a general rule for drawing legal documents from the earliest times, one which one is taught when one first becomes a pupil to a conveyancer, never to change the form of words unless you are going to change the meaning . . .'[11] Different words in a consolidation Act may be given the same meaning because derived from different Acts.[12] Clearly the original drafters of these different Acts would not have been able to apply the principle enunciated by Blackburn J.

The concept that an Act is to be read as a whole is also applied to a group of Acts if they are *in pari materia*. That is the description given to Acts which deal with the same subject-matter on the same lines. Such Acts are sometimes described as forming a code, but this does not mean they are codifying Acts in the technical sense. They are 'to be taken together as forming one system, and as interpreting and enforcing each other'.[13] In other words they are to be construed as one, whether or not the relevant enactment expressly requires this.[14] It is however necessary to remain realistic. A drafter who produces an amending Bill does not always have the time or industry to read through the whole of a mass of preceding legislation to make sure the current drafting is in full accordance with it. 'The broad principle laid down by Lord Mansfield in *R. v Loxdale* as to the exposition of one statute by the language of another must be taken with a pinch of salt when a long series of Acts is being dealt with.'[15]

[9] *Tillotson (Oswald) v IRC* [1933] 1 KB 134 at 155.
[10] *Doe d. Angell v Angell* (1846) 9 QB 328 at 355.
[11] *Hadley v Perks* (1866) LR 1 QB 444 at 457.
[12] *MRS Environmental Services Ltd v Marsh* [1997] 1 All ER 92 at 102.
[13] *R. v Palmer* (1785) Leach 352.
[14] *Chief Adjudication Officer v Foster* [1993] AC 754 at 769.
[15] *Littlewoods Mail Order Stores v I.R.C.* [1961] Ch. 597, *per* Harman LJ at 633.

A number of linguistic canons are best known in their Latin form. One of these, previously mentioned, is *noscitur a sociis*, meaning 'it is recognized by its associates'.[16]

English words derive colour from those which surround them. Sentences are not mere collections of words to be taken out of the sentence, defined separately by reference to the dictionary or decided cases, and then put back into the sentence with the meaning which you have assigned to them as separate words . . .[17]

Where a term is ambiguous, reference to a nearby passage may resolve the ambiguity. The Financial Services Act 1986 Sch. 1 para. 9 refers to a contract the purpose of which is 'to secure a profit or avoid a loss'. The question arose whether 'secure a profit' meant obtain a profit or arrange security for a profit. The court decided the point by reference to a note included in paragraph 9 which disapplied the paragraph 'where the profit is to be obtained' in a specified manner.[18]

The Latin phrase *ejusdem generis* (of the same kind or nature), has been attached to a principle of construction whereby wide words associated in the text with more limited words are taken to be restricted by implication to matters of the same limited character. The principle may apply whatever the form of the association, but the most usual form is a list or string of genus-describing terms followed by wider residuary or sweeping-up words. Section 43 of the Customs Consolidation Act 1876 read: 'The importation of arms, ammunition, gunpowder, *or any other goods* may be prohibited by proclamation or Order in Council'.[19] Although the italicized words are completely general, it is obvious that some limitation is intended. Otherwise why did not the drafter simply say 'The importation of any goods may be prohibited'? It was held that the *ejusdem generis* principle applied. Sankey J. refrained from describing what the genus was, being content to hold that the substance in question, pyrogallic acid, was outside it.

The rank principle lays down that where a string of items of a

---

[16] Two detailed applications of this principle, the *ejusdem generis* principle and the rank principle, are treated separately below.

[17] *Bourne v Norwich Crematorium Ltd.* [1967] 1 WLR 691, *per* Stamp J at 696.

[18] *City Index Ltd. v Leslie* [1992] QB 98.

[19] Emphasis added.

certain level is followed by residuary words, it is presumed that the residuary words are not intended to include items of a higher rank. Thus in the phrase 'an officer or examiner of the court or some other person' in RSC Ord. 39 r. 4(a) the residuary words were held not to include judges.[20]

The *reddendo singula singulis* principle (render each to each) concerns the use of words distributively. Where a complex sentence has more than one subject, and more than one object, it may be the right construction to render each to each by applying each object to its appropriate subject. A similar principle applies to verbs and their subjects, and to other parts of speech. Section 1 of the Immigration Act 1971 lays down general principles. It begins: 'All those who are in this Act expressed to have the right of abode in the United Kingdom shall be free to live in, and to come and go into and from, the United Kingdom without let or hindrance . . .' The phrase 'to come and go into and from' the United Kingdom appears clumsy. Applied *reddendo singula singulis,* it is to be read as if it said 'to come into the United Kingdom and go from it'. Why was it not put that way in the Act? Because the drafter wished to keep the evocative phrase 'come and go'.

Many statutory propositions are implied rather than being directly expressed, which calls for accurate inference by the reader. The maxim *expressum facit cessare tacitum* embodies the principle that no inference is proper if it goes against the express words Parliament has used. 'Express enactment shuts the door to further implication.'[21] The question arose whether the Indecency with Children Act 1960 s. 1(1), which makes it an offence to commit an act of gross indecency with a child under the age of fourteen, contains an implication requiring proof of knowledge by the accused that the child is under that age. It was held by the Divisional Court that such an implication did not arise in view of the fact that in the wide-ranging Sexual Offences Act 1956 it is expressly stated when knowledge of the relevant age is required. The 1960 Act was passed to fill a lacuna in the 1956 Act 'wherein the specific defence which was sought to be advanced had been provided for in certain sections but pointedly omitted in others'.[22]

---

[20] *Re Brickman's Settlement* [1981] 1 WLR 1560.
[21] *Whiteman v Sadler* [1910] AC 514, *per* Lord Dunedin at 527.
[22] *B. v Director of Public Prosecutions* [1998] 4 All ER 265 at 274.

The difficulty of statutory interpretation is illustrated by the fact that this decision was reversed by the House of Lords on the ground that the Sexual Offences Act 1956 is a 'ragbag' of various provisions drawn from different statutes, and is therefore incapable of supporting the implication drawn so precisely by the Divisional Court.[23]

The last of these Latin maxims, *expressio unius est exclusio alterius* (to express one thing is to exclude another) is an aspect of the principle *expressum facit cessare tacitum* discussed above. Known for short as the *expressio unius* principle, it is applied where a statutory proposition might have covered a number of matters but in fact mentions only some of them. Unless these are mentioned merely as examples, or out of excess of caution, or for some other sufficient reason, the rest are taken to be intended to be excluded from the proposition. In particular the *expressio unius* principle is applied where a formula which in itself may or may not include a certain class is accompanied by words of extension or exception naming only some members of that class. The remaining members of the class are then taken to be excluded from these words. Section 2(3) of the Immigration Act 1971 states that for the purposes of s. 2(1) of the Act the word 'parent' includes the mother of an illegitimate child. The class to which this extension relates is the parents of an illegitimate child. Lord Lane CJ said: 'Under the rule *expressio unius exclusio alterius*, that express mention of the mother implies that the father is excluded'.[24]

The methodology

I conclude this chapter with a brief recapitulation of the methodology to be used in applying the four categories of interpretative criteria, or guides to legislative intention. The essence of the method is to move from the general to the particular. The interpretative criteria are general in nature. What is required in an actual case is a method of applying the relevant interpretative

---

[23] B. *(a minor) v Director of Public Prosecutions* [2000] 1 All ER 833.
[24] R. *v Secretary of State for the Home Department, ex p Crew* [1982] Imm. A.R. 94.

criterion or criteria to the specific enactment in question and the specific facts of the instant case.

The first step in the required method is to identify, in relation to the enactment, the factual outline and the legal thrust. As I have said, the usual legal effect of an enactment is that, when the facts of a case fall within an indicated area called the factual outline, specified consequences called the legal thrust ensue. Typically, the legal thrust in criminal law is the treatment of the facts as an offence, while in civil law it is the treatment of the facts as a cause of action.[25]

The next step is to identify the relevant interpretative *factors*. The term 'interpretative factor', in relation to an enactment, is used to denote a specific legal consideration which (1) derives from the way a general interpretative criterion applies to the text of the enactment and the facts of the instant case (and to other factual situations within the relevant factual outline), and (2) serves as a guide to the construction of the enactment in its application to those facts. The principle to be followed was stated by Lord Reid as follows:

When doubt arises, rules of construction are relied on. They are not rules in the ordinary sense of having some binding force. They are our servants not our masters. They are aids to construction, presumptions or pointers. Not infrequently one 'rule' points in one direction, another in a different direction. In each case we must look at all relevant circumstances, and decide as a matter of judgment what weight to attach to any particular 'rule'.[26]

No doubt when Lord Reid put the word rule in quotation marks here he meant to acknowledge that, as I have explained, many of the interpretative criteria are not rules. The task in a particular case is to determine (by reference to general criteria) the specific factors which, in the light of the facts of the instant case, are relevant in construing the enactment for the purposes of that case.

Where, as frequently happens, factors tend in different directions the interpreter then has to evaluate or 'weigh' them. This is the next step in the process. As respects a particular construction of the enactment, an interpretative factor may be either positive (tending in favour of that construction) or negative (tending away

25 For further details see Ch. 1.
26 *Maunsell v Olins* [1974] 3 WLR 835 at 837.

from it). Usually a factor which is positive in relation to one of the opposing constructions will be reflected in a corresponding factor which is negative in relation to the other. A common case is whether a literal construction ('Construction L') or a strained construction ('Construction S') shall be applied to the enactment. The positive factor in favour of Construction L that it gives effect to the literal meaning is opposed by the negative factor against Construction S that it fails to do this.

Where the interpretative factors do not all point one way, it is necessary for the court to assess the respective weights of the relevant factors and determine which of the opposing constructions they favour *on balance*. This is the final step unless, in the light of the various factors, the court decides that it prefers a third construction not put forward by either of the opposing parties. The relevant factors may be numerous, with no single one overriding. As Lord Scarman said of the principle of no deprivation without compensation, 'the principle is not an overriding rule of law: it is an aid *amongst many others*, developed by the judges in their never ending task of interpreting statutes . . .'[27] So for instance it is wrong for judges to say, as they often do, that doubt as to a penal enactment must always be resolved in favour of the accused. In this, as in every other case of disputed statutory interpretation, the court's task is to identify *all* the relevant factors and then conduct a balancing exercise.[28]

----

[27] *Secretary of State for Defence v Guardian Newspapers Ltd* [1985] AC 339 at 363 (emphasis added).
[28] For a summary of this chapter see pp. 214–15 below.

13

The nature of judgment

So far in this book we have looked mainly at cases where finding the legal meaning of an enactment is rendered problematic by a drafting defect or other avoidable cause of ambiguity or obscurity. In this chapter and the next we successively consider types of enactment which, though often criticizsed as ambiguous or uncertain, in fact are not. Here the reason why the enactment's legal meaning is unclear does not lie in anything defective in the drafting. It lies in the fact that the enactment's perfectly normal and correct wording calls for the exercise by a state functionary either of *judgment* or *discretion*. The outcome is uncertain only because different functionaries may legitimately pronounce different results, since human minds are not alike. The functionary may be an administrative official of central or local government or a judicial officer such as a judge, magistrate, or tribunal member.

At one extreme, where the decision is to be taken in exercise of a fully open discretion, the power of the decision maker is one which is completely unfettered.[1] At the other extreme, where the decision is to be taken in exercise of a duty to arrive at a judgment, there is no room whatever for individual choice (even though different decision-takers may legitimately arrive at different outcomes). Discretion is free, except for limitations placed upon it (expressly or impliedly) by the defining formula. Judgment is necessarily confined, because its sole purpose is to arrive at a conclusion of fact or law which accurately reflects reality. Discretion, by its nature, necessarily offers choice; judgment registers (or should do) a functionary's honest assessment of a situation offering no choice. Discretion analytically offers a variety of outcomes; judgment but one.

Here is a simple illustration. If at the holding of a race J were

---

[1] Judges dislike being placed in this position. Goddard LJ said of the Courts (Emergency Powers) Act 1939 that the court 'is really put very much in the position of a Cadi under the palm tree. There are no principles on which he is directed to act. He has to do the best he can in the circumstances, having no rules of law to guide him': *Metropolitan Properties Co. Ltd. v Purdy* [1940] 1 All ER 188 at 191.

deputed to stand at the finishing line and note down the order in which the runners ended the race, this would be a matter of judgment not discretion. J would not think he had any discretion in the matter, though in a close finish different judges in his position might honestly reach different conclusions.

Sharpening our analysis

With the growing political importance in western society of judicial or quasi-judicial functions (whether exercised by the executive or the judiciary), we need to sharpen our analysis of their elements. This most obviously presents itself as a matter of terminology, by the accurate use of which we helpfully allot to specific terms a clear working significance. Assuming the allocation to be correctly conceived we do well to respect it and apply it consistently, for that helps argument and analysis and furthers the deployment of law as a useful social tool.

One aspect of this necessary scrutiny concerns the insufficiently perceived distinction between discretion and judgment. Broadly, the first is subjective, the second objective. This chapter and the next examine in detail the difference between judgment and discretion as exercisable by state authorities. Although the conclusions have wider import, in terms the discussion is mainly limited to the field of legislation in jurisdictions where the common law or Global method of statutory interpretation prevails. We are concerned with cases where an enactment confers on a state functionary the duty or power to reach a judgment or exercise a discretion. Like a jaguar and a donkey, these are very different animals. Unlike a jaguar and a donkey, they are frequently confused.

Whether the task, in relation to a particular enactment, is to arrive at a judgment or exercise a discretion the operation can be accomplished only by taking a decision, so what we are talking about here is an aspect of the rules of decision-taking.[2] Nowadays these rules are often worked out and applied in judicial review proceedings, but that must not confuse us. They do not essentially

---

[2] In relation to public law, these rules are set out in detail in *Bennion Code*, s. 329.

belong to judicial review. To think they do is to confuse procedure with substance; these rules of decision-taking are substantial not procedural.

If a decision which requires judgment or discretion is not taken correctly, it can be challenged in the courts and perhaps quashed. This can happen if the decision-taker has mistaken a jaguar for a donkey, or vice versa. It can also happen if, because the relevant enactment is not clearly evaluated or the difference is not fully understood, the decision-taker confuses the characteristics of the two beasts. Such confusion may earlier have been experienced by the drafter of the enactment in question.

The context may be more complex than this. For example the decision-taker may (1) need to exercise judgment in determining whether required conditions are satisfied; and then, if they are, may (2) be called on to judge whether or not to exercise a discretion, and then (3) to decide in what way to do so. This may arise unprompted, or on the application of a person interested. The time for it may be at large, or tied to a specific event or period.

In the remainder of this chapter we look at the nature of judgment.

The nature of judgment

One example of judgment arises when a judge or magistrate assesses rival testimonies to arrive at a finding of fact: 'confronted with two conflicting stories and little else, he has to base his decision, mainly if not entirely, on his impression of the witnesses'.[3] A more complex example of judgment is the process of arriving at the legal meaning of a doubtful enactment in its application to given facts. To this conundrum there is, in the Dworkinian sense, only one right answer. However arriving at that answer may involve several decisions. One or more acts of judgment may be required in deciding what the relevant facts are. Other acts of judgment may be needed when it comes to examining and assessing the wording of the enactment in question. Both aspects are present when we seek to identify the factual outline and the legal thrust. However the point to grasp is that none of the judgments

---

[3] Lord Devlin, *The Judge* (Oxford: OUP, 1979), 3.

that are required to be made offer any looseness of outcome or scope for variation. True, different persons with different minds may reach different views on what the correct outcome is—but that is a distraction. It helps to avoid that distraction if for the purpose of analysis we assume that only one decision taker is involved.

The function of judgment is to assess a situation which requires a definitive answer. Here certain criteria are stated or implied to determine the choice of result. These criteria are inflexible, notionally demanding one answer, and one only. For example, in a given situation the criterion of 'justice' notionally calls for a single verdict. Justice is an absolute. When you apply an absolute to a conundrum there can in theory be only one result. If people arrive at different results it must be due to human fallibility or variability. That echoes Dworkin's view (unpopular in many academic quarters) that even on a difficult question of law there is but one correct answer. 'No aspect of law as integrity has been so misunderstood', Dworkin says, 'as its refusal to accept the popular view that there are no uniquely right answers in hard cases at law.'[4]

An example of what this means, and of how difficult it can be to get it right, is furnished by the famous but mistaken House of Lords decision in *Pepper (Inspector of Taxes) v Hart*.[5] In that case the question was what was a 'proper proportion' of certain expenses. The relevant decision was to be taken initially by a tax inspector, but the taxpayer had rights of appeal. This was essentially a simple question of judgment on the facts of the individual case, but the Appellate Committee of the House of Lords decided, mistakenly in my view, that the phrase 'a proper proportion' was ambiguous and that the ambiguity should be settled by referring to Hansard to find out how Ministers had said the phrase was intended to be construed.[6]

The effecting of judgment, or judgment-forming, means one must relate the particular facts to the abstract concept in question,

---

[4] *Law's Empire* (Oxford: Hart Publishing, 1998), 266.

[5] [1993] AC 593.

[6] The matter is dealt with at length in my article 'How they all got it wrong in *Pepper v Hart*' (1995) *British Tax Review* 325. In the article I got it wrong myself by saying that deciding on 'a proper proportion' was a matter of judgment or discretion. I now realize it is emphatically a question of judgment, and that discretion does not come into it.

often expressed as a broad term (such as 'proper proportion'). In this sense, concerned with formal logic, the *OED* defines 'judgment' as the action of mentally apprehending the relation between two objects of thought.[7] Whately said '[j]udgement is the comparing together in the mind two of the notions or ideas which are the objects of apprehension'.[8] For various reasons, legislative drafters are forced to strive for brevity. Broad terms assist in this. By use of a word or phrase of wide meaning, legislative power is delegated to the interpreters whose function is to work out the detailed effect. Doubt is necessarily created. Until the details lurking within the broad term are authoritatively worked out, it must be uncertain what they are. The statute user has to apply his own judgment, though it will be a judgment of what considerations a court would deploy if the point were litigated.

Broad terms

A broad term may consist either of a single word or a phrase. In its judgment the court may decide not to apply it to its full extent, so Scott J. said of the phrase 'pending land action' in the Land Charges Act 1972 s. 17(1) 'those words are very broad and cannot be given their full literal meaning'.[9] A broad term may perform the function of a verb, adverb, adjective, or substantive. If a substantive, it is what was described in an early case as a *nomen generale*.[10] Other descriptions include 'open-ended expression'[11], 'word of the most loose and flexible description'[12], and 'somewhat comprehensive and somewhat indeterminate term'.[13] The drafter selects a broad term which is either a processed term or an unprocessed term.[14] Either way the term is likely to have a core of certain meaning and a penumbra of uncertainty. It may be mobile or static. Its meaning will be coloured by the context, and the

---

[7] *Oxford English Dictionary* (2nd edn., 1992), meaning 9.
[8] *Logic* (2nd edn., London, 1827), p. 59.
[9] *Regan & Blackburn Ltd. v Rogers* [1985] 1 WLR 870 at 873.
[10] *Hunter v Bowyer* (1850) 15 LTOS 281.
[11] *Express Newspapers Ltd. v McShane* [1980] 2 WLR 89 at 94.
[12] *Green v Marsden* (1853) 1 Drew 646.
[13] *Campbell v Adair* [1945] JC 29.
[14] I refer to previous processing by court decision under the doctrine of *stare decicis*—see below.

legislative purpose. An implied intention that an unqualified broad term shall be construed as if a narrowing provision had accompanied it will not be found where the absence of such a provision is explicable only on the ground that it was not intended. Thus the House of Lords declined to treat the term 'accommodation' in the Housing (Homeless Persons) Act 1977 ss. 1 and 4 as qualified by an implied epithet such as 'appropriate' or 'reasonable'. If Parliament had intended such a narrowing of its meaning it would surely have said so.[15] In fact however, Parliament often does not 'say so', but leaves it to implication.

When drafters elect to attain brevity by using a broad term, they look for one which has been processed. If the courts have already worked out the meaning of a term, and that meaning corresponds to the drafter's intention, the term is suitable for present adoption. Then, instead of there being uncertainty about whether subsequent interpreters will apply the legal meaning desired, the drafter may feel reasonably sure that the established meaning will be followed in the present case. Usually, the processed term will be one used in previous legislation. Only rarely will a term whose meaning has been worked out solely at common law present itself as suitable for adoption by the legislature. The drafter of A. P. Herbert's Divorce Act, the Matrimonial Causes Act 1937, used a processed verb when he expressed as a ground of divorce that the respondent 'has deserted the petitioner without cause' for three years. The verb 'deserted', used by itself, is a typical broad term. There are many acts which might be held to fall within it. One is a simple refusal of sexual intercourse. But it had been earlier held that such a refusal did not constitute 'desertion' within the meaning of an earlier Act.[16] When the point was raised under the 1937 Act Tucker LJ took the same line: 'I think the Legislature in . . . refraining from defining desertion must be taken as accepting the tests which had hitherto been applied in the courts . . .'[17]

Doubt may arise whether use of a processed term in a new Act brings in the processed meaning or the ordinary (dictionary) meaning where these differ. Often there is no significant difference.

---

[15] *Puhlhofer v Hillingdon L.B.C.* [1986] AC 484.
[16] *Jackson v Jackson* [1924] P. 19.
[17] *Weatherley v Weatherley* [1946] 2 All ER 1 at 8.

Where there is a difference, the point may turn on whether the new Act is *in pari materia* with the earlier Acts in which the term appeared. The rule was thus laid down by Lord Buckmaster:

It has long been a well-established principle to be applied in the consideration of Acts of Parliament that where a word of doubtful meaning has received a clear judicial interpretation, the subsequent statute which incorporates the same word or the same phrase *in a similar context* must be construed so that the word or phrase is interpreted according to the meaning that has previously been ascribed to it.[18]

Here two points should be noted. First, it is not the practice of legislative drafters (who tend to be over-cautious) to attract processing expressly by saying in the new Act that the term has the same (undefined but processed) meaning as in the previous Act. This renders unrealistic the remark by Lord Simon of Glaisdale that '[i]f Parliament wishes to endorse the previous interpretation it can do so in terms'.[19] Secondly, the courts will be reluctant to attach previous processing to the term in its new use if they think that processing was defective.[20] While the borrowing by the drafter of a term already processed may be convenient, it can give rise to a conceptual difficulty. A word or phrase used in an Act is to be construed in accordance with the purpose of that Act. Decisions on its meaning may be misleading if the term is borrowed for another Act with a different purpose.[21]

Doubt arises from the drafter's use of a broad term only where its meaning is to some extent essentially uncertain. There are terms which are broad in the sense that they cover many different cases, but whose meaning is certain in virtually every case: for example 'mammal' or 'moving'. It is anyway unlikely that the application of a statutory broad term will be doubtful in *every* case. Selection by the drafter of such a term would be an error, since it would mean that the entirety of the legal rule in question was founded upon uncertainty; which does not accord with the nature of law. A modern Act whose application was uncertain in every case would certainly be considered ill-drawn. It follows that

[18] *Barras v Aberdeen Steam Trawling and Fishing Co.* [1933] AC 402 at 411 (emphasis added).
[19] *Farrell v Alexander* [1977] AC 59 at 90.
[20] See, e.g., *Royal Crown Derby Porcelain Co. v Russell* [1949] 2 KB 417 at 429.
[21] See, e.g., *Hanlon v The Law Society* [1981] AC 124.

what we are in practice concerned with is the broad term whose application to some cases is clear and to others doubtful. A penumbra is defined as a partial shade bordering upon a fuller or darker one; in other words a twilight. This is a good description here because we are all familiar with the difficulty caused by a phrase such as 'during the hours of darkness'. Midnight (except in the Arctic Circle) is clearly within this broad term, and noon equally clearly outside it. But there are periods around dawn and sunset during which it must be debatable whether darkness has ceased or fallen.

The drafter tries to choose phrases whose penumbra of doubt is as small as possible. At common law, burglary was committed when a dwelling-house was broken and entered by night with intent to commit a felony. Night was understood as the period between sunset and sunrise. A later common law refinement held it not to be 'night' if there was sufficient light from the sun by which to tell a person's face. Finally, when statute intervened, night was precisely if arbitrarily defined as the period between 9 p.m. and 6 a.m. So although the penumbra remained in nature, it vanished from the law of burglary.

An unnecessarily wide penumbra betokens bad drafting. The standard example used in juristic discussions of what Hart calls the 'open texture' of language is the notice reading 'No vehicles allowed in the park'. We can depict the uncertainty this causes by a diagram in which the inner circle depicts the core of certain meaning while the space between the circles marks the penumbra of doubt about what is allowed in the park. Outside this penumbra the meaning is once again certain—in the opposite sense. We may take three doubtful cases. There could be genuine argument with the park-keeper over whether it is allowed to take into the park a ridden bicycle, a motorized bath chair, or a sit-on motor mower. Other doubtful objects can readily be imagined, and we can vary the condition of the ones mentioned. Does it make a difference if the bicycle is pushed instead of ridden, or the motor mower belongs to the council managing the park? Is an ambulance allowed in to take away the victim of an accident on the slide? Suppose a car chassis, minus wheels and engine, is carried in by mischievous youths? The possibilities of doubt are endless. Greater precision can be achieved by detailed wording, but then we end up with the closely printed park notice that nobody reads.

Even the park-keeper may not read it, and so lack conviction in trying to repel the practical villains: motorists and motor cyclists. Modern legislative drafters go into as much detail as they consider practicable. For the rest, they rely on ellipsis—or select broad terms with the smallest penumbra of doubt.

Broad terms can be divided into two types. First, there is the case where the content of the term is static or constant, in both place and time. The circumstances that fall within it are basically the same wherever they happen, and at whatever historic moment. An example is the term 'accident' (see below). Secondly, there is the mobile term. What falls within it may differ according to time or place (or both). For instance one person may or may not be regarded as belonging to another person's 'family' according to the place, or the period, in which they live.[22] We now consider the two categories in turn, examining examples from decided cases. We shall see later that failure by the drafter to understand the distinction between the categories can have important consequences.

Static broad terms

The static term 'accident' has been frequently employed in legislation. One famous example was in the Workmen's Compensation Acts, which gave a workman a right to compensation for 'an accident arising out of and in the course of his employment'. This is a multiple broad term of epic proportions. Many thousands of judicial decisions proved necessary to process it. This operation began with the very first case to reach the House of Lords under the Workmen's Compensation Act 1909. It concerned a workman suffering from a form of heart disease induced by natural causes, an aneurism. The aneurism might have burst and killed the workman at any time—even while he was asleep in bed. In fact it did so while he was at work, engaged in manual labour of a by no means strenuous kind. Was this an 'accident'? Yes, said the House of Lords in a judgment we are not surprised to find lacked unanimity. The fact was that the purpose of the Act plainly required the term 'accident' to be given a wide meaning. As Kennedy LJ said in

[22] See p. 59 above.

another case, when holding that it even covered the murder of a cashier by a thief:

> An historian who described the end of Rizzio by saying that he met with a fatal accident in Holyrood Palace would fairly, I suppose, be charged with a misleading statement of fact . . . But whilst the description of death by murderous violence as an 'accident' cannot honestly be said to accord with the common understanding of the word, wherein is implied a negation of wilfulness and intention, I conceive it to be my duty rather to stretch the meaning of the word from the narrower to the wider sense of which it is inherently and etymologically capable . . .[23]

This neatly illustrates the difference between the case where the drafter has selected a term which is etymologically capable of the wide meaning it should bear and the case where he has erred by making his wording narrower than the object. Other examples of static broad terms are the following, dealing first with the term 'repairing' and then with the term 'supply'.

Rules made under the Railway Employment Prevention of Accidents Act 1900 protected workers engaged in 'relaying or repairing' the permanent way. Did this include the routine oiling and maintenance of apparatus working the points? The House of Lords, by a majority of three to two, held that it did not.[24] The wording was narrower than the object, a frequent drafting defect. The literal meaning, applied here, defeated the claim of one who on policy grounds clearly should have been covered. Today a purposive construction would be applied, and the claimant would succeed.

Section 1(1) of the Finance Act 1972 introduced a brand new tax in these words: 'A tax, to be known as value added tax, shall be charged . . . on the *supply* of goods and services in the United Kingdom. . . .'. Griffiths J. said: 'There is no definition of "supply" in the Act itself, but it is quite clear from the language of the Act that "supply" is a word of the widest import'.[25] Many more instances could be given of static broad terms, but this is not necessary. The terms are 'static' in the sense that, by processing, detailed rules can be worked out which will be of universal application despite differences of time or place. I turn now to the *mobile* broad term.

[23] *Nisbet v Rayne and Burn* [1910] 2 KB 689.
[24] *London and North Eastern Railway v Berriman* [1946] AC 278.
[25] *Customs and Excise Commissioners v Oliver* [1980] 1 All ER 353 at 354.

Mobile broad terms

Section 4(1) of the Obscene Publications Act 1959 provides a defence against a charge of publishing an obscene article 'if it is proved that publication of the article in question is justified as being for the public good on the ground that it is in the interests of science, literature, art or learning, or of other objects of general concern'. Lord Wilberforce said that the phrase *other objects of general concern* 'is no doubt a mobile phrase; it may, and should, change in content as society changes'.[26]

Changes of this kind may occur in time or in place. Often they occur in both. Since an ongoing Act is always speaking[27] it must be worded so as to accommodate them. The drafter of the Obscene Publications Act 1959 assumed that, throughout the life of the Act, science, literature, art and learning would be of general concern. It was safe therefore to specify them (and helpful to do so, since they gave shape and colour to his proposition). But other topics were to be judged not on what was of general concern in 1959 but on what was of general concern at the time of an alleged offence. If the Act lasted 50 years, and a prosecution was brought at the time of its golden jubilee, the drafter intended the case to be judged by what was of general concern in 2009 not 1959. Let us take some other examples, first of changes in time and then in place.

Suppose it is desired to impose control over firearms, but exempt any antique weapon. The broad term 'antique' is vague. The drafter might seek precision by referring instead to a weapon 'manufactured more than 100 years before the passing of this Act'. But that would be illogical. If the Act were passed in 1968 a gun made 105 years earlier would be exempt. By 1978 however, a gun made 105 years earlier would not be exempt, because it would have been made only 95 years before the passing of the Act. What is wanted is a rolling period, so that at any moment the Act will exempt guns which at that moment are 100 years old. The drafter of the Firearms Act 1968 s. 58(2) did not adopt this course. Instead, he provided a flurry of broad terms: 'Nothing in this Act relating to firearms shall apply to an antique firearm

26 *R. v Jordan* [1976] 2 WLR 887, 893. 27 See Ch. 5.

which is sold, transferred, purchased, acquired or possessed as a curiosity or ornament'. No definitions were provided for 'antique', 'curiosity' or 'ornament'. The question of the legal meaning of 'antique' in s. 58(2) came before the Divisional Court.[28] The prosecutor appealed from magistrates' acquittal of a defendant in relation to three guns 'dating from possibly 1886, and after 1905 and 1910'. He told the court that prosecuting authorities needed guidance on what was 'antique' for this purpose. Eveleigh LJ said it was a question of fact, but guns manufactured in the twentieth century 'could not be antique' in 1980. The court directed the magistrates to convict in relation to the guns made after 1905 and 1910. Regarding the gun possibly made in 1886, Eveleigh LJ said that the magistrates were entitled to come to their conclusion, though he would not have done so himself. This judgment seems to put excessive weight on the arbitrary division of time into centuries.

Is 'book' a mobile term? It might not seem so. Everyone knows what a book is. Or do they? Section 9 of the Bankers' Books Evidence Act 1879 defines 'banker's book' as including ledgers, day books, account books, 'and all other books used in the ordinary business of the bank'. In 1879 it was no doubt unthinkable that banks would keep their records in anything but bound books. One cannot blame the drafter for failing to envisage the invention of microfilm. Yet in seeking to make copies of all bank records admissible in evidence he might have managed to find a phrase of more general meaning. The Divisional Court had no hesitation in coming to the drafter's rescue.[29] They treated 'book' as a mobile term wide enough to embrace microfilm—and indeed 'any form of permanent record kept by the bank by means made available by modern technology'. It did not worry Caulfield J. that a microfilm 'is not normally called a book'. Had he foreseen the development of computer use by banks he might have hesitated over using the word 'permanent'.

Social change has frequently to be accommodated by the mobile term. When 'single woman' was first used in Affiliation Acts (requiring the father to pay) it referred solely to an unmarried woman. The growing frequency with which marriages broke up

[28] *Bennett v Brown* (1980) *Times*, 12 April.
[29] *Barker v Wilson* [1980] 1 WLR 884.

led to its ultimate extension to a married woman living apart from her husband—even where they shared a roof.[30] It follows that a judicial decision on the meaning of a term may be disregarded if the popular meaning changes. The Rent Acts gave protection, where the tenant died, to a member of the tenant's 'family'. In 1950 it was held by the Court of Appeal that this did not include the tenant's common law husband.[31] In another case 25 years later the same court reversed its ruling.[32] Bridge LJ said:

If the language can change its meaning to accord with changing social attitudes, then a decision on the meaning of a word in a statute before such a change should not continue to bind thereafter, at all events in a case where the courts have constantly affirmed that the word is to be understood in its ordinary meaning.[33]

By this Bridge LJ clearly referred to the fact that a mobile term is to be applied to facts arising at a particular time in accordance with its meaning at that time. This is so where that conforms to the purpose or policy of the Act. Where it does not do this, it may be necessary to apply the original meaning of the term.[34]

Another legal matrimonial term of long standing is 'cruelty' as a ground of divorce. Here we see the effect of a social change attributable to advancing civilization. As the times become less rough and barbarous, and the standard of comfort advances, people will put up with less hardship. What was once part of the give-and-take of marriage becomes 'cruelty'. Mental torture enters the scene, alongside physical ill-treatment. There is a similar progression with broad terms like 'riotous', 'disorderly', 'inde-cent', and 'insulting' as descriptions of public behaviour. A dog may now be held 'dangerous' within the meaning of the Dogs Act 1871 even though its behaviour is something less than savage or ferocious.[35]

Here are two examples of broad terms which are geographic-ally mobile, that is whose content varies from place to place.

Section 59 of the Highways Act 1980 gives a highway authority power to recover compensation from an operator responsible for

---

[30] *Watson v Tuckwell* (1947) 63 TLR 634.
[31] *Gammans v Elkins* [1950] 2 KB 328.
[32] *Dyson Holdings Ltd v Fox* [1976] QB 503.
[33] p. 513.
[34] As with the term 'engine', discussed on p. 60 above.
[35] *Keddle v Payn* [1964] 1 WLR 262.

damage caused by 'excessive' weight passing along the highway, or other 'extraordinary' traffic thereon. Both these broad terms are modified by reference to the average maintenance expenses of highways in the neighbourhood of the one in question. Here the geographical variability of the term is expressed in the statute.

In the other example the variability is not expressed, but has been held by the courts to be implied. Section 74(4) of the Licensing Act 1964 (reproducing earlier legislation) empowers justices to extend permitted licensing hours for the sale and consumption of alcoholic liquor on a 'special occasion'. No definition of this term is provided. In a case decided under earlier legislation, Lord Coleridge CJ said 'the question what is a special occasion must necessarily be a question of fact in each locality'. He added: '[e]ach locality may very well have its own meaning to those words, and it is for the justices in each district to say whether a certain time and place come within the description.'[36] Thus the Saturday before a bank holiday may be a 'special occasion' in a seaside holiday resort but not in an industrial town.[37]

Noticing the distinction

Not only should the interpreter be alert to the distinction between the static and mobile broad term, but at an earlier stage the drafter needs to be aware of it too. It is really a distinction between static and mobile concepts. If the concept for which the drafter needs a term is static, then he should select a static term, and vice versa. If he fails in this he may create unnecessary difficulties of interpretation. The commonest error, and the most troublesome, is where the drafter with insufficient imagination thinks his concept is fixed when it is in fact mobile. The Canadian Criminal Code made it an offence to trade or traffic in 'any bottle or syphon' which had upon it the trade mark of another person, or fill it with any beverage for sale, without his consent.[38] It is obviously possible for beverages to be sold in other forms of container,

---

[36] *Devine v Keeling* (1886) 50 JP 551, 552.
[37] *R. v Corwen Justices* [1980] 1 WLR 1045.
[38] Cited Elmer Driedger, *The Construction of Statutes* (Toronto: Butterworths, 1974), 86.

such as cartons. By looking only at the conditions prevailing at the time he was writing, and failing to exercise his imagination, the drafter made his text unnecessarily and unjustifiably narrow. He could easily have written 'container' instead of 'bottle or syphon'. We saw earlier how a similar difficulty arose in connection with bankers' books. The reverse error, of using a mobile term for a static concept, creates unnecessary vagueness. It would not have been sensible to say 'container' instead of 'bottle' in a provision intended to guard against danger from broken glass.

As we have seen, the wider the penumbra of doubt attached to a broad term the greater the range of judgment effectively delegated to the interpreter. There is an important class of cases where, because the limiting framework is virtually non-existent, this form of delegation occurs practically across the whole field. In effect the legislator abdicates completely. For his judgment is substituted that of the interpreter, guided only by vague concepts such as what is 'reasonable' or 'just' or 'fit and proper'. There are many examples of this form of delegation. Here is one, drawn from the Consumer Credit Act 1974. In this instance the interpreter is an official, the Director General of Fair Trading. Section 25(1) states that a licence to carry on a credit or hire business shall be granted on the application of any person if he satisfies the Director General that he is 'a fit person to engage in activities covered by the licence'. If this stood alone, as it well might have done, it would empower the Director General to set his own standards of fitness. Parliament thought it right to lay down guidelines however, and the section goes on to instruct the Director General to have regard to specified factors—such as whether the applicant has a record of dishonesty or violence.

For obvious reasons, Parliament has been more ready to entrust unfettered decision-making to judges than officials. In the early days of divorce law for example, the court was empowered in relation to the children of dissolved marriages to 'make such provision as it may deem just and proper' with respect to their custody, maintenance and education.[39] The modern tendency is for judges to receive (and indeed expect) more detailed guidance from the legislator. When the grounds for divorce were recast in 1969–70 elaborate criteria were laid down for maintenance,

---

[39] Matrimonial Causes Act 1859, s. 35.

including the absurd requirement to put the parties as nearly as possible in the position they would have been in if the marriage had not broken down.[40] This could not last, and was speedily abandoned—but not before it had inflicted great harm on divorcing husbands.

Sometimes, as we have seen, guides to the interpretation of the broad term are stated expressly in the legislative text. Even where this is not done, the meaning is not left completely at large. Under the *noscitur a sociis* principle, terms are recognized to gain colour from their context.[41] The context may not furnish much assistance however. The Housing Act 1980 laid down the repairing covenants that are to apply where the secure tenant of a flat exercises his statutory right to acquire a long lease.[42] It enabled the landlord to charge the tenant a 'reasonable' proportion of the cost of non-structural repairs. Often when the broad term 'reasonable' is used, as with the concept of a 'reasonable' rent, the factors by reference to which it is to be applied are obvious. Here they are not. The Act imposed on the landlord the duty to repair whether or not it was 'reasonable' that he should be saddled with this. It then enabled him to transfer to the tenant such part of the duty as might be 'reasonable'. If, from an objective viewpoint it was wholly unreasonable in a particular case to saddle the landlord with the cost of any repairs, how could it be 'reasonable' to transfer only a part of the cost to the tenant—and how could one judge which part? The courts are forced to grope for a meaning in such cases.

Although where judgment is required there is notionally one right answer, in practice there is what in one case Lord Bingham of Cornhill CJ called 'the area of judgment'.[43] In that case the Criminal Cases Review Commission might properly have found either that there was or that there was not a 'real possibility' within the meaning of the Criminal Appeal Act 1995 s. 13(1)(a) that the conviction would not be upheld. This 'area of judgment' may overlap two alternative categories, e.g. two broad terms. In

---

[40] Matrimonial Proceedings and Property Act 1970, s. 5(1) and (2), succeeded by the Matrimonial Causes Act 1973, s. 25(1).
[41] For this principle see p. 110 above.
[42] See Sch. 2, paras 13 to 17.
[43] *R. v Criminal Cases Review Commission, ex p Pearson* [1999] 3 All ER 498 at 523.

another case the Court of Appeal held that there was such an overlap between the broad terms 'special educational provision' and 'non-educational provision' in the Education Act 1996 s. 319.[44] Sedley LJ referred[45] to 'the limits of possible meaning' of the term 'special educational provision'. These led, he said,[46] to a 'potentially large area of judgment' resulting in the fact that it would be acceptable to reach a judgment that given treatment fell within the range of special educational provision or fell within the range of non-educational provision.

The width of this 'area of judgment' depends on the degree of precision with which the standard to be used for forming the judgment is defined.

> the criterion so established may itself be so imprecise that different decision-makers, each acting rationally, might reach differing conclusions when applying it to the facts of a given case. In such a case the court [of review] is entitled to substitute its own opinion for that of the person to whom the decision has been entrusted only if the decision is so aberrant that it cannot be classed as rational: *Edwards (Inspector of Taxes) v Bairstow* [1956] AC 14.[47]

Even so, as I have said, notionally there is only one correct answer arising from judgment-forming, as opposed to the exercise of discretion, where there must be at least two. When the question arose whether a certain act was an abuse of process Lord Diplock, stressing that the question was one of judgment, said 'I disavow the word discretion'.[48] In pronouncing on the meaning of 'substantial' in the Fair Trading Act 1973 s. 64(3) (which allows a merger reference to be made where services are supplied 'in a substantial part of the United Kingdom'), Lord Mustill said: 'Even after eliminating inappropriate senses of "substantial" one is still left with a meaning broad enough to call for the exercise of judgment . . .'[49] Where the exercise of judgment is required, the term

---

[44] *Bromley London Borough Council v Special Educational Needs Tribunal* [1999] 3 All ER 587.
[45] At 591. [46] At 596.
[47] *South Yorkshire Transport Ltd. v Monopolies and Mergers Commission* [1993] 1 WLR 23, *per* Lord Mustill at 32; cited by Auld LJ in *R. v Ministry of Defence, ex p Walker* [1999] 3 All ER 935 at 942.
[48] *Hunter v Chief Constable of West Midlands* [1982] AC 529 at 536.
[49] *R. v Monopolies and Mergers Commission, ex p South Yorkshire Transport Ltd.* [1993] 1 WLR 23 at 32.

'evaluate' may be used. In the case of a statutory application to an authority, e.g. under the Housing Act 1985 s. 62(1), it may be necessary for the authority to judge whether the applicant has the necessary mental capacity to be a householder. Lord Griffiths said that Parliament 'must have intended the local housing authority to evaluate the capacity of the applicant'.[50]

As indicated in the above discussion on the 'area of judgment', a court or other adjudicating authority needs in arriving at a judgment on the legal meaning of an enactment to have regard to the phenomenon of differential readings. This is the name given to the situation where different minds arrive at different assessments. Often this involves what can only be called impression. Lord Nolan said of one enactment that the matter 'is one of impression which may present and has presented itself differently to different minds'.[51] The problem is not confined to language; differential readings may apply to the legal policy governing the enactment, or any other intangible factor. Thus in relation to the conviction under the War Crimes Act 1991 of the war criminal Anthony Sawoniuk, who was then in his eighties, Lord Bingham of Cornhill CJ differed sharply with the trial judge Potts J. on what advice should be given to the Home Secretary regarding the prisoner's release date. Lord Bingham felt the policy of the Act required mercy, so that Sawoniuk should be able to look forward to release in his lifetime. Potts J. thought he should die in prison.[52]

There may be more than one relevant concept, and the various concepts may conflict. Here weighing and balancing of the concepts becomes necessary. There is a point beyond which analysis cannot get:

Even when judicial reasoning is based on the cumulative effect of several independent premises, a time inevitably comes when all that the judge can say is 'I have weighed the pros and cons which I have stated and I now give judgment for so and so in accordance with the principle I have formulated after weighing the stated pros and cons'. The important thing

[50] *R. v Oldham Metropolitan Borough Council, ex p Garlick* [1993] AC 509 at 520.
[51] *R. v Secretary of State for the Environment, ex p Camden London Borough Council* [1998] 1 All ER 937 at 944.
[52] *The Times*, 25 June 1999; BBC Radio Four 'Today' programme, 24 June 1999.

is that it is of the essence of the judicial process that the pros and cons should first be weighed.[53]

Differential readings

It is notorious that different judicial minds may, and frequently do, conscientiously arrive at differential readings. Nothing can be done about this; it is part of the human condition. One cause lies in a difference of values, or what Neil MacCormick called the bedrock:

> Judges evaluating consequences of rival possible rulings may give different weight to different criteria of evaluation, differ as to the degree of perceived injustice, or of predicted inconvenience which will arise from adoption or rejection of a given ruling. Not surprisingly, they differ, sometimes sharply and even passionately, in relation to their final judgment of the acceptability or unacceptability all things considered of a ruling under scrutiny. At this point we reach the bedrock of the value preferences which inform our reasoning but are not demonstrable by it. At this level there can simply be irresoluble differences of opinion between people of goodwill and reason.[54]

The legal meaning of a broad term which is to be applied in relation to particular facts is determined as a matter of judgment in the light of the interpretative criteria. Here differential readings are commonly arrived at. For example the House of Lord considered the broad term 'token' in the Gaming Act 1968 s. 34(3)(b) (which refers to a 'token' which is exchangeable for other items).[55] The majority held as a matter of judgment that a toy teddy bear exchangeable for another form of prize was not a 'token', Lord Lloyd saying 'In my judgment "token" in s. 34(3)(b) is used in its ordinary sense, and does not include an exchangeable teddy bear.'[56] However Lord Hoffmann, dissenting, held that the form of the object was immaterial, since 'the identifying characteristic of a "token" must be the right to exchange it for something else'.

[53] Rupert Cross, *Precedent in English Law* (3rd edn., London: Butterworths, 1977), 196–7.
[54] *Legal Reasoning and Legal Theory* (Oxford: Clarendon Press, 1978), 105–6.
[55] *R. v Burt & Adams Ltd.* [1998] 2 All ER 417.
[56] p. 420.

In the end judges can find no better words to use for this phenomenon of differential readings than 'instinct' or 'feel'. There is 'an instinctive feeling that the event or act being weighed in the balance is too remote'.[57] 'As Lord Pearce once said: "I do not know, I only feel".'[58] However there is evidence that some judges are predisposed to reach certain conclusions on some matters. In a study of House of Lords decisions arrived at in 1993[59] David Robertson showed statistically that Lord Templeman 'was so strongly opposed to tax evasion that his presence on a panel [of the Appellate Committee] must have pleased the Revenue Authorities. Equally strong . . . was the tendency for criminal appeals to go to the defendant when Lord Bridge was on the bench'.[60] As pointed out in Chapter 1, in recent times, with the increasing appointment of judges from among persons of the female sex or with non-indigenous ethnic backgrounds, the likelihood of differential readings has increased.

The idea of judicial subjectivism, and its separation from objectivity, can be taken too far. It is true that the weight to be attached to a particular factor is not a precise resultant of the combination of the general criterion and the facts of the instant case: our law is not so mechanistic and predetermined as that. Yet it is not accurate to say that the weight to be attached to a factor is a purely subjective matter, entirely dependent on the idiosyncrasies of particular judges. In balancing rival considerations in notional scales it is expected that any judge in the system would arrive at much the same (even though not identical) weighting. One judge who consistently arrived at weightings markedly different from those of the rest would be regarded as a maverick. The reason for that is that such weights are never assessed in a vacuum. Each judge comes to the task of exercising judgment equipped with both experience and ability. The experience (compounded of learning and practice) shows him or her in a particular case how other judges have weighed similar factors. The ability equips the judge for the difficult intellectual task of assembling and then assessing the factors bearing on the decision. Justice requires that

[57] *Lamb v London Borough of Camden* [1981] QB 625, *per* Watkins LJ at 647.
[58] *Rost v Edwards* [1990] 2 QB 460, *per* Popplewell J at 478.
[59] *Judicial Discretion in the House of Lords* (Oxford: Clarendon Press, 1998).
[60] p. 36.

the process, though far from mechanistic, shall in some sense be uniform.

This chapter has explored the nature of judgment. The next chapter considers the rather different nature of discretion. The two concepts are constantly muddled by judges and others, which does harm to our legal processes and their social utility.[61]

[61] For a summary of this chapter see p. 215–16 below.

14

The nature of discretion

After the discussion in the previous chapter of the nature of judgment we turn now to examine the nature of discretion, a wholly different cerebral concept.

At any point within a given range

Discretion is applied where the empowering enactment leaves it to the chosen functionary to make a determination at any point within a given range, for example in fixing the court's sentence, following conviction of an offence, somewhere among the array of punishments prescribed by the relevant criminal statute as available on conviction of that offence. However it is also possible for a statutory discretion to relate only to two alternatives. If asked to give leave to appeal a judge may either grant leave or refuse it. That is discretion not judgment because the decision is left wholly to the judge, and no one else can say there is some other 'correct' answer so that the judge's decision is wrong. This becomes more obvious where there is no right of appeal from the judge's exercise of the discretion. Power becomes absolute when no loftier authority is empowered to pronounce upon the validity of its exercise.

David Robertson mistakenly defines discretion as arising whenever a judicial decision 'could have been different'.[1] This is the language of a political scientist rather than a lawyer. It confuses true discretion with true judgment. As Lord Justice Sedley said when reviewing Robertson's book, 'By discretion he does not mean what a lawyer means . . . He means the entire process of choosing between or among available outcomes. Since his target audience must in large part be lawyers, this might seem an unfortunate failure of communication . . .'[2]

For an enactment to bestow a discretion on a person (D)

---

[1] *Judicial Discretion in the House of Lords* (Oxford: Clarendon Press, 1998), 6.
[2] Sir Stephen Sedley, *Cambridge Law Journal*, Vol. 58, Nov. 1999, 627.

involves a built-in looseness of outcome. In reaching a decision, D is not required to assume there is only one right answer. On the contrary D is given a choice dependent to a greater or lesser extent on personal inclination and preference. The discretion may be open, when it is completely at large. Alternatively it may be confined, to be exercised within limits laid down expressly or by implication. The gift of open discretion bestows total freedom of choice on the recipient. The dictionary definition says it accords liberty or power of deciding, or of acting according as one thinks fit, amounting to an uncontrolled power of disposal.[3] In 1399 the rolls of Parliament[4] recorded the puissance of royal will as the 'Mercy and grace of the Kyng as it longes to hym in his owene discretion'.

In law discretion has been defined as the power of a court of justice, or person acting in a judicial capacity, to decide, within the limits allowed by positive rules of law, as to the punishment to be awarded or remedy to be applied, or in civil causes how the costs shall be borne, and generally to regulate matters of procedure and administration.[5] Balcombe LJ said of the question whether a judge should permit a litigant's McKenzie friend to be present in chambers proceedings: 'this must be a matter for the discretion of the judge'. He added that he could see no ground upon which the Court of Appeal could possibly interfere with a judge's exercise of this discretion.[6] That would indicate a fully open discretion, but in fact there are of course some limits, as where the judge is proved venal or has made a basic error. 'It is well known that [the Court of Appeal] will not intervene in an exercise of discretion by a trial judge unless he has erred on a matter of principle.'[7]

The most obvious way for an enactment to confer a discretion is by the use of the term 'may'. This confers on a person power or authority to take a certain decision. Unless more is to be gathered, the decision is at large; in other words the discretion bestowed is

---

[3] *Oxford English Dictionary* (2nd edn., 1992).   [4] III 451/2.
[5] *Oxford English Dictionary* (2nd edn., 1992).
[6] *Re G (a minor) (chambers hearing: assistance) (Note)* (1991) [1999] 1 WLR 1828 at 1829; cited by Lord Woolf MR in *R. v Bow County Court, ex p Pelling* [1999] 4 All ER 751 at 755.
[7] *Copeland v Smith* [2000] 1 All ER 457, *per* Buxton LJ at 461.

open.[8] In former times it was the practice for statutes instead to employ the phrase 'it shall be lawful' to bestow this type of authority.

Implied restrictions

Case law has grown up to indicate implied restrictions on the apparently unlimited power conferred by open discretion. Often these spring from principles laid down by the courts under the head of legal policy. Thus where a tribunal set up under the Tribunals Of Inquiry (Evidence) Act 1921 to investigate shootings by British soldiers in Londonderry exercised its discretion to withhold anonymity from witnesses in a way that was unfair because it unnecessarily risked endangering their lives this was held unlawful.[9]

Similarly it is the policy of the law to protect children and young persons against parents and others who, motivated by cultural or religious values deriving from countries outside the United Kingdom, seek to subject them to coercion by such means as forced marriages or forced residence overseas. This was laid down in a 1999 case[10] which, said Singer J.[11]

throws into sharp focus these difficult situations, most frequently involving minority ethnic and religious groups within our community . . . My hope is that practitioners who may not be fully aware of these issues may become so; that the likely attitude of the English courts may be made clear to parents and families in the relevant communities; and that perhaps greater vigilance and protection may be afforded by local authorities.

Singer J added that parents of such children need to understand that 'they may face considerable difficulties if they hope on the

[8] See *R. v. Governor of Brixton Prison, ex p Enaharo* [1963] 2 QB 455 at 465; P. B. Maxwell, *The Interpretation of Statutes* (12th edn., Bombay: Tripathi, 1969), 234–5; W. F. Craies, *A Treatise on Statute Law* (7th edn., London: Sweet & Maxwell, 1971), 229; Bennion, *Statute Law* (2nd edn., 1983), 199; *Bennion Code*, p. 34.
[9] *R. v Lord Savill of Newdigate and others, ex p A and others* [1999] 4 All ER 860.
[10] *Re K. R. (a child) (abduction: forcible removal by parents)* [1999] 4 All ER 954.
[11] At 960.

one hand to bring them up in an English educational system and society but at the same time to retain every aspect of their own traditions and expectations'.

In some instances the courts have laid down that 'may' is to be interpreted as 'shall'. Here the apparent power is converted to a duty. The effect is to convert a discretion into an obligation to exercise judgment, the judgment in question being one of determining whether the conditions required for the exercise of the duty have arisen.

Guidelines

The laying down of guidelines is often, though not always, the sign of a discretion. The Parliamentary Constituencies Act 1986 Sch. 2 contains rules for the guidance of members of Boundary Commissions. Rule 7 provides that the Commissions need not aim to give effect to the earlier rules in all circumstances 'which emphasises that they are discretionary'.[12] Hence 'the practical effect is that a strict application of the rules ceases to be mandatory, so that the rules, while remaining very important indeed, are reduced to the status of guidelines'.[13] The practice is growing of including in an Act which uses a broad term requiring the exercise of discretion some indication of how Parliament intends the discretion to be exercised. This is an important category of cases where rules of construction are laid down by statute.[14]

Apart from itself containing guidelines, an Act may authorize or require them to be laid down by a Minister or other authority. Thus the Local Authority Social Services Act 1970 s. 7(1) requires a council 'to act under the general guidance of the Secretary of State'.[15] Such guidance has to be followed unless there is a good reason to deviate from it.[16] In one case the relevant guidelines

---

[12] Colin R. Munro, *Studies in Constitutional Law* (2nd edn., London: Butterworths, 1999), 100.

[13] *R. v. Boundary Commission for England, ex p Foot* [1983] QB 600, *per* Donaldson MR at 624.

[14] See Ch. 9.

[15] For another example see Housing Act 1985 s. 71 and comment thereon by Lord Griffiths in *R. v Oldham Metropolitan Borough Council, ex p Garlick* [1993] AC 509 at 516.

[16] *R. v Islington London Borough Council, ex p Rixon* [1997] ELR 66.

were set out in a document entitled *Working Together Under the Children Act 1989*.[17] Where these envisaged that at a case conference the parent would be accompanied by a lawyer, and stated that the minutes should be sent to all who attended, it was held unlawful for an authority to adopt a contrary policy.[18] Where, under powers conferred by an enactment, a Minister or other authority issues guidelines as to the construction of that or any other enactment, and the court on judicial review finds that the guidelines are incorrect in law, it may make a declaration to that effect.[19]

The mere fact that a statutory power to exercise discretion is in terms unfettered does not prevent the court from laying down guidelines as to its exercise.[20] A court should not however lay down guidelines where the need for them has not been made 'entirely apparent', since the risk is then that cases will be treated as matters of law on the interpretation not of the enactment but the guidelines.[21] Judicial guidelines should not fetter a statutory discretion by confining its exercise to rare or exceptional cases if no such restriction is indicated in the enactment conferring the discretion.[22]

Guidelines are now sometimes laid down by the Judicial Studies Board.[23] In a combined judgment covering eight cases, of which the first was *Heil v Rankin and Another*,[24] the Court of Appeal handed down revised guidelines in this area in the light of the Law Commission Report *Damages for Personal Injury: Non-Pecuniary Loss*.[25] Lord Bingham of Cornhill CJ said that the issue of the JSB guidelines had been a welcome development and that it was highly

---

[17] HMSO, 1991.

[18] *R. v Cornwall County Council, ex p L* (1999) *Times*, 25 Nov.

[19] *R. v Secretary of State for the Environment, ex p Tower Hamlets London Borough Council* [1993] QB 632 (provision of the Code of Guidance to Local Authorities on Homelessness, issued under the Housing Act 1985 s. 71, held to be wrong in law).

[20] *Ramsden v Lee* [1992] 2 All ER 204 at 211 (concerning the discretion conferred by the Limitation Act 1980 s. 33).

[21] *Thompson v Brown Construction (Ebbw Vale) Ltd.* [1981] 1 WLR 744 at 752.

[22] *R. v Lee* [1993] 1 WLR 103 (discretion conferred by Children and Young Persons Act 1933 s. 39(1) to prohibit publication of identity of juvenile defendants).

[23] See for example their *Guidelines for the Assessment of General Damages in Personal Injury Cases* (4th edn., London: Blackstone, 1998).

[24] (2000) *Times*, 23 March.　　　[25] 1999, Law Com. No. 257.

desirable that they should issue a new edition reflecting the revised guidelines as soon as possible.[26]

Distinguishing discretion from judgment

The Chronically Sick and Disabled Persons Act 1970 s. 2(1) requires an authority to ascertain the 'needs' of certain persons as a preliminary to deciding what benefits they should receive. Swinton Thomas LJ said of the argument that an assessment of need involved a discretion that it was fundamentally flawed, adding: 'A need is a question of assessment and judgment, not discretion.'[27] He neatly showed the distinction between judgment and discretion by holding that while a local authority could not take its own financial means into account when deciding, as a matter of judgment, whether a person had 'needs' it could do so when deciding, as a matter of discretion, how it was to meet those 'needs'.

What is judicially described as discretion often turns out to be judgment. In one case Lord Bingham of Cornhill CJ said that under the Police and Criminal Evidence Act 1984 s. 78 the court had a 'discretion' to refuse to allow evidence to be given if its admission would have such an adverse effect on the fairness of the proceedings that the court ought not to admit it. But, as Lord Bingham acknowledged later in the report, that is truly a matter of judgment not discretion.[28] Unfortunately judges not infrequently blur the distinction between judgment and discretion. Thus Lord Keith of Kinkel said of a local authority's duty under the Education Act 1944 s. 55(1) to determine whether free school transport was 'necessary': '[t]he authority's function in this respect is capable of being described as a "discretion", though it is not, of course, an unfettered discretion but rather in the nature of an exercise of judgment'.[29] It is in fact nothing else but an exercise of judgment.

[26] The JSB has also published a collection of specimen directions to the jury for Crown Court judges: see *Crown Court Bench Book* (May 1999). In effect these lay down the legal meanings of a large number of criminal enactments.

[27] *R. v Gloucestershire County Council, ex p Barry* [1996] 4 All ER 421 at 438.

[28] *Nottingham City Council v Amin* (1999) *Times* 2 Dec.

[29] *Devon County Council v George* [1989] AC 573 at 604.

Even though the existence of such conceptual questions prevents the effect of an enactment requiring judgment or discretion from being known with certainty until they are answered by a decision of the relevant authority (an official or the court), this does not in itself mean that the enactment's drafting is unsatisfactory, or that it is ambiguous or obscure. On the contrary, the posing of such questions is an essential part of legislative functioning. The Broadcasting Act 1990 s. 92(2)(a) restricts radio advertising which is of a nature which is judged by the Radio Authority to be 'political'. It was held that the term 'political' is not here ambiguous merely because it is a broad term of indeterminate meaning. In view of the wide variety of possible advertisements, it was not possible for Parliament to provide a clear definition of the term 'political'. So it left the decision to the judgment of the regulatory authority, which had expertise in the field and was able to respond to changing circumstances.[30]

In a recent case Lord Hope of Craighead said in relation to the European Convention on Human Rights:

In some circumstances [that is where the margin of appreciation applies] it will be appropriate for the courts to recognise that there is an area of judgment within which the judiciary will defer, on democratic grounds, to the considered opinion of the elected body or person whose act or decision is said to be incompatible with the Convention. This point is well made in *Human Rights Law and Practice* (1999) p. 4, para. 3.21, of which Lord Lester of Herne Hill QC and Mr David Pannick QC are the general editors, where the area in which these choices may arise is conveniently and appropriately described as the 'discretionary area of judgment'.[31]

This is indeed to muddle judgment and discretion. As I hope to have shown, there can no such thing as a discretionary area of judgment. Properly understood the two concepts are as different as chalk and cheese, or a jaguar and a donkey. The correct analysis in the case mentioned by Lord Hope is that, within the area where the margin of appreciation applies, the court does not interpose its own judgment to displace the judgment exercised by the

---

[30] R. *v Radio Authority, ex p Bull* [1995] 4 All ER 481, following R. *v Broadcasting Complaints Commission, ex p Granada Television Ltd.* [1995] EMLR 163 at 167 (meaning of 'privacy').

[31] R. *v Director of Public Prosecutions, ex p Kebilene and others* [1999] 4 All ER 801 at 844. See n. 35 on p. 158 below.

local body in question. The position is similar where what is in issue is the exercise of a discretion.

Changing the law

I deal finally with the case where the decision-taker changes the law by his or her decision. A judgment which states and applies what the law is would not be expected itself to change the law. Most decision-takers have no power to do this anyway, so for them the question does not arise. However some senior judges do claim to be possessed of a power to change rules of common law. Other senior judges disagree, and would disclaim this alleged power. As stated in Chapter 3, in 1952 Viscount Simonds savagely criticized Denning LJ for his wish to engage in judicial legislation, which in a famous phrase Simonds described as 'a naked usurpation of the legislative function'.[32] Many judges of today would still agree with Simonds.

This disagreement at the highest levels of the judiciary presents problems for the analyst. A recent instance is the decision of the House of Lords in *Kleinwort Benson Ltd. v Lincoln City Council*.[33] It arose out of the wish of some local authorities to evade the full rigour of the Government's capping system by entering into contracts for interest rate swaps. Under these the parties gambled on interest rates by reference to a notional capital sum. One party agreed to pay to the other interest over a specified period at a fixed rate. The other agreed to pay, in relation to the same period and capital sum, interest at a floating rate geared to the money market's fluctuating rate. In essence this was a gamble on how the money market would perform over the given period. At the time they were entered into, the general view of the legal profession was that such contracts by local authorities were valid. However in a 1991 decision[34] the House of Lords held them to be ultra vires and void. The bankers Kleinwort Benson then sought to recover payments they had made to some local authorities in the mistaken belief that swaps contracts were valid.

---

[32] See p. 43 above.
[33] [1998] 4 All ER 513.
[34] *Hazell v Hammersmith and Fulham London Borough Council* [1991] 2 AC 1.

At first instance Langley J., following well-established law, held that their statement of claim disclosed no cause of action. The Appellate Committee of the House of Lords, by a majority of three to two, reversed Langley J. They purported to overturn, as if by parliamentary legislation, the long-standing rule of the common law that payments made under a mistake of law are irrecoverable (the mistake of law rule). One of the majority, Lord Goff, boldly described what they were doing as the 'abrogation' of this rule.[35] He described his thought processes quite openly. He was considering whether the mistake of law rule 'should remain part of English law'.[36] What was in issue at the heart of the case was, he said, 'the continued existence of a long-standing rule of law, which has been maintained in existence for nearly two centuries in what has been seen to be the public interest'. It was, he went on, for the House to consider whether this rule should be maintained, 'or alternatively should be abrogated altogether or reformulated'.[37] The boldness, if not impudence, of this move is accentuated by the fact that a past Lord Chancellor had asked the Law Commission to examine the mistake of law rule with a view to its reform by legislation. In response the Law Commission produced a report and draft bill, which still awaits consideration by Parliament.[38] What Lord Goff had to say about this was:

I am very conscious that the Law Commission has recommended legisla-tion. But the principal reasons given for this were that it might be some time before the matter came before the House, and that one of the dissentients in [*Woolwich Building Society v IRC (No 2)* [1993] AC 70] (Lord Keith of Kinkel) had expressed the opinion [at 154] that the mistake of law rule was too deeply embedded to be uprooted judicially. Of these two reasons, the former has not proved to be justified, and the latter does not trouble your Lordships *because a more robust view of judicial development of the law is, I understand, taken by all members of the Appellate Committee hearing the present appeals.*[39]

Another recent example of judicial legislation by the House of Lords is *Director of Public Prosecutions v Jones and Another.*[40]

---

[35] At p. 525.   [36] Ibid.   [37] p. 526.

[38] See *Restitution: mistakes of law and ultra vires public authority receipts and payments* (Law Com. No. 227) (1994).

[39] p. 532 (emphasis added). The decision was followed in *Nurdin & Peacock plc v D B Ramsden & Co. Ltd. (No 2)* [1999] 1 All ER 941.

[40] [1999] 2 All ER 257.

This concerned a demonstration consisting of around twenty-one persons congregating on the highway near Stonehenge. The House of Lords, again by a majority of three to two, here purported to revolutionize the common law of highways. It was clearly established, by long authority, that the right of the public is limited to passing and repassing along the highway, together with uses incidental to that. In *Jones* Lord Irvine of Lairg LC decided this was too constricted for modern conditions: 'to limit lawful use of the highway to that which is literally "incidental or ancillary" to the right of passage would be to place an unrealistic and unwarranted restriction on commonplace day-to-day activities'.[41] The Oxford English Dictionary[42] defines 'warranted' as 'allowed by law or authority; approved, justified, sanctioned'. That is an apt description of the rule overturned by this decision, so the Lord Chancellor was saying what was the exact opposite of the true position.

Under the rules of equity as laid down by the courts, manifest disadvantage is a necessary ingredient in a case of presumed undue influence. In *CIBC Mortgages plc v Pitt* [1994] 1 AC 200 the House of Lords 'signalled that it might not continue to be a necessary ingredient indefinitely'.[43] This is judicial legislation (or the threat of it) of the most inconvenient kind. How is the legal adviser able to advise a client when it has been announced that the existing law is liable to be changed by the judiciary at an unspecified and unknowable time?

In so far as a court purports to ascertain and declare an uncertain or disputed legal rule and apply it in the instant case, the decision by which it does this is properly called an exercise of judgment in the sense we are discussing. That is the usual case. If however the court purports to go beyond this and deliberately *alter* the relevant law, it is exercising a discretion. Whether in juridical truth such a discretion to alter the law truly exists continues to be a matter of debate and controversy; but while some senior judges act on the basis that it does exist analysts must find a slot for it.

---

[41] pp. 263–4.
[42] 2nd edn., 1992.
[43] *Per* Nourse LJ in *Barclays Bank plc v Coleman and Another* [2000] *The Times* 5 Jan.

Conclusion

It is important that legislators who bestow a power to exercise judgment or discretion, and judges or officials upon whom they bestow it, should know and observe the clear difference between the two. Judgment leads to but one result; discretion has a range. In the United States Douglas J. said that absolute discretion, like corruption, marks the beginning of the end of liberty.[44] We need to be able to recognize it when we see it.[45]

[44] *New York v United States* (1951) 342 US 882 at 884.
[45] For a summary of this chapter see pp. 216–17 below.

15

The European Union and the HRA

In Britain the operation of the common law or Global system of statutory interpretation, which is the main subject of this book, has been modified in the case of certain enactments by two Westminster Acts, the European Communities Act 1972 and the Human Rights Act 1998 (known for short as the HRA). For completeness this chapter gives some account of their effect. They revolutionized the unwritten British constitution by handing immense powers to unelected judges, both of the European and homegrown variety.

Scrapping the unwritten Constitution

What follows is a jeremiad, defined by the *Oxford English Dictionary* as a lamentation; a writing or speech in a strain of grief or distress; a doleful complaint; a complaining tirade; a lugubrious effusion.

In Britain, periodical free elections by secret ballot long procured a legislative chamber (the House of Commons) composed of representatives of the people who were yet required to exercise their own judgment and not take orders from anyone. They had access to the views of their constituents, but in deciding from day to day on what legislation to enact possessed a sovereign power of free decision. For their resulting Acts of Parliament they would be criticized by the media, and within a year or two called on to face their masters the people in a general election. Meanwhile the sovereign power of the British nation was effectively theirs. What Parliament could do by way of legislation was in constitutional terms unlimited.

In particular, unlike the legislatures of other nations, Britain's Westminster Parliament was not in any way confined by the detailed conditional clauses of a written constitution, usually written by different people in the distant past and required in the present to be construed by uncontrolled and unelected judges.

This ideal situation of the British lasted for a long while, but was too good to last for ever. As always, the path to Hell was paved with good intentions. At the end of the Second World War the blinded British, dazzled and bemused by the brutal physical assault they had undergone, which was underlined by the horrors of the Holocaust and the terrors of the Japanese Kamikaze, joined other surprised and confused Europeans in saying it must never happen again.

The way to stop it happening again seemed to the confused British people of that time and their leaders to be to draw up broad human rights clauses and back them by international law enforced by judges. The consequence was the Convention for the Protection of Human Rights and Fundamental Freedoms agreed by the Council of Europe on 4 November 1950 ('the Convention'). Over a wide field, this treaty turned appointed European judges into legislators. So far as its vague clauses were, or were held to be, given overriding effect, the undemocratic result was to elevate these salaried functionaries, working their steady way to retirement and a pension, above elected representatives of the people. Who could have expected that the victors in a war against the opponents of democracy would engineer what was, as it turned out, a dire reverse for democracy? Yet history teems with such quirks. Things rarely turn out in the way well-meaning people expect.

For half a century the full effects of this catastrophe were staved off in Britain. Discontented litigants could go to Strasbourg to claim their 'rights' under the Convention, but that was too difficult and expensive for most of them. Insidiously however the drip, drip, drip of ignorant critical comment went on, and at last the dam gave way. Now we have the Convention incorporated into our law by the HRA. In effect we at last have a written constitution—just like everyone else. So in this important area the British constitutional genius is extinguished, and uncomprehending conformity rules.

The result is that our elected representatives must now constantly look over their shoulders at unelected judges. It is the latter who will in future decide whether or not Parliament's laws infringe the vague and woolly requirements of the Convention, almost all made up of broad terms.[1] If the judges hold that they

---

[1] For an extensive analysis of the juridical nature of broad terms see Ch. 13.

do so infringe, Parliament (meaning the Executive) feels itself obliged to change the laws. The HRA provides a fast-track procedure to achieve it. All this is a very great shame, indeed a betrayal. Formerly, decisions on what were or were not just and righteous laws were properly and democratically left to our elected representatives, with all the inbuilt safeguards there were against abuse. Now we have the unhappy situation that no one can rely on what a law says for fear of what might happen if it were challenged in the courts on HRA grounds. In the highly civilized state that is modern Britain, few if any true abuses will thereby be avoided. What will for sure happen is that the nature and civic usefulness of law will be undermined and quite possibly eventually destroyed.

Having said all that by way of introduction, I must now forget such jeremiads and resume the attempts of this book at being useful in a practical way. Section 3(1) of the Human Rights Act 1998 lays down that so far as 'possible' United Kingdom legislation (whenever enacted) must be read and given effect in a way which is compatible with rights ('the Convention rights') set out in the Convention. Why did Parliament lay down this rule (which I call the compatible construction rule) since it was already the law—at least on the general view of the meaning of 'possible'?[2] It raises certain questions. What is 'possible' supposed to mean here? Does it mean corresponding to the literal meaning, or does it allow for a strained meaning—and if so to what extent?

As I have said in earlier chapters, the interpretative method generally used in the countries we are dealing with is securely based in the common law. In Britain today however there is increasing osmosis between the common law and the civil law (based on Roman law). That adds, in ways not yet fully worked out, to the number of different interpretative criteria or guides to legislative intention that are available to British judges and others seeking to arrive at the legal meaning of a Westminster enactment. Under the common law system, as we have seen, it is taken to be the legislator's intention that a particular enactment shall be construed according to such of the accepted criteria as are relevant; and that where they conflict (as they often do) the problem shall be resolved by weighing and balancing the interpretative

---

[2] See *R. v Khan* [1997] AC 558. See also *Bennion Code*, s. 270.

factors concerned.[3] The task normally is to choose between two opposing constructions of the enactment, each put forward by either side.[4] As I have said elsewhere,[5] the clue should not be missed that viewed in this way statutory interpretation keys into the whole system of our law; indeed that whole system is subject to the scheme of interpretation and in turn supports it. Study of our interpretative method in relation to statutes forms the best and most useful introduction to the entire British legal system.

Construing European enactments

Within the United Kingdom, a European Community law may have direct effect or be transposed into specifically British legislation. If it has direct effect it must be construed by a British court in the same way as it would be construed by the Court of Justice of the European Communities (CJEC). If it is transposed, the position is more complex. A Community law is said to be transposed into the national law of a member state when that state alters its national law so as to give effect to the Community law.[6] There are various methods of transposition. A member state 'may incorporate the provisions of the [Community law] into an existing legislative code, adopt a separate law or refer in a separate law to provisions of the general civil law'.[7] The first of these three methods is known as 'copyout', where legislation is enacted by which the exact terms of the directive are simply transposed as they stand into the national law. The copyout technique has disadvantages and some dangers.[8] Its defects were shown for example as respects the Unfair Contract Terms Act 1977, where '[t]here was no harmonising amendment of the 1977 Act and the problems of "fit" have been left to the courts to sort out'.[9]

---

[3] See Ch. 9.   [4] For the opposing constructions see Ch. 2.
[5] *Bennion Code*, p. 2.
[6] See Alec Samuels, 'Incorporating, Translating or Implementing European Union Law into UK Law' [1998] *Stat. L.R.* 80.
[7] *Faccini Dori v Recreb Srl* (Case C-91/92) [1995] All ER (EC) 1, *per* Advocate General Lenz at 6 (para. 8).
[8] For a discussion of these see Lynn E. Ramsey, 'The Copy Out technique: More of a Cop Out than a Solution?' [1996] *Stat. L.R.* 218.
[9] Jack Beatson, 'Has the common law a future?'. See 6th Report of the Select Committee on the European Communities, *Unfair Contract Terms*, HL Paper 28, Jan. 1992, p. 96 (evidence of Professor Treitel).

Where copyout is not used, the Community law in question will not be treated as properly or correctly transposed unless the substantial effect of the national law, in whatever form, is seen to be the same as that of the Community law in question. Provided the substantial effect is the same, the transposition will be accepted by the CJEC even though an identical effect may not be achieved.[10] Where a required transposition has not been effected by the state the position regarding remedies is subject to the rule in European jurisprudence that a breach has vertical but not horizontal effect. Here is an example. Council Directive 85/337/EEC (OJ1985 L175/40) requires member states to ensure that, before development consent is given for quarrying, an assessment of significant environmental effects is carried out. The Planning and Compensation Act 1991 Sch. 2 para. 2(6)(b) purports to give a deemed planning consent without the need for such an assessment. *Held.* This deemed consent must be treated as ineffective. Sedley LJ said:

The question is whether the possibility of giving that Directive direct effect by disapplying the deeming provision is precluded by the consequence that to do so would impermissibly alter the legal relations between two persons, the applicant and the developers, neither of whom is part of the state. In other words, is this the forbidden territory of horizontal direct effect?

The Court of Appeal answered in the negative, holding that in treating the deemed consent as ineffective it was giving the directive a vertical effect which clothed the planning authority with a power of control over the development which it should have been given by the state.[11]

In construing Community law operating by any method in the United Kingdom the system of interpretation to be used by our courts is that practised by the CJEC and not our own system based in the common law.[12] In one case Evans-Lombe J. said:

[10] *Johnson v Chief Adjudication Officer (No. 2)* (Case C-410/92) [1995] All ER (EC) 258 at 276 (para. 21).
[11] *R. v Durham County Council and Others, ex p Huddleston* (2000) *Times* 15 March.
[12] See Richard Wainwright, 'Techniques of Drafting European Community Legislation' [1996] *Stat. L.R.* 7; James O'Reilly, 'Coping with Community Legislation—A Practitioner's Reaction' [1996] *Stat. L.R.* 15; Thomas A. Finlay QC (former Chief Justice of Ireland), 'Community Legislation: How Big a Change for the National Judge?' [1996] *Stat. L.R.* 79.

The origin of [the Unfair Terms in Consumer Contracts Regulations 1994, SI 1994/3159] is Council Directive (EEC) 93/13. It is clear, therefore, that the words 'good faith' are not to be construed in the English law sense of absence of dishonesty but rather in the continental civil law sense.[13]

Of the CJEC method of interpretation Lord Diplock said:

The [CJEC], in contrast to English courts, applies teleological rather than historical methods to the interpretation of the Treaties and other Community legislation. It seeks to give effect to what it conceives to be the spirit rather than the letter of the Treaties; sometimes, indeed, to an English judge, it may seem to the exclusion of the letter. It views the Communities as living and expanding organisms and the interpretation of the provisions of the Treaties as changing to match their growth.[14]

As indicated in this dictum, the CJEC adopts a purposive or teleological interpretation of statutes rather than a mainly literal interpretation.[15] Straightforward construction of the words used is eschewed in favour of a 'creative' stance. As Justice Scalia of the United States Supreme Court put it, this method of construction renders democratically adopted texts mere springboards for judicial lawmaking.[16]

The British doctrine of purposive construction, comprised within the common law or Global method, is markedly more literalist than the European variety, and permits strained construction only in comparatively rare cases.[17] It is increasingly obliged to give way to the European system, as Lord Clyde acknowledged:

The adoption of a construction which departs boldly from the ordinary meaning of the language of the statute is . . . particularly appropriate where the validity of legislation has to be tested against the provisions of European law. In that context it is proper to give effect to the design and

---

[13] *Director General of Fair Trading v First National Bank plc* [2000] 1 All ER 240 at 250.

[14] *Henn and Darby v D.P.P.* [1981] AC 850 at 905.

[15] See *Pinna v Caisse d'allocations familiales de la Savoie* (Case 359/87) [1989] ECR 585, *per* Advocate-General Lenz at 605–6 (para 29). See also *Coloroll Pension Trustees Ltd v Russell* (Case C-200/91) [1995] All ER (EC) 23, *per* Advocate-General Van Gerven at 42 (n. 18): 'it is clear that a teleological interpretation . . . is usual.'

[16] Antonin Scalia, *A Matter of Interpretation: Federal Courts and the Law*, 1997 (Princeton: Princeton University Press, 1997), 25.

[17] See *Bennion Code*, s. 311.

purpose behind the legislation, and to give weight to the spirit rather than the letter.[18]

The CJEC method may be called Developmental construction because in advancing the 'spirit' it is always ready to depart from the text, if the court deems this necessary.[19] It uses the text merely as a starting point, with the aim of developing the particular piece of Community law in the way the nations of the European Union are presumed to intend within the context of the grand design.[20] This harks back to the civilian system of drafting legislation, as compared to the common law drafting method. As Lisbeth Campbell has pointed out, by a clever analogy with computer science terminology the product of the former method, when expressed (as it often is, but by no means invariably) in broad general principles, has been called *fuzzy law*. By contrast the elaborate, detailed product of common law drafting can be called *fussy law*.[21] Another difference is that the Developmental method pays far less regard to precedent than the common law method does. Developmental construction was thus described by Lord Denning:

[European judges] adopt a method which they call in English by strange words—at any rate they were strange to me—the 'schematic and teleological' method of interpretation. It is not really so alarming as it sounds. All it means is that the judges do not go by the literal meaning of the words or by the grammatical structure of the sentence. They go by the design or purpose . . . behind it.[22]

In 1983 Bingham J. echoed this:[23]

The interpretation of Community instruments involves very often not the process familiar to common lawyers of laboriously extracting the meaning from words used but the more creative process of supplying flesh to a

---

[18] *Cutter v Eagle Star Insurance Co Ltd* [1998] 4 All ER 417 at 426.

[19] Similarly the term 'dynamic or evolutive interpretation' has been used in relation to the Convention: see D. J. Harris, M. O'Boyle, and C. Warbrick, *Law of the European Convention on Human Rights* (London: Butterworths, 1995), 7.

[20] For a trenchant criticism of Developmental construction see Sir Patrick Neil QC (now Lord Neill of Bladen QC), *The European Court of Justice: a case study in judicial activism* (Aug. 1995), referred to at p. 156 below.

[21] See Lisbeth Campbell, 'Drafting Styles: Fuzzy or Fussy?' *E Law—Murdoch University Electronic Journal of Law*, vol. 3, no. 2 (July 1996).

[22] *James Buchanan & Co. Ltd. v Babco Forwarding & Shipping (UK) Ltd.* [1977] 2 WLR 107 at 112.

[23] Now Lord Bingham of Cornhill CJ.

spare and loosely constructed skeleton. The choice between alternative submissions may turn not on purely legal considerations, but on a broader view of what the orderly development of the Community requires. These are matters which [the Court of Justice of the European Communities (CJEC)] is very much better placed to assess and determine than a national court.[24]

The then Prime Minister's private secretary, Sir Charles Powell, remarked in 1991 that the CJEC had by 'interpretation' widened the powers conferred by the Single European Act on the Commission and the European Parliament.[25] In 1995 Sir Patrick Neill QC[26] wrote an account containing extensive complaints about Developmental construction of Community legislation by the CJEC.[27] After discussing in detail a number of decisions of the CJEC.[28] he concluded that the CJEC sees itself as 'a court with a mission', namely that of pushing the Community (now the European Union) forward towards the goals enshrined in the preambles to the various treaties. With this aim it has gone far beyond literal interpretation, and even beyond purposive construction as comprised in the common law method. Neill warned: 'A court with a mission is not an orthodox court. It is potentially a dangerous court—the danger being that inherent in uncontrollable judicial power.'[29]

The CJEC method of Developmental construction also embraces the principles enshrined in the European Convention on Human Rights. 'There is no dispute that since [the Environmental Protection Act 1990] gives effect to a directive, it must be interpreted according to the principles of Community law, including its doctrines of fundamental human rights'.[30] A Community law provision may be drafted so as not to deal comprehensively with a

[24] *Commissioners of Customs and Excise v ApS Samex* [1983] 1 All ER 1042 at 1056.
[25] *The Times*, 12 Nov. 1991.
[26] Now Lord Neill of Bladen QC.
[27] *The European Court of Justice: a case study in judicial activism* (Aug. 1995), published by European Policy Forum.
[28] These included cases before and after the accession of the United Kingdom, beginning with *Van Gend en Loos v Nederlandse Administratie der Belastingen (Netherlands Inland Revenue Administration)* [1963] ECR 1 (Case 26/62).
[29] Loc. cit., 48. Lord Neill told me in May 1998 that he thought the CJEC 'is now much more cautious'.
[30] *R. v Hertfordshire County Council, ex p Green Environmental Industries Ltd and another* [2000] 1 All ER 773, *per* Lord Hoffmann at 780.

matter, leaving space for certain details to be laid down by a UK enactment. Here the latter is to be given a purposive construction which so far as possible gives effect to the Community law provision. For example Roch LJ said:

The [CJEC] has decided that where the transfer of an undertaking takes place an employee is entitled to decide not to continue the contract of employment or employment relationship with the transferee. The [Council Directive (EEC) 77/187 (the acquired rights directive)] cannot be interpreted as obliging the employee to continue his employment relationship with the transferee. Where the employee decides not to continue with the transferee, the court has left it to member states to provide whether in such cases the contract of employment or employment relationship must be regarded as terminated either by the employee or the employer.[31]

There is a presumption that a UK enactment is compatible with a Community law provision unless and until it has been declared incompatible by a competent court.[32] There is also a presumption that the common law is not displaced by implication. This is a general presumption applicable to all UK legislation, and applies even where that legislation is supplementary to Community law.[33]

A question sometimes posed is whether the legislative drafter intends the user always to adopt a literal interpretation, or where necessary adopt a purposive but strained interpretation (common law or Global construction), or even on occasion arrive at a Developmental interpretation departing altogether from the text. I would say the answer is this. Nowadays, the drafter never intends the first course. In the case of a common law enactment not affected by European considerations, or delegated legislation made thereunder, the drafter intends the second course. In the case of Community legislation, the drafter intends the third course.

It will be apparent from the argument so far that we have for some time had available, in relation to different items of legislation operating within the United Kingdom, two distinct methods of statutory interpretation: the common law or Global method

---

[31] *The Chancellor, Masters and Scholars of the University of Oxford v Humphreys and another* [2000] 1 All ER 996 at 1023.

[32] *Factortame Ltd v Secretary of State for Transport* [1990] 2 AC 85, *per* Lord Bridge at 142: see *R. v Secretary of State for Health and others, ex p Imperial Tobacco Ltd. and others* [2000] 1 All ER 572, *per* Lord Woolf MR at 584.

[33] *The Chancellor, Masters and Scholars of the University of Oxford v Humphreys and another* [2000] 1 All ER 996.

and the Developmental method. These have many features in common, and are different mainly in the extent to which they allow or require a strained construction and the respect they pay to precedent.

The compatible construction rule

Now under the Human Rights Act 1998 we have a third method of statutory interpretation, which I call the compatible construction rule. This contemplates two kinds of interpretation: an interpretation of the Convention right in question and an interpretation of the enactment being judged by reference to it. In determining the ambit of a Convention right a court must take into account relevant decisions etc. of the European Court of Human Rights and the European Commission of Human Rights,[34] though one must not overlook the margin of appreciation afforded to individual countries.[35] Subject to this, it would be problematic to arrive at a legal meaning of a Convention right different from that likely to be found by the European Court of Human Rights. The situation is complicated enough without permitting there to be two markedly different legal meanings for one Convention right.

It has been suggested that the two concepts in the compatible construction rule, 'read and given effect', may each produce different outcomes, that under it an enactment may be 'read' in one way but 'given effect' in another.[36] I believe this is not the case. To read an enactment in a particular way is to give it that *legal meaning*.[37] If the court's 'reading' of an enactment is that the legal meaning is X then the court must 'give effect' to X. Too much

[34] Human Rights Act 1998 s. 2.

[35] This allows a state 'a certain measure of discretion, subject to European supervision, when it takes legislative, administrative or judicial action in the area of a Convention right': see the work cited in n. 19 above at p. 12 and the detailed exposition at pp. 12–15. See also *R. v Director of Public Prosecutions, ex p Kebilene and others* [1999] 4 All ER 801, *per* Lord Hope of Graighead at 843–4 and David Pannick, 'Principles of Interpretation of Convention rights under the Human Rights Act and the discretionary area of judgment', [1998] *PL*, 545 at 548–51. On the latter see p. 143.

[36] Geoffrey Marshall, 'Two kinds of compatibility: more about section 3 of the Human Rights Act 1998' [1999] *PL*, 377.

[37] See Ch. 1.

should not be read into the use by the drafter of two terms where one would have done: it follows an old proclivity.[38] All that the compatible construction rule is talking about in using the two terms is the legal meaning the court is to arrive at.

The compatible construction rule refers to 'compatibility' between United Kingdom legislation and the Convention rights. Here we must appreciate that a Convention right may be absolute or qualified, and the two types need different handling. I will now give three examples of the working of the rule.[39]

Example 1. Article 3 of the Convention, which states that no one shall be subjected to torture, is absolute. Suppose A has been held on remand for two years under enactment E1, which expressly authorizes remand in custody but imposes no time limit. A argues that 'torture' in Article 3 includes mental torture and says he is suffering this from his long detention. He argues for a legal meaning of enactment E1 which incorporates an implied proviso precluding detention on remand for an unreasonably long period. The other side deny such an implication, and those then are the opposing constructions. If the court finds that Article 3 does embrace mental torture, the questions on the compatible construction rule are: (1) Is the other side's construction compatible with the absolute right conferred by Article 3? (2) If the answer is no, is it 'possible' to read enactment E1 with the implication desired by A?

Example 2. Article 7(1) of the Convention says that no one shall be held guilty where the act in question did not constitute a criminal offence under national or international law at the time it was committed. It is qualified by Article 7(2), which says that this shall not prejudice trial and punishment for an act which, at the time it was committed, was criminal according to the general principles of law recognized by civilized nations. Suppose B has been convicted of an offence created by enactment E2 (national law) which is not an offence under international law and was not an offence under national law at the time B's act was done. E2 is expressed to be retrospective to before that time. Article 7(1) has been contravened unless the conviction is saved by Article 7(2).

[38] See Ch. 8
[39] These three examples are further considered later in this chapter.

Here the court has to decide the difficult question whether, although B's act was not an offence under international law, it was criminal according to the general principles of law recognized by civilized nations. If the answer is no the question arises of whether it is 'possible' to read enactment E2 in a way which is compatible with Article 7(1).

Example 3.[40] Enactment E3 makes it an offence to destroy a British passport. C, charged with committing this offence at a demonstration against British immigration laws, admits committing the act but pleads that he did it as free expression within Article 10(1) of the Convention. By his act he was, he argues, 'imparting information and ideas' as mentioned in Article 10(1). This is another qualified right, since Article 10(2) places limitations on its exercise. The only relevant limitation here is that relating to the prevention of disorder. The questions for the court are: (1) Was enactment E3 passed for the prevention of disorder? (2) If so, was that 'necessary in a democratic society' within the meaning of those words in Article 10(2)? (3) If the answer to (1) or (2) is no, can enactment E3 possibly be 'read' subject to an exception which would exonerate C?

Geoffrey Marshall called the compatible construction rule 'a deeply mysterious provision'.[41] That is a just description. Francesca Klug has examined its legislative history.[42] I gratefully adopt her citations and will not repeat them. One thing the legislative history shows is that there was much vagueness and confusion in the minds of the Act's promoters about the intended meaning of the rule. This renders the legislative history largely useless here, because it is inconsistent and one can prove almost anything by citations from it. In his Tom Sargent Memorial Lecture on 16 December 1997[43] Lord Irvine of Lairg LC said that in applying the compatible construction rule the courts must strike a balance, going neither too far nor not far enough. Elsewhere he said 'the

[40] This is based on the example given in the article referred to in n. 367 above.
[41] 'Interpreting interpretation in the Human Rights Bill' [1998] *PL*, 167.
[42] 'The Human Rights Act 1998, '*Pepper v Hart* and All That' [1999] *PL*, 246 at 252–5.
[43] This is so far unpublished except on the Internet, though parts of it were quoted in debates on the Bill for the 1998 Act: see the article cited in the previous footnote at p. 254. See also the article cited in the next footnote.

courts will be required to uphold the Convention rights unless the legislation itself is so clearly incompatible with the Convention that it is impossible to do so'.[44] He added that our courts may interpret Community law by 'straining the meaning of words or reading in words which are not there' and that this 'shows the strong interpretative techniques that can be expected in Convention cases'. All that suggests the compatible construction rule may require the Developmental method to be used in Convention cases, but this is left unclear.

An additional criterion, which may be called the fundamental rights criterion, is imported by the following dictum of Lord Hope of Craighead in *R. v Director of Public Prosecutions, ex p Kebilene and others*.[45]

In *A-G of Hong Kong v Lee Kwong-Kut* [1993] AC 951 at 966 Lord Woolf referred to the general approach to the interpretations of constitutions and bills of rights indicated in the previous decisions of the Board, which he said were equally applicable to the Hong Kong Bill of Rights Ordinance 1991. He mentioned Lord Wilberforce's observation in *Minister of Home Affairs v Fisher* [1980] AC 319 at 328 that instruments of this nature call for a generous interpretation suitable to give to individuals the full measure of the fundamental rights and freedoms referred to, and Lord Diplock's comment in *A-G of the Gambia v Momodou Jobe* [1984] AC 689 at 700 that a generous and purposive construction is to be given to that part of a constitution which protects and entrenches fundamental rights and freedoms to which all persons in the state are to be entitled. The same approach will now have to be applied in this country when issues are raised under the Human Rights Act 1998 about the compatibility of domestic legislation and of acts of public authorities with the fundamental rights and freedoms which are enshrined in the Convention.

In drafting the compatible construction rule it seems there was a failure to understand the current British method of statutory interpretation, which I am calling the common law or Global method.[46] To begin with, the drafting overlooks the crucial fact

---

[44] 'The Development of Human Rights in Britain under an Incorporated Convention on Human Rights' [1998] *PL*, 221 at 228.

[45] [1999] 4 All ER 801 at 838–9.

[46] The drafter of the New Zealand provision did no better. In the article mentioned in n. 36 above Geoffrey Marshall refers (p. 377 n. 4), to its wording as 'wherever an enactment can be given a meaning that is consistent with [the Bill of Rights]'. This is simply s. 3(1) of the 1998 Act in a slightly different guise.

that the latter requires a two-stage approach.[47] It is not a matter
of deciding at first sight whether words are ambiguous or obscure,
and if so going on to decide what they mean. This is an error
constantly made. The true rule is that there are two stages: (1) It
must be decided, on an *informed* basis, whether or not there is a
real doubt about the legal meaning of the enactment. (2) If there
is, the interpreter moves on to the second stage, which is resolving
the doubt. As Lord Upjohn said, 'you must look at all the admissible surrounding circumstances before starting to construe the
Act'.[48]

Next, the basic rule of statutory construction must be applied,
namely that the enactment shall be construed in accordance with
the various general guides to legislative intention laid down by law
and that where these conflict the problem shall be resolved by
weighing and balancing the interpretative factors concerned. The
1998 Act now provides an addition, which I am calling the
compatible construction rule, to these general guides. What the
drafter of the compatible construction rule should have done was
to say that the general guides are in future to be taken to include
the strong principle that it is highly desirable that legislation
should be taken to conform to the Convention (while Parliament
reserves the right to say in a particular case that it intends to
depart from it).[49] It is my submission that that is what Parliament
must be taken as really intending by the compatible construction
rule, and that it should be applied accordingly. I also submit that
the rule should be applied using the Developmental method. The
CJEC uses that method when taking notice of the Convention,
and consistency here is essential.

In the light of all this, I return to the three examples set out
above (pages 159–60).

Example 1. Assuming the answer to question (1) is no, the
answer to question (2) must be found by assembling the interpretative factors either way. It could be argued that in favour of

[47] The same applies to the Developmental method.
[48] *R. v Schildkamp* [1971] AC 1 at 23. The two-stage approach is fully
explained in *Bennion Code*, s. 204.
[49] In *R. v Director of Public Prosecutions, ex p Kebilene* [1999] 4 All ER 801 at
837 Lord Cooke of Thornden said that section 3(1) provides a major new canon of
interpretation imposing 'a strong adjuration'.

the other side's construction are such factors as the following: it corresponds to the plain meaning of E1, it represents the intention of Parliament, it protects the public to keep A in custody, it is administratively convenient, and so on. A's main argument is of course that his construction complies with the Convention, but he could add the following: in the case of a penal provision he should be given the benefit of any doubt, there is a presumption against restraint of the person, and so on. His trump card in arguing that the necessary proviso should be treated as implied is that even before the 1998 Act courts often found implications of this sort. The court must now weigh each figurative bundle of factors and decide which is heavier. One imagines A would succeed.

Example 2. Is it 'possible' to read enactment E2 in a way which is compatible with Article 7(1)? If the provision stating that E2 is retrospective is worded so as to show that Parliament intended to override the Convention, the answer is no. Otherwise the answer will depend on how the interpretative factors balance out on either side. If E2 was passed before the compatible construction rule was thought of, the weight of the 'bundle' of factors on B's side must be treated as increased by the addition of that rule. By how much it is increased is, as always, a matter for the court's judgment. What matters is that the court should apply the right test.

Example 3. Is it 'possible' to read enactment E3 in a way which is compatible with Article 10(1)? In posing this example Geoffrey Marshall suggested inserting after the words 'to destroy a British passport' the words 'except by anyone intending to express or communicate an idea or opinion'.[50] He then raised the question whether the compatible construction rule requires such an addition to be made whenever this is needed for compliance with the Convention. That would be too easy a way out. One must go through the steps required by the Developmental method as applied by the compatible construction rule.

---

[50] See the article referred to at n. 36, p. 380.

Conclusions

My conclusions from the above discussion are as follows.

Section 3(1) of the Human Rights Act 1998 (the compatible construction rule) should be taken as requiring the enactment in question to be construed according to the Developmental method, thus bringing in the wider European system of purposive construction. So, while not exactly providing a third method of statutory interpretation; it drastically alters existing methods. The fact that this powerful new criterion has been added to the existing guides to statutory interpretation contained in the common law or Global method reopens all precedents. No pre-1998 Act court decision on the legal meaning of an enactment to which a Convention right is relevant can now stand unexamined. Even though it truly reflected the intention Parliament had when passing the enactment, the decision needs to be looked at again in the light of s. 3(1). Parliament's original intention is no longer the sole deciding factor. While it retains its importance, it must now be reassessed in the light of the new rule. For pre-1998 Act enactments the interpretative criteria can therefore be ultimately reduced to 'legislative intention plus compatible construction rule', to which must now be added the fundamental rights criterion mentioned above (page 161). One likely result is that there will be less room for implication.[51]

The new compatible construction rule overrides the classic idea that the sole test of legal meaning is the legislator's intention. Ex post facto, it adds a new slant. This notional override of intention will not apply to post-1998 Act enactments, for here Parliament in forming its intention must be taken to have the compatible construction rule in mind and wish it to be taken into account (unless of course Parliament in a particular case expresses a contrary intention).[52]

---

[51] Colin R. Munro suggests that an effect of s. 3(1) will be to displace 'the normal presumption in favour of implied repeal': *Studies in Constitutional Law* (2nd edn., London: Butterworths, 1999), 169 n.

[52] For a summary of this chapter see pp. 217–18 below.

16

The jurisprudential basis of the common law method

The preceding chapters may have convinced any doubters that statutory interpretation is not a question of just going by the words alone (literal interpretation) or applying rules of thumb (the literal rule, mischief rule or golden rule), but something much more difficult and pluralistic. It lies in picking out relevant factors from a number of possible criteria, and then where necessary performing a balancing act. I am speaking here of the system I call the Global or common law method. The Developmental method, based in Europe, has a different basis, as shown in the previous chapter.

Seeking background support for my thesis concerning the validity of the common law or Global method, I aim in this chapter to widen the treatment earlier given by providing some politico-philosophical colouring based on Ronald Dworkin's seminal book *Law's Empire*. His cool, densely argued, elegant work is impossible to summarize, and I will not try. Instead I shall write for those who have read the book (as all common lawyers should), while scattering clues for those who have not yet given themselves that treat.

As I have said,[1] there is in our British jurisprudence an increasing osmosis between common law and civil law. For this and other reasons there is a growing need to seek out and grasp the jurisprudential basis of the current common law method of statutory interpretation, based as it is on principles prevailing through most of the English-speaking world.

This need is strengthened by the fact that it is now understood that the whole basis of our law is interpretative. In 1986 Dworkin wrote: 'Law is an interpretive concept'.[2] Andrei Marmor said in 1995 that in the previous fifteen years interpretation had become

---

[1] See p. 7 above.
[2] *Law's Empire* (1st edn., Oxford: Hart Publishing, 1998), 410. In what follows I adopt Dworkin's American spelling and usage when quoting directly from his book.

one of the main intellectual paradigms of legal scholarship.[3] In 1998 Peter Birks called for a partnership in interpretative development of our law.[4] But without some consideration of jurisprudential theory there is a gap in any realistic treatment of interpretation, whether from the academic's or the practitioner's viewpoint (why should they be different?). Even if the common law criteria I have described in the preceding chapters and elsewhere are correct, who is to say that particular judges or officials will obey them? Have they the learning to do so? If they do obey them, will it be willingly and constructively or reluctantly, with the constant taking of petty objections? Will they on the other hand disregard them, perhaps in that ignorance so many judges and officials of today revel in (thinking themselves too stressed and busy to take account of learning)? Above all, on what basis do they, and ought they to, approach and apply this common law method?

When people organize themselves into a sovereign state the result is to project combined, concentrated, physical force which is used where necessary to coerce people who are within the state or under its jurisdiction. Dworkin's book *Law's Empire* starts from the proposition that the rule of law, indeed civilization itself, requires that this organized state coercion shall always be controlled and regulated by democratic law. That indeed is a prime function of such law. The state's force must not be used or withheld, no matter how useful that would be to ends in view, no matter how beneficial or noble those ends, except as licensed or required by individual rights and responsibilities flowing from past political decisions about when this collective force is justified.[5] The reference to 'past political decisions' here is a reference to (1) decisions of legislators framed as valid legislation and (2) decisions of courts that have the effect of making law. In the case of Britain and other common law countries these decisions together make up the statute book and the common law respectively.

---

[3] *Law and Interpretation, Essays in Legal Philosophy* (Oxford: Oxford University Press, 1995), p. v.

[4] Peter Birks, 'The academic and the practitioner' 18 *Legal Studies* (1998), 397 at 407.

[5] p. 93. In this and the following footnotes page references, unless the contrary is indicated, refer to *Law's Empire*.

Dworkin's book goes on to tackle three basic questions: (1) Is the form of coercion imposed by the state on citizens in reliance on its legal system justified, considering that it amounts to enforcing judgments that 'flow from' a collection of legislative and judicial decisions necessarily originating in the past, sometimes the distant past? (2) If there is a justification, what is it? (3) What reading of 'flow from'—what notion of consistency with past decisions—best serves that justification?[6]

Dworkin's entire argument predicates a state 'community'. He is 'defending an interpretation of our own political culture, not an abstract and timeless political morality'.[7] The argument rests on our community's particular values and its own 'climate of public opinion'.[8] This community is a 'fraternity'.[9] Dworkin wishes legal interpreters (that is officials and judges), by their decisions, to place the political history of 'our' community in the best possible light.[10] Statutory interpretation must make the community's legal record the best it can from the point of view of political morality.[11] We should try to conceive our political community as an association of principle.[12] Interpretative decisions should subserve principles that provide the best justification available for the doctrines and devices of our law as a whole.[13] They should represent democracy as it really is and reflect the nation's character.[14] They should embrace popular convictions and national traditions, and show the nation's constitutional history in its best light.[15] They should respect long-standing traditions of the community's political and constitutional culture.[16] They should be a credit to law.[17]

Considering the nature of the system of law that serves this 'community', Dworkin gives us three conceptions as rivals for best fitting current legal practice: conventionalism, legal pragmatism, and law as integrity. Bravely disdaining relativism, he rejects the first two and comes down in favour of the last.[18] Conventionalism is dismissed because it offers no answers in difficult cases where there is a gap in the legislation or it is obscure, leaving the judge to decide as he thinks fit, and because under it 'judges would not

---

[6] p. 94.   [7] p. 216.   [8] p. 349.   [9] p. 263.
[10] p. 248.   [11] p. 411.   [12] pp. 263, 411.
[13] p. 400.   [14] p. 399.   [15] p. 398.
[16] pp. 377–8.   [17] p. 391.   [18] p. 94.

think themselves free to change rules adopted pursuant to the reigning legal conventions just because on balance a different rule would be more just or efficient'.[19] Pragmatism would allow judges to make such changes, but goes too far in jettisoning the past and giving judges free rein to abandon legal certainty and decide each case in a way they think best suits current conditions. 'Law as integrity denies that statements of law are either the backward-looking factual reports of conventionalism or the forward-looking instrumental programs of legal pragmatism. It insists that legal claims are interpretive judgments and therefore combine back-ward-and-forward-looking elements; they interpret contemporary legal practice seen as an unfolding political narrative. So law as integrity rejects as unhelpful the ancient question whether judges find or invent law; we understand legal reasoning, it suggests, only by seeing the sense in which they do both and neither.'[20]

I next need to explain some concepts Dworkin uses. First, he occasionally cites principles in terms of what a super-judge whom he calls Hercules would decide. Hercules is 'an imaginary judge of superhuman intellectual power and patience who accepts law as integrity'.[21] Hercules has an infinite amount of time at his disposal, and scrupulous respect for the constraints of the law.

If Hercules had decided to ignore legislative supremacy and strict prece-dent whenever ignoring these doctrines would allow him to improve the law's integrity, judged as a matter of substance alone, then he would have violated integrity overall. For any successful general interpretation of our legal practice must recognise these institutional constraints.[22]

Next, Dworkin employs specific meanings of 'fairness', 'justice' and 'procedural due process'. 'Fairness . . . is a matter of finding political procedures—methods of electing officials and making their decisions responsive to the electorate—that distribute politi-cal power in the right way. That is now generally understood, in the United States and Britain at least, to mean procedures and practices that give all citizens more or less equal influence in the decisions that govern them.'[23] 'Justice is a matter of the correct or best theory of moral and political rights, and anyone's conception of justice is his theory, imposed by his own personal convictions,

---

[19] p. 148. It seems that law as integrity would not permit this either.
[20] p. 225.   [21] p. 239.   [22] p. 401.
[23] pp. 164–5.

of what these rights actually are'.[24] Procedural due process is a matter of the right procedures for judging whether some citizen has violated laws laid down by the political procedures.[25]

Dworkin employs specific meanings of 'principle' and 'policy'. Equality of concern for citizens is a matter of principle, not policy. 'Though integrity, by definition, is a matter of principle, Hercules must prefer an account of any single statute that also shows a high order of consistency in policy'.[26] 'A law subsidising contraception might be justified either out of respect for presumed rights that are violated when contraceptives are unavailable, which is a matter of principle, or out of concern that the population not grow too rapidly, which is a matter of policy, or both.'[27]

In Dworkin's view law as integrity is 'a distinct political virtue'.[28] It 'supposes that people have legal rights—rights that follow from past decisions of political institutions and therefore license coercion—that go beyond the explicit extension of political practices conceived as conventions. Law as integrity supposes that people are entitled to a coherent and principled extension of past political decisions even when judges profoundly disagree about what this means.'[29] In other words law as integrity takes rights seriously. It regards justice and fairness as leading principles: 'each citizen respects the principles of fairness and justice instinct in the standing political arrangement of his particular community, which may be different from those of other communities, whether or not he thinks these the best principles from a utopian standpoint'.[30] Dworkin does not claim that our political practices enforce integrity perfectly. 'Our commitment to integrity means, however, that we must report this fact as a defect . . . and that we must strive to remedy whatever inconsistencies in principle we are forced to confront'.[31] 'Members of a society of principle accept that their political rights and duties are not exhausted by the particular decisions their political institutions have reached, but depend, more generally, on the scheme of principles those decisions presuppose and endorse.'[32]

---

[24] p. 97. One might add that justice is fundamentally a matter of the right deployment of the state's coercive power.
[25] p. 165. The same must also apply to judging legal claims by citizens.
[26] pp. 447–8.   [27] p. 339.   [28] p. 166.
[29] p. 134.   [30] p. 213.   [31] p. 217.
[32] p. 211.

The claims of law as integrity can be divided into two more practical principles, the principle of integrity in legislation (which asks those who create law by legislation to keep that law coherent in principle) and the principle of integrity in adjudication (which asks those responsible for deciding on the legal meaning of legislation to see and enforce it as coherent in that way).[33] I will concentrate here on integrity in adjudication, because my main concern in this book is to examine how judges construe and apply legislation.

According to Dworkin, integrity in adjudication explains how and why the past must be allowed some special power of its own in court, contrary to the pragmatist's claim that it must not; and why judges must conceive the body of law they administer as a whole rather than as a set of discrete decisions they are free to make or amend one by one, with nothing but a strategic interest in the rest.[34] If a judge's own sense of justice condemned what a statute required

he would have to consider whether he should actually enforce it ... or whether he should lie and say that this was not the law after all, or whether he should resign. The principle of integrity in adjudication, therefore, does not necessarily have the last word about how the coercive power of the state should be used. But it does have the first word, and normally there is nothing to add to what it says.[35]

Integrity in adjudication instructs judges to identify legal rights and duties, so far as possible, on the assumption that they were all created by a single author—the community personified—expressing a coherent conception of justice and fairness.[36] It does not aim to recapture, even for present law, the ideals or practical purposes of the politicians who first created it. It aims rather to justify what they did and said in an overall story worth telling now.[37] It assumes that judges are in a very different position from legislators.

It does not fit the character of a community of principle that a judge should have authority to hold people liable in damages for acting in a way he concedes they had no legal duty not to act ... Judges must make their common-law decisions on grounds of principle, not policy: they

---

[33] p. 167.   [34] p. 167.   [35] p. 219.
[36] p. 225.   [37] pp. 227–8.

must deploy arguments why the parties actually had the 'novel' legal rights and duties they enforce . . .[38]

The political history of a community is *pro tanto* a better history . . . if it shows judges making plain to their public, through their opinions, the path that later judges guided by integrity will follow, and if it shows judges making decisions that give voice as well as effect to convictions about morality that are widespread through the community.[39]

For convenience law is divided into compartments such as contract, tort etc. 'Law as integrity has a . . . complex attitude toward departments of law. Its general spirit condemns them, because the adjudicative spirit of integrity asks judges to make the law coherent as a whole, so far as they can, and this might be better done by ignoring academic boundaries and reforming some departments of law radically to make them more consistent in principle with others. But law as integrity is interpretive, and compartmentalization is a feature of legal practice no competent interpretation can ignore.[40]

No aspect of law as integrity has been so misunderstood as its refusal to accept the popular view that there are no uniquely right answers in hard cases at law.[41]

Hercules knows that the law is far from perfectly consistent in principle overall. He knows that legislative supremacy gives force to some statutes that are inconsistent in principle with others, and that the compartmentalization of the common law, together with local priorities, allows inconsistency even there. But he assumes that these contradictions are not so pervasive and intractable that his task is impossible. He assumes that some set of reasonably plausible principles can be found, for each general department of law that he must enforce, that fit well enough to count as an eligible interpretation of it.[42]

The judge 'tries to impose order over doctrine, not to discover order in the forces that created it. He struggles toward a set of principles he can offer to integrity, a scheme for transforming the varied links in the chain of law into a vision of government now speaking with one voice, even if this is very different from the voices of leaders past. He might fail . . . but his failure is not ensured by anything even the most careful and sensitive history teaches.'[43] 'A successful interpretation must not only fit but justify the practice it interprets.'[44]

---

[38] p. 224.   [39] p. 248.   [40] pp. 251–2.
[41] p. 266.   [42] p. 268.   [43] p. 273.
[44] p. 285.

Towards the end of his book Dworkin says: 'If [the reader] leaves my argument early, at some crucial abstract stage, then I have largely failed for him. If he leaves it late, in some matter of relative detail, then I have largely succeeded. I have failed entirely, however, if he never leaves it at all.'[45] While I fundamentally agree with Dworkin's argument, there are two respects in which, I hope at a suitably late stage, I would leave it so far as it relates to statutory interpretation.

My first departure from Dworkin's thesis rejects the vagueness and subjectivity of the standards to which he links law as integrity. He says judicial decisions should place the political history of our community 'in the best possible light'. Statutory interpretation must make our community's legal record 'the best it can from the point of view of political morality'. Integrity must observe principles that 'provide the best justification available for the doctrines and devices of our law'. These examples of vagueness are taken from passages from *Law's Empire* quoted above. Many more could be cited. Dworkin's assumption seems to be that a judge will draw on his or her own unformulated instincts and experiences for the necessary juristic standards: 'anyone's conception of justice is his theory, imposed by his own personal convictions'.[46] That will not do.

Linked to this criticism is a rejection of Dworkin's view that there are no objective rules of statutory interpretation. 'A judge must ultimately rely on his own opinions in developing and applying a theory about how to read a statute.'[47] That is heresy. Dworkin devotes much space in analysing the well-known will case of *Riggs v Palmer*,[48] which turned on the question whether the law of succession would say that a man who murdered his grandfather is entitled to succeed under the grandfather's will. Dworkin does not, as the common law method does, treat this question as falling to be determined by the principle of legal policy that a person should not profit from his own wrong. Yet under the common law method this principle, like many others, is generally applicable in statutory interpretation.[49] I suggest therefore that Dworkin's theory of integrity in law should be modified by

---

[45] p. 413.   [46] See p. 168 above.   [47] p. 334.
[48] (1889) 115 N.Y. 506, 22 NE 188. See *Bennion Code*, p. 596.
[49] See p. 97 above and *Bennion Code*, s. 349.

stipulating that, when it comes to applying it to statutory interpretation in the common law world, it must be linked to the detailed prescriptions of the common law method rather than resting on the vagaries of individual judges.

The other way in which I think Dworkin's theory needs modification concerns its relation to 'our' community. The simple idea that a body of law serves one culture and one community no longer applies in the multicultural, pluralistic Britain of the twenty-first century. So a particular item of our law now needs to be interpreted according to the demographic group in which it holds sway, whether the European Union, the nations who have ratified the European Convention on Human Rights, the United Kingdom, or a devolved area inside the United Kingdom. Thus for example Lord Slynn said of the Convention on Human Rights that it has to be construed according to 'what is acceptable throughout Europe'.[50]

I will end this chapter with a look at a passage from the recent book by the political scientist David Robertson already referred to.[51]

Even if a code cannot be expected to be complete, one might hope to paper over its cracks by a separate set of rules for interpretation of the code. Most jurisdictions do in fact have such auxiliary codes. There have been several interpretation Acts in recent British legal history, and the common law contains several rules of interpretation, some stemming from its formative days. Most such auxiliary codes do little more than provide judges with a ragbag of acceptable ways of expressing their discretionary judgments.[52]

It is difficult to know what this is intended to mean in the British context. We do not have a code, so how can we have an 'auxiliary' code. Auxiliary to what? As explained above,[53] the sole purpose of our Interpretation Acts since the first one in 1850 has been to lay down definitions etc. so that the language of Acts can be a little shorter. Common law Interpretation Acts do nothing to 'provide judges with a ragbag of acceptable ways of expressing

[50] *Fitzpatrick v Sterling Housing Association Ltd.* (1999) *The Times* 2 Nov.
[51] See p. 137 above.
[52] David Robertson, *Judicial Discretion in the House of Lords* (Oxford: Oxford University Press, 1998), 9–10.
[53] p. 88.

their discretionary judgments'. Then what is meant by saying that the common law contains 'several rules of interpretation', some stemming from its formative days. Is this a reference to 'the thousand and one interpretative criteria' which have taken me a 1,000-page textbook to expound?[54] I was so intrigued by these questions that I asked Dr Robertson if he would kindly explain. I need not say any more about Interpretation Acts, whose true nature, described above, was in those discussions accepted by Dr Robertson.[55] On the other point I quote his reply:

> The more important point is your second one, and it is difficult to answer, in as much as there is a real puzzle here. It may be what social scientists like me call a 'level of analysis problem'. At one level, the level of overt and public judicial argument, my summary stands. There are a few, well known basic rules of interpretation, which are not always consistent with each other. These are the old standards 'the mischief rule', 'the plain meaning rule', the idea of teleological interpretation, rules giving benefit of doubt to the tax payer in financial legislation, rules insisting on a presumption towards the accused in cases of criminal interpretation and so on. Judges seldom go beneath or beyond this level in their overt references. The recent classics of jurisprudence, Hart's *The Concept of Law* and Dworkin's *Taking Rights Seriously*, when discussing statutes, go no further . . . However underneath this level is the hugely complex and detailed mass of rules and techniques you analyse.

This is very interesting. For purposes of argument I would like to give these two levels of analysis descriptive labels which are not pejorative. I suggest 'the concise analysis' for the first and 'the detailed analysis' for the second. The first question that suggests itself is this. Is the concise analysis a mere précis of the detailed analysis, or are they different in nature? One would expect them to be of the same nature, assuming the detailed analysis is correct. The latter is not entirely made up of detail; the detail clothes a skeleton including major features (spine, pelvis, skull etc.). The concise analysis should correspond to this skeleton, but does it?

Then we need to ask whether Dr Robertson is correct in saying what he does about judges, and about Hart and Dworkin. I rather think he is right. Certainly Dworkin's 'heresy' cited above[56] bears

---

[54] See the citation on p. 12 above.

[55] Dr Robertson has seen the references to him and his book made in this chapter and does not object to their publication.

[56] p. 173.

it out. If he is right, then the first question I have just put matters rather a lot. Unhappily, I suspect the answer to it is that the concise analysis does not correspond to the skeleton. The reason is that few of the people who matter have made a conscious effort to make sure that the concise analysis they hold to is correct or, if it once was correct, is still correct today. Too many analysts in jurisprudence, even Hart and Dworkin, seem to think it scarcely matters at all what real judges really do about statutory interpretation, and whether for that they should be congratulated or reprimanded.

Which brings me back to what Dr Robertson said about judges. He said they seldom go beneath or beyond the concise level in their overt references, and in our correspondence I felt bound to agree with him. However they do *sometimes* go beyond that level. That accounts for the monstrous length of my main textbook *Statutory Interpretation*. Except in the rare cases where it expounds rules laid down by Act of Parliament, almost every word of that book, bones, muscles, tissue, liver and lights, derives from something judges in common law countries at some time, right up to the present day, have decided or said. That is why I call our system the common law method of statutory interpretation. It is the common law in action, as that great Chancery lawyer Lord Wilberforce said.[57]

---

[57] *Express Newspapers Ltd v McShane* [1980] AC 672 at 684. For a summary of this chapter see pp. 218–19.

17

The common law system in America

We have so far assumed that throughout the length and breadth of the common law world there is, as one would expect, an agreed system of statutory interpretation. Broadly that is indeed the case, but we now need to recognize and deal with the fact that in the United States, a prominent common law country, there is some disunity on this point. It seems largely to arise because the United States has a written constitution whereas England, where the common law was born and first developed, does not.

A twofold approach

Americans distinguish interpreting their constitution from interpreting other enacted law, with a tendency to develop different rules for the two processes. This is foreign to the common law technique, based on the concept of legislative intention, of ascertaining in the same way the legal meaning of legislation of any kind, though some English judges are now drifting in that direction even without the aid of a written constitution. The English Lord Justice Buxton referred in 2001 to a rule of construction of 'striking force', which he said has recently come to be referred to as the principle of legality.[1] It was, he explained, expressed by Lord Hoffmann[2] as follows:

Parliamentary sovereignty means that Parliament can, if it chooses, legislate contrary to fundamental principles of human rights. The Human Rights Act 1998 will not detract from this power. The constraints upon its exercise by Parliament are ultimately political, not legal. But the principle of legality means that Parliament must squarely confront what it is doing and accept the political cost. Fundamental rights cannot be overridden by general or ambiguous words. This is because there is too great a

[1] R. (on the application of Morgan Grenfell & Co Ltd) v Special Commissioner [2001] 1 All ER 535 at 539–40.
[2] In R. v Secretary of State for the Home Department, ex p Simms [2000] 2 AC 115 at 131.

risk that the full implications of their unqualified meaning may have passed unnoticed in the democratic process. In the absence of express language or necessary implication to the contrary, the courts therefore presume that even the most general words were intended to be subject to the basic rights of the individual. In this way the courts of the United Kingdom, though acknowledging the sovereignty of Parliament, apply principles of constitutionality little different from those which exist in countries where the power of the legislature is expressly limited by a constitutional document.

Interpreting a written constitution

A truth rarely recognized, and never so far as I know acted on by modern constitution makers, is this. Any written constitution is gravely incomplete unless it contains full instructions on exactly how it is intended by the framers to be interpreted and applied. Without such instructions the text is at large, and at the mercy of future interpreters. The original United States constitution contained no instructions of this kind. The Ninth Amendment went a little way by asserting that the enumeration in the constitution of certain rights 'shall not be construed to deny or disparage others retained by the people'. The Eleventh Amendment says the judicial power allocated by the constitution shall not be construed to extend to suits by foreigners. However such provisions as these do not meet the case, since they are narrowly limited in their effect.[3]

What happened in the United States in the absence of such rules has been described by one Supreme Court justice as 'a sheer judicial power-grab'.[4] He asked where the courts get the authority to

---

[3] Those who drew up the United States constitution were said to have been divided between 'a global rejection of any and all methods of constitutional construction and a willingness to interpret the constitutional text in accordance with the common law principles that had been used to construe statutes': H. Jefferson Powell, 'The Original Understanding of Original Intent' 98 *Harvard Law Review* (1985) 885, 887. I am obliged to Professor Mary Ann Glendon for this reference.

[4] Antonin Scalia, *A Matter of Interpretation: Federal Courts and the Law* (Princeton: Princeton University Press, 1997 (hereafter referred to as *A Matter of Interpretation*)), 29. In the struggle over the presidential election in 2000 the seven-justice Florida Supreme Court said in their unanimous judgment: 'Twenty-five years ago this court commented that the will of the people, *not a hyper-technical reliance upon statutory provisions*, should be our guiding principle in election cases' London *Times*, 23 Nov. 2000 (emphasis added).

impose rules giving the Supreme Court the role of a federal law-giver.[5] The answer, as we find today in England, is that judges, being human, will usurp power if there is no one to stop them.[6] Professor Laurence H. Tribe says there is a problem of self-referential regress whenever one seeks to validate, from within any text's four corners, a particular method of giving that text meaning.[7] So the method of interpretation must be specified externally if it is to have effect. This rarely if ever happens, because framers of a particular text are usually inexperienced in constitution making. They do not perceive its necessity. They are normally not inclined to seek instruction from history books on what they are about, important thought they must know it is. So the people suffer.

Where there is no written constitution there can of course be no interpretative rules laid down by the constitution. England, placed in this situation, could over the years have provided such rules by legislation, but by and large has not done so. The alternative, which was followed, was trustfully to leave it to the judges to provide the interpretative rules on a case by case basis, under the doctrine of precedent or *stare decisis*. These judicial dicta came to be regarded as a part of the common law, but they are not enough in themselves. Being enunciated *ad hoc* in individual cases they lack coherence. It needs someone to draw them together. As an experienced parliamentary draftsman I attempted this task, publishing the entire corpus in the form of a 1000-page statutory code.[8] For most judges this code was too much to absorb, so they continued to rely on the *disjecta membra*[9] of the busy workaday courts, served up to them by equally uncomprehending advocates.

It is a feature of the common law that ultimately in democracies its theory does not admit of rival views. While scholars may dispute over the content of a particular rule, the judges will not hear of this conflict. Our living lady the common law is not to be subjected to dissection in her lifetime: she is an indivisible whole. As I said earlier, we in England regard the common law as what

[5] Ibid.
[6] For one example see Bennion, 'A naked usurpation?' 149 NLJ (1999) 421.
[7] *A Matter of Interpretation*, 76.
[8] See *Bennion Code*.
[9] Literally scattered remains, an alteration of Horace's *disjecti membra poetæ* 'limbs of a dismembered poet'.

the House of Lords has said it is, or would say it is if the point
came before them. Other common law countries substitute for
the House of Lords their own highest court. As I have indicated,
the problem with this is the familiar one of induction, defined as
the process of inferring a general law or principle from the observation of particular instances.[10] What is essential to this process
is the inference from the particular to the general, from the
known to the unknown. The process contains the seeds of
disunity, for even expert opinions may differ on what is the true
content of an induced rule. I have set out my own detailed view
of the content in my textbook *Statutory Interpretation*, and in
condensed form in the preceding chapters of the present book.
That some scholars may think I have not got it quite right in
particular details (no one is infallible) does not affect the principle, which is that broadly (apart from the special factors I have
referred to related to the interpretation of constitutions) there is
consensus on what this particular code contains or should be
regarded as containing if the authorities had only drawn it up
and set it out.

One obstacle to arriving at this consensus lies in the fact that
many legal scholars and teachers in the common law countries
have still not woken up to the fact that legislation has assumed the
dominant role in their systems. As Professor Mary Ann Glendon
has said in relation to the United States:

Although more than a century has passed since legislative enactments
displaced case law as the principal starting points for legal reasoning, we
still operate with craft habits formed in an age when, as Roscoe Pound
once put it, a lawyer could count on his fingers the statutes with an
enduring effect on private law . . . Most of our fellow citizens, no doubt,
would be astonished if they knew how little training the average law
student receives in dealing with enacted law, or how completely the
profession has neglected the art of legislative drafting (the other side of
the coin of interpretation).[11]

---

[10] *Oxford English Dictionary* 2nd edn.
[11] Comment in *A Matter of Interpretation*, 95–114 at 95–6. I have been making
the same plea for England since 1968, with little effect.

Textualism

In the United States, consensus is also hindered by the fact that today there is open disagreement between the proponents of what is called textualism and those who believe in the living constitution (or a similar manifestation as respects ordinary legislation). Leading the former school is Antonin Scalia, an Associate Justice of the US Supreme Court since 1986. He believes that judges have no authority to pursue broader purposes or write new laws.[12] He thinks they should not regard democratically adopted texts as springboards for judicial lawmaking.[13]

Stressing that textualism does not mean blind adherence to literalism, Scalia cites a case where a statute relating to drug trafficking provided for an increased term of imprisonment if the defendant had used a firearm. Here the accused had offered a drug dealer an unloaded firearm in exchange for cocaine. By six to three the Supreme Court held him guilty.[14] Dissenting, Justice Scalia said, surely rightly, that 'using' a firearm must mean using it for what firearms are normally used for, namely shooting or threatening to shoot.

In the view of Justice Scalia, textualism has been undermined by the growing resort to legislative history, which he dates from the 1940s.[15] Earlier, textualists had started resorting to legislative history in order to put the finding of legislative intent beyond judicial manipulation. After reciting the old joke that one should consult the text of the statute only when the legislative history is ambiguous, Scalia goes on:

Alas that is no longer funny. Reality has overtaken parody. A few terms ago I read a brief that *began* the legal argument with a discussion of legislative history and then continued ... 'Unfortunately, the legislative debates are not helpful. Thus we turn to the other guidepost in this difficult area, statutory language'.[16]

Commenting on the Scalia position, Professor Gordon S. Wood says that when construing statutes English common-law judges try to fit them into the body of the law, so that knowing the text of a

---

[12] Ibid. 23.   [13] Ibid. 25.
[14] *Smith v United States* (1993) 508 US 223; cited in *A Matter of Interpretation*, 23–4.
[15] Ibid. 30.   [16] Ibid. 31.

statute is not the same as knowing the law. This he says means that judicial interpretation of texts requires extensive knowledge of the whole legal system 'and involves the continual creation of new legal meanings'. Hence, says Wood, English judges have been accused of acting as legislators almost as often as have American judges.[17] He concludes that in view of the great social changes that have occurred since the US Constitution was framed Scalia's insistence on textualism 'seems scarcely commensurate with the severity of the problem and may in fact be no solution at all'. The judges' interpretative power can be limited only by changing the judicial culture 'or by appointing to the bench only those judges having the attitude you want'.[18] Both solutions seem forlorn hopes, in England as well as America.

However Scalia's doctrine of textualism won a telling triumph when he persuaded the Supreme Court to follow the letter of the law in the disputed presidential election of 2000. Governor Bush defeated Vice-President Gore because a divided U.S. Supreme Court decided by a majority to follow Scalia's lead and ignore judicial creativity by the Florida Supreme Court. The U.S. Supreme Court struck a blow for textualism and certainty over the doctrine held by some judges of 'let's make it up as we go along and try to make things better in the way we happen to see it at this moment'.

In doing that many will think the Supreme Court of the United States struck a blow for true democracy and followed and rein-forced the spirit of the common law.[19]

---

[17] *A Matter of Interpretation,* 59–60.
[18] Ibid. 62–3.
[19] For a summary of this chapter see p. 219–20.

18

Techniques of law management

Handling statutes is not just a matter of interpretation. The handler needs to understand the entire nature of an enactment, and the nuts and bolts which hold related enactments together. This means that officials, lawyers and judges must know how to deploy essential techniques when dealing with legislation, if they are to handle it properly. They can scarcely do so if they have not been taught the techniques, which on the whole does not happen. These techniques can be called 'law handling' or 'law management'. It is not difficult to teach or learn them, for like much else they mainly spring from common sense This final chapter briefly describes these techniques, so far as they apply to legislation in the common law world. To command them is the surest way to thread the legislative maze and understand the statute book.

It is basic to the argument of this book that law requires to be taught and learnt from primary texts and full analysis rather than nutshells or other predigested materials, and that society needs lawyers to be deeply educated both in the liberal and the practical mode. Law is there to serve the public. It cannot work and develop as it should unless there is sufficient academic input. One aspect of this concerns the constantly needed improvement of the technical body of law and legal techniques, as opposed to its substantive content. Politicians talk of law reform, but limit this to crude (if important) substance. There are notoriously no votes, and therefore no politicians' interest, in reform of the technical areas, sometimes called lawyers' law. Legal academics speak of research and the money that requires, but there is less discussion about furthering law's social purpose. In a broad sense, this must be directed to technical improvement of the *corpus juris* or body of law, and the techniques of handling it. The policy of law is all-important, but it is necessary to ensure that law works as planned by those who frame it.

Ability effectively to *manage* the relevant law is central to any lawyer's or law student's functioning. It is a complex intellectual skill, to which neither academia nor the legal profession has so far paid full attention. This neglect extends to the development and refinement of the skill both in practice and by academic research, and to its teaching. There is an element of vicious circle here: what is little taught is not much researched. This central intellectual skill is what Americans call 'lawyering'. It needs, deserves, and is capable of, improvement both in its practice and its teaching.

There is a professional as well as an academic requirement in the sphere of law management. It was pointed out in the report of the first consultative conference of the Lord Chancellor's Advisory Committee on Legal Education and Conduct that little information is available on what lawyers actually do.[1] The report raised the question whether today's lawyers are doing their work properly and suggested that concerns about quality of service need to be addressed by the Advisory Committee's review. In her paper to the conference, Ann Halpern said that in practice as a solicitor she found a lack of ability to solve clients' problems manifested in 'people not recognising or dealing with the full range of legal issues that arise'.[2]

Professor William Twining has said that direct learning of 'skills' should be made a central component of every stage of legal education and training.[3] Gold, Mackie and Twining have pointed out that 'one cannot draft, persuade, interrogate, advise or manage in law without first having intellectually manipulated the relevant materials'. They went on: 'while it is clear that much cognitive skill work is done in the teaching programmes of the universities and professional training programmes around the Commonwealth, it is characteristically done indirectly, providing no specific instructional materials'.[4]

A central area where intellectual manipulation of materials is required concerns the application of a legal rule to a particular set of facts, which may be called basic lawyering. As Gold has put it, the practitioner must often need to 'identify and evaluate legal

[1] *Review of Legal Education: First Consultative Conference*, Discussion Group 3, 9 July 1993.
[2] See paper cited in n. 1 above, p. 3.
[3] W. Twining, 'Legal Skills and Legal Education', 22 *Journal of the Association of Law Teachers* (1988) 4.
[4] N. Gold, K. Mackie and W. Twining, *Learning Lawyers' Skills* (London: Butterworths, 1989) vi.

issues and apply the law'.[5] Elsewhere Gold characterized the skill as that required to 'identify and evaluate relevant facts' and 'identify and evaluate legal issues efficiently'.[6] It is also necessary to know how to work out the resolution of the issues, producing an answer to the question What is the result of applying the law to these facts? As Gold says:

The development of refined, analytical skills is clearly at the root of effective lawyering. Given a fact pattern, a lawyer must know what legal propositions might apply. He must be able to pursue lines of questioning in order to determine other relevant facts not yet laid bare. [It is necessary to] know how to push back that which lies on the surface in order to uncover both legal and factual material which lies below . . . Legal rules guide, direct and ultimately determine the results in particular cases; nevertheless, they always exist for some reason, however vague and unclear. A lawyer is therefore called upon to determine the intent, purpose and goal of legal rules. Underlying rules there may be specific principles or policies to which an adjudicator will give effect. Oftentimes rules form part of an over-arching theory . . . Knowledge required of the lawyer is therefore the well orchestrated co-ordination of information and intellectual skill . . . [Training materials] must specify in clear, concrete terms the specific analytical skills required to *manage* legal information in as proficient a manner as is possible . . .[7]

Yet remarkably, legal educational materials in use today do not spell out this information. Indeed there seems to be no accepted name for this overall skill, vital though it is. The omission may be significant: what is not perceived to exist is not named. I first used the term 'law management' in a proposal submitted to the Council of Legal Education for England and Wales in March 1992.[8] I suggested that the legal research topic in the Bar vocational training course should be expanded to include the handling and manipulation of legal sources, and should then be renamed law management. This was not acted on.

Obviously 'management' is here used in a sense different from

[5] Gold, 'Are Skills Really Frills?', Papers of the Tenth Commonwealth Law Conference, Cyprus, May 1993, 185 at 190.
[6] Gold, 'The Professional Legal Training Program: Towards Training for Competence', 41 *The Advocate* (Canada) (1983) 247 at 251.
[7] Ibid. at 248. Emphasis added.
[8] 'Law Management: A Proposal to add Law Management to the Inns of Court School of Law Vocational Course'.

that meant in terms such as 'practice management' or 'managing your work'. These are practical skills, while law management is an intellectual skill employed in practice. This is the sense used by Macaulay when he said 'In the management of the heroic couplet Dryden has never been equalled'.[9] It embodies at least four of the 24 legal skills listed in the 1988 Marre Report as needing to be taught to students either at the academic or vocational stage.[10] In the Marre Committee's words, and retaining their numbering, these are:

(2) An ability to identify legal issues and construct a valid and cogent argument on a question of law.

(4) An ability to understand the underlying policy of, and social context of, any law.

(5) An ability to analyse and elucidate an abstract concept.

(12) An efficient grasp of techniques for applying the law, *i.e.* problem solving skills.

Several other skills listed by *Marre* are relevant to law management without being comprised in it, for example the ability to carry out legal research making intelligent use of all source material. Ordinary advocacy skills, though not included, are also relevant. The borderline between formulating a legal proposition and putting it across by advocacy can be difficult to draw, since advocacy begins with the way the proposition is worked out and drawn up even before the courtroom door is reached. An American committee on legal education listed the following advocacy skills:

that an argument is addressed not to its author, but to a specific tribunal and must for effectiveness move in terms of what will appeal to and persuade that tribunal. Or: the principle of 'limited span of attention' of any tribunal, with corollaries: the value of simplicity of thread; the value of points which cumulate instead of scattering; the extra-interest which the statement of facts arouses, and the importance of making that statement frame the issue favorably, and of an arrangement which drives forward. Or again: the value to a legal thesis of a phrasing in language both simple and familiar; or the power, in an answering argument, of a

---

[9] *Edinburgh Review*, 26 Jan. 1828.
[10] *A Time for Change*, Report of the Committee on the Future of the Legal Profession, Chairman Lady Marre (1988) para. 12.21.

positive thesis which neither accepts the ground chosen by the other party nor loses momentum by a succession of denials or explanations.[11]

These skills are useful, but they are not law management. Essentially, we are talking not about how to dress up an argument to achieve maximum persuasiveness but how to work out its substantive intellectual content in the first place. This is a basic lawyering technique that applies to all areas of law, in virtually all jurisdictions. While specific knowledge of a particular area will also be needed for full effectiveness, the lawyer can go a long way in unfamiliar areas simply by using the basic technique. It is a technique for use with specialized legal rules, whether familiar or not, as well as general rules applicable to all law. Hence it ministers to the needed versatility of lawyers operating in fields such as general practice or litigation. It helps overcome practice problems created by facts such as that no student taking an academic course can cover more than a small proportion of the area, or that real-life problems are not neatly packaged with a topic label but messily cut across boundaries.[12]

I have written elsewhere of how the purposes of law can be set out in tree form proceeding downwards from the widest generality to the narrowest specialization.[13] Legal knowledge, including possession of skills, can be treated in the same way. Take an example from commercial law. In his 1991 memorial lecture for the late Clive Schmitthoff, Sir Roy Goode explained how he began teaching this subject with the idea that it was necessary for him to 'cover the field'. Twenty years later he accepts that it is more important to instil in his students the basic principles of commercial law: 'Better that they should understand the fundamental concepts, so that they would know how to analyse the legal effects of a fact situation not the subject of any previous reported case, than that they should become bogged down in the minutiae of technical law. . .'[14] What Goode does not mention is that in order

---

[11] 'The Place of Skills in Legal Education', Report of Committee on Curriculum, Association of American Law Schools (Chairman, Karl N. Llewellyn), 45 *Columbia Law Rev.* (1945) 345 at 373 n.

[12] For checklists of court techniques in relation to the legal meaning of enactments see *Bennion Code*, pp. 1019–23.

[13] *Bennion Code*, p. 734.

[14] Roy Goode, 'The Teaching and Application of Fundamental Concepts of Commercial Law' in P. B. H. Birks (ed.), *Examining the Law Syllabus: Beyond the Core* (Oxford: Oxford University Press, 1993) 55 at 57.

successfully 'to analyse the legal effects of a [commercial] fact situation' the student or practitioner needs general law management skill as well as specific knowledge of commercial law fundamentals.[15] For this field the legal knowledge tree can be set out in the following way:

Law management

|

Commercial law

|

Sale of goods

|

Goods must be of reasonable quality

What needs to be grasped is that in any such tree, no matter what the area of law in question, *the top branch will always be law management.*

The facts in question in a law management exercise may be actual or hypothetical. They will be actual where the lawyer or student is asked to advise, litigate or comment on particular facts. They will be hypothetical where the task is one such as the drafting of a contract or legislative text or preparing a moot argument. Either way, facts are the starting point. Then one needs to find the legal key that unlocks the case. While a case report is useful for illustration, especially where, as with say *Salomon v Salomon & Co. Ltd.* [1897] AC 22, it illustrates a number of different points, we need to beware of limiting tuition to law's pathology and remember its facilitating function.[16] Law management techniques are needed for both solving and avoiding problems, since each depends on exposing the legal thrust applicable to the factual situation. Law reports show that judges and practitioners can make mistakes.[17] It is a function of law management to spot these. They

---

[15] For an example in relation to vocabulary (or jargon): see *Brady v Brady* [1989] AC 755.

[16] At the first consultative conference of the Lord Chancellor's Advisory Committee on Legal Education and Conduct it was pointed out that 'lawyers often concentrated on solving problems rather than avoiding them', concluding that 'a more strategic and creative use of law was needed instead of this pathological approach': see *Review of Legal Education: First Consultative Conference*, Discussion Group 3, 9 July 1993.

[17] '[T]he reasoning of the judge(s) may be dodgy or patently bad': Len Sealy, 'Company Law through the Cases' in P. B. H. Birks (ed.), *Examining the Law Syllabus: Beyond the Core* (see n. 14 above), 37 at 38, citing *Houldsworth v City*

may be used to throw doubt on an adverse decision, or suggest ways round it. Legislative drafters also err, and this too can be turned to account if noticed.[18] How then can we define law management? I offer the following.

Law management is the general skill, applied in the context of particular facts (whether actual or hypothetical) and supplemented where necessary by detailed knowledge of the particular area of law in question in a case, of identifying the legal issues involved, formulating the relevant legal rule(s) and, by intellectual manipulation of the materials (witness statements, case reports, legislative enactments etc.), reaching the legal resultant (or arguable legal resultant) of applying the rule(s) to the facts. All this needs to be accompanied by the working out and formulation of explanations and arguments.

Very often, the law that is to be 'managed' must first be found out by research. There is reason to believe that accurate indwelling (i.e. memorized) legal knowledge is sparse among many practising lawyers.[19] One reason for this is no doubt the recent growth in the opposition of teachers to rote learning.[20] Another factor is the increase in the volume, complexity and variety of primary laws. In these circumstances teaching of correct categorization assumes greater importance. Primary laws can be categorized in various ways, of which the following are perhaps the most important.

• The division between substantive and procedural law.
• The division between statute law and judge-made law.
• The division between law laid down by the United Kingdom legislature and courts and law laid down by institutions of the

of Glasgow Bank (1880) 5 App. Cas. 317 (reversed by Companies Act 1989 s. 131(1)) and *Rayfield v Hands* [1960] Ch. 1.

[18] '[I]t is particularly bad that so much legislation is drafted in disregard (or ignorance) of the common law rules that it is designed to co-exist with': Len Sealy again (in work cited in n. 17 above, p. 39).

[19] Research published by the Royal Commission on Criminal Justice showed that of 187 solicitors responding to a questionnaire '52 per cent. wrongly believed that the Appeal Court can impose a more severe sentence on an appellant . . . and advise [*sic*] their clients accordingly': 137 *Sol. J*, 14 May 1993, 444.

[20] At the first consultative conference of the Lord Chancellor's Advisory Committee on Legal Education and Conduct, 9 July 1993, Discussion Group 1 'agreed that it was essential to ensure that the course did not become a matter of rote learning, as some courses were at present': See *Review of Legal Education*, the report of proceedings at the conference.

European Union and other international bodies or groupings such as the European Court of Human Rights.

- Sub-divisions within these categories, e.g. statute law can be divided into Acts, regulations, orders, by-laws etc.

There are complex interactions between laws in the various divisions and subdivisions, with some laws overriding others. Policy considerations obtrude. As we have seen in earlier chapters, the literal meaning of a law is sometimes modified by reference to the policy underlying it or to general legal or public policy. Teachers may ignore this aspect. Sir Roy Goode said:

> Commercial law continues to possess an astonishingly large number of unresolved conceptual problems. . .The sad fact is that we have tended to take the easy way out, to teach the rule and neglect the concept, to analyse the case and the statutory provision and ignore the philosophical framework. Key policy issues . . . pass us by.[21]

Another complicating factor concerns the nature of techniques that need to be applied. As we have seen, the rules, principles, presumptions and linguistic canons which under the common law or Global method are applicable to the interpretation of UK legislation, and therefore form part of the technique of law management, are not the same when it comes to the interpretation of a treaty given legislative effect or an EU directive. This also applies to the doctrine of precedent as it applies to a decision of the Appellate Committee of the House of Lords at Westminster as compared to a decision of the CJEC at Luxembourg or the European Court of Human Rights at Strasbourg. As the inevitable integration continues of English jurisprudence, based on common law, with Continental jurisprudence, based on civil law, so will it be necessary to unify the respective law management principles. Meanwhile they have to be applied separately, according to the source of the legal rule in question. So both need to be taught and learnt.

It is often not realized that in arriving at the legal result of applying the rule to the facts a lawyer has to unlock and release some part of the endeavour originally put into the composing of the judgment or enactment in question. Considerable intellectual

---

[21] 'The Teaching and Application of Fundamental Concepts of Commercial Law' (in work cited in n. 14 above, p. 55 at pp. 60–1).

effort goes into the composing operation. It is wasted if proportionate labour does not go into construing and applying the product; moreover the law applied may not be the law intended. Deployment of this original effort means that, for those who know how to take advantage of it, a high degree of precision may be possible in the application process. This is particularly true of British legislation. Atiyah and Summers point out that in the United Kingdom, unlike the United States, the legislature gives its instructions in the form of 'exceptionally precise and detailed commands, drafted with great technical skill'.[22]

The same cannot always be said of legislative passages in judgments. In answer to my suggestion in a seminar that it would be advantageous for judges to cast appropriate portions of their judgments in legislative form, the Australian judge Kirby J. said they would not do this because 'the discursive nature of their judgments is the historic basis of the development of the common law'.[23] However there seems no reason why a judgment could not contain both a brief 'legislative' passage and an accompanying discursive explanation.[24] Judges ought not to shrink, in the name of the developing common law, from being precise as to the legal propositions they are laying down in their judgments.

Despite the most intensive effort, it is often found by the 'law manager' that the result of applying the rule to the facts is real doubt. An important element in law management techniques is the ability to assess the nature and extent of this uncertainty. The nuances involved are well summed up by the American committee previously cited: 'consistent discrimination among competing case-law formulations in terms of "safe, pretty safe, not safe enough", is as much a needed lawyer's skill to be made habitual as is discrimination in terms of "sound, probably sound, dubiously sound, unsound", or in terms of "technically tenable or untenable; and if tenable, then compelling, adequately persuasive, risky, or too risky" '.[25] The art of assessing the degree of such uncertainty

---

[22] P. S. Atiyah and R. S. Summers, *Form and Substance in Anglo-American Law* (Oxford: Clarendon Press, 1987), 318.

[23] *Proceedings of the Tenth Commonwealth Law Conference*, Cyprus, 4 May 1993, session 1.2.

[24] For a detailed proposal that judicial sub-rules should be couched in this way by 'interstitial articulation' see Bennion, *Statute Law* (3rd edn., London: Longman, 1990), 305–10.

[25] See work cited in n. 11 above at p. 361.

is difficult for students to master. Ann Halpern has said of her contract students: 'They never seemed to be willing to assess whether their ideas, arguments, interpretations would succeed or what the risks might be in promoting a particular argument. This habit is one I recognise in practice.'[26]

Finding the legal result (certain or doubtful) of applying the legal rule to the facts may not be the end of the story. What the law *says* is the result may not be so in reality. For example the law laying down a particular offence may say that a person guilty of it is liable to imprisonment for a term not exceeding three months, but if caught in fact a particular criminal may be expected to end up with nothing worse than a conditional discharge or even a police caution. The law may say that the facts surrounding a particular marriage give grounds for divorce, whereas what is really called for on the part of the legal practitioner is mediation or conciliation.

In relation to common law and other 'unwritten' law, the technique of law management involves framing and presenting a legal rule based on case law in the light of the facts of the instant case. Even in relation to statute law, the handling of case law which glosses the relevant legislation is an important skill. In relation to case law, English judges expect to have put before them the case as reported in the semi-official Law Reports unless it is reported only in some other medium. This means that textbook summaries of a decision are rarely acceptable, so advocates must use an appropriate technique for arguing the point of law effectively. Before they can adopt this, they need a technique for extracting the relevant legal rule from the reports. While there may be no dispute about the content of that rule, this does not mean it is easy to find, or to state in the form best suited to the practitioner's case.

Points of law based on reported cases may form a comparatively small proportion of the new practitioner's early experience. However it is vital that he or she knows how to handle them when they do arise, and also knows how to spot the latent point of law which can turn out to be crucial. At the apprenticeship stage Bar pupils are likely to be asked to devil in cases in the High Court or above where law-handling skills are of first importance. This is a

---

[26] See paper cited in n. 1 above, p. 18.

very difficult area for the inexperienced practitioner. How far, if at all, can it be assumed that the judge knows the law? In what form should legal propositions be laid before the court? If a skeleton argument is put in, how far does oral argument need to go to supplement this? How far will the court permit it to go? And so on.

The student needs to learn how to tease out and state the legal rule which is relevant on the facts. If possible it needs to be so formulated that it is stated (still of course accurately) in a form that goes no wider than the facts. The art of doing this is central to an advocate's function. One useful technique is to state the rule in the combined form of factual outline and legal thrust.[27] The basis of the doctrine of precedent is that like cases must be decided alike. This requires a correct identification and statement of the factual outline that triggers the legal thrust of the rule on actual facts such as are before the court.

The concept of the *ratio decidendi* of a case involves postulating a general factual outline. This is part of the rule laid down or followed by the case, since a legal rule imports a factual situation to which it applies. When relying on a reported case as a precedent it is the first function of the court, and therefore of an advocate advising the court, to generalize the facts of that case. Thus in the famous case of *Donoghue v Stevenson* [1932] AC 562 the relevant generalized fact was not a sealed bottle of ginger-beer but a product intended to reach the consumer without intermediate examination. The relevant factual outline proceeds from this to identify the situations which, in relation to the legal rule in question, are material on the actual facts of the instant case. Thus if a man charged with murder claims to be acquitted because what he admittedly killed was a person who through brain damage was permanently unconscious, the relevant factual outline is concerned only with whether the crime of murder extends to the killing with malice aforethought of a person who is in a persistent vegetative state. It is the function of the court, and therefore of an advocate advising the court, accurately to identify this area of relevance.

Instruction is also needed in such matters as the nature of an obiter dictum, the distinction between binding and persuasive authority, whether a decision has been affirmed, the difference

[27] See Ch. 1 above.

between extempore and reserved judgments, arguing a case of first impression, persuading an appellate court that the lower court got the law wrong, the status of dissenting judgments, overruling *per incuriam* decisions, and arguing for or against development of rules of common law or equity to meet changes in social conditions, technology, etc. Here the actual way in which judges currently handle precedent greatly needs academic examination and comment, since it differs markedly from the classic treatment of *stare decisis*. There is a present tendency, for example, to place undue emphasis on obiter dicta, often randomly selected. The almost universal practice of our judges today in relying solely on what advocates choose to place before them in the way of legal argument (it was not always so) seriously endangers the consistency of legal rulings and the proper development of the law.

The theoretical concept of the *ratio decidendi* is taught early, but instruction is needed in extracting it in an actual case (particularly where there are several judgments), finding ways to support it (e.g. by citing a judicial dictum), arguing for or against its extension by analogy when it does not fit the actual facts, distinguishing it where necessary, and applying the processes outlined above. It may be important to identify the *ratio decidendi* to determine whether the decision is binding on a later court.[28] In practice it is not so much the *ratio decidendi* of an individual case that is likely to be important, but the legal rule for which a line of cases can be cited as authority (the two may of course amount to the same thing). A useful exercise is to *codify* the relevant rule, citing the case(s) on which the rule as codified is said to be based. The traditional concentration by law teachers on extracting the *ratio decidendi* of an individual case might usefully be redirected to framing the codified rule for which one or more cases stand as authority.

What may be called the codifier's approach can be very useful in case work. When reading a decided case, whether it concerns written or unwritten law, or a mixture of the two, the student or practitioner should do so at several levels. Apart from reading it for what it actually says and decides, it is helpful (particularly for students and inexperienced practitioners) to read it critically. The arguments presented by the advocates and in the judgments

---

[28] See, e.g. *AB v. South West Water Services Ltd* [1993] 1 All ER 609 at 620 ('the point formed no part of the ratio of the case and it is not binding on us').

should be tested and assessed, a point to which I return below. Where an argument is being constructed on the basis of the case, its place as an element in what could be a codified rule should be worked out. This may be pure common law codification or 'mixed' codification embracing both written and unwritten law.

The critical approach to the reading of decided cases, where the arguments presented by the advocates and in the judgments are tested and assessed, may be called the appellant's approach. I give it this name because the reader is placed in the position of a possible appellant from the decision. This is an exercise which can of course be done even where the case was decided by a 'final' court such as the House of Lords: it may be useful to detect weaknesses and flaws even though there is no possibility of appealing the decision. The purpose of doing so relates to the *argument* that may be deployed in the practitioner's instant case by reference to the decision being examined. For instance, the practitioner may need to distinguish the binding decision.

For students at the academic level, the critical approach to decided cases is a necessity, since the essence of academia is criticism. This reminds us that law management is not just a humdrum tool. While confined to finding out how the law and particular facts mesh, it involves an awareness of a range of linguistic, sociological, jurisprudential and other considerations that might influence a court's decision on those facts.

English courts require an advocate to cite primary sources of legislation as officially issued. Quite apart from techniques of statutory interpretation, there are many practical aspects to the handling of the relevant statutory materials once they have been found by research. This is an area where there is considerable ignorance among practitioners and even judges. Basically this arises from long-standing refusal to recognize what is seen by Professor Carol Harlow as the need 'to give statute its true place as the centre of gravity of the legal system'.[29] No one can be sure of arriving at and presenting the correct rule derived from an Act without knowledge of such matters as the following, some of which have been explained in previous chapters:[30]

---

[29] See work cited in n. 14 above, p. 69.   [30] See Index.

(*a*) enactment and assent procedure, including the way Bills are drafted and amended;

(*b*) the structure of an Act, including the juridical nature of the long title, preamble (if any), recitals (if any), purpose clause (if any), sections, sidenotes, provisos, headings, short title, Schedules, punctuation and format;

(*c*) geographical extent of an Act, including relevant rules of private international law (conflict of laws);

(*d*) the persons and things to whom or which an Act applies, again including private international law rules;

(*e*) the various ways an Act may be brought into force, including differential commencement and the vexed question of retrospectivity;

(*f*) the vital matter of transitional provisions, so often overlooked in practice;

(*g*) ways in which Acts are amended, whether textually, indirectly or by implication;

(*h*) repeals, whether express or implied, including savings.

Next comes the technique of isolating the part of the Act which is relevant in the case, known as an 'enactment'. As we have seen, the relevant enactment, very often no more than a single sentence (or even part only of a sentence), is the unit of inquiry upon which the decision will turn. There is a practical technique (known as selective comminution) for isolating this without violating Parliament's actual language. There is a further technique (interstitial articulation) for expanding the official words of an enactment with detail either drawn from reported cases on the enactment or put forward by the advocate in advancing argument. Where there is dispute about the legal meaning of the enactment, there is a technique of putting forward the opposing constructions of the enactment, between which the court is invited by each side to choose. The task is then one of ascertaining and weighing the relevant interpretative factors.

The isolating technique mentioned above also applies to statutory instruments (SIs), and for this purpose it may be necessary to combine in one formulation materials drawn both from Acts and SIs. This can be done by composite restatement.[31] In handling an

---

[31] This is explained in Bennion, *Statute Law* (2nd edn, 1983), Ch. 27.

SI it is necessary to bear in mind, in relation to the parent Act, the matters specified above. In relation to the SI itself the user needs to be aware of such matters as commencement, amendment and revocation of SIs, parliamentary control, the rule of primary intention, the general interpretative principle, the *Padfield* approach, severability and the doctrine of ultra vires.[32]

This final chapter adds support to the argument that lawyers need a liberal education based firmly on primary sources. In describing the nature and uses of the essential technique of law management, which uses only such sources, it shows one way in which the contribution of academic research and theory is needed; and could indeed be enhanced. I propose a teaching syllabus on the following lines. It should begin by explaining various *techniques* of the law, leading to an account of how necessary is the technique of law management. It involves a synthesis of presently disparate and separately taught techniques such as fact management, legal research, legal method, problem solving (to a limited extent only since there are other areas of problem solving in law), handling case law (finding the *ratio decidendi*, applying the doctrine of precedent, etc.), applying the rules, principles, presumptions and linguistic canons governing statutory interpretation, and using the techniques of advocacy (again to a limited extent only, relating to the preparation and marshalling of argument on points of law).

Then it is necessary to describe in brief and simple terms the various *types* of law on which law management techniques must operate. As well as common law and statute law these include European law (consisting of Community law, law of other elements within the European Union such as the European Convention on Human Rights, international law in Europe, and the emerging common law of Europe). The syllabus could then be innovative in showing that many criteria are uniform for the interpretation both of statute law and case law, since both are informed by the principles of *legal policy*, including concern for human rights and international treaty obligations. Going on with how the court *decides* a case, the syllabus would continue the innovative note by synthesizing the way in which a court handles common law and statutory issues.

---

[32] See Index.

Next the nature of *legal rules* would be dealt with. For law management to operate successfully it is necessary to understand the nature of the various types of legal rule. Some are more precise than others; some operate more or less flexibly; some are open to development or to the argument that they should be discarded by the court as obsolete or unsuitable. Then would follow a treatment of the *factual outline* laid down by the legal rule in question and the concomitant *legal thrust* when the facts of a particular case fall within the outline. Next would come a section on what is called by some law schools *fact management*. This involves ascertaining the facts of the case, distinguishing relevant from irrelevant facts, and assessing the ways in which the facts should be established (by agreement, evidence, judicial notice, admissions etc.), gathering evidence, and taking witness statements. These matters would be gone into only so far as necessary for discussing law management aspects.

The next topic is identification of the legal *issues* that arise on the facts. This is often a difficult task, yet needs to be performed precisely and accurately. There are special techniques for stating the issues in an opinion, pleading, skeleton argument or judgment. It is then necessary to deal with *case law* techniques such as how to read a case report, arriving at the *ratio decidendi* and applying the doctrine of precedent. Case law presents a problem not so acutely found with legislation, namely how to work out the correct statement of the relevant legal rule. Here a textbook often needs to be relied on, though this is not popular with judges. They prefer to act on the words of fellow judges, often diffuse and contradictory. These need very careful handling by the practitioner and a sound method for presenting them to the court with accompanying argument.

Then would follow a discussion of the techniques for the management of legislation of various types. This includes selective comminution, for isolating the precise statutory words on which an argument needs to be constructed. Another technique concerns the identification of the opposing constructions which the two sides may wish to place upon an enactment. A further technique, interstitial articulation, is concerned with filling out gaps in legislation by sub-rules. These may, and often should, be worked out in judgments. Earlier, the advocate may advance his or her case by formulating them.

Next it is necessary to show how to handle a *multi-law* case, where more than one system is relevant. This brings in conflict of laws (otherwise known as private international law) and the vital question of the overriding of national law by European Community law and the effect of the Human Rights Act 1998.

The final stages of the syllabus would be concerned with the techniques that govern the constructing of legal arguments, opinions, pleadings and judgments once the work of extracting the legal conclusions has been completed. The syllabus should cover the judicial function as well as that of advocates and other practitioners. There is much room for improvement in the way judges carry out their functions in relation to law management. The syllabus will be found useful for training judges.

I end by stressing that this proposed syllabus is designed very much with the needs in mind of students burdened with ever-widening courses. I do not expect law management to be erected into yet another subject in a crowded curriculum. Rather I contemplate that it will be treated as a necessary accompaniment to student work on most if not all individual subjects and aspects of the legal system. While there are other important legal skills (such as negotiating skills) I believe they all ultimately depend on an achieved ability to find out how the law applies to particular facts.[33]

---

[33] For a summary of this chapter see pp. 220–2.

Chapter Summaries

Chapter 1: Basic concepts I: common law statutes; the enactment; legal meaning; factual outline and legal thrust; implied ancillary rules

- The laws that govern the common law countries are now mostly enactments of a democratic parliament, mediated by common law principles of interpretation.

- In the case of the United Kingdom, mother of the common law, the position is now complicated by European involvement.

- The term 'statute law' means: (1) law in statutory form ('legislation'); (2) the area of knowledge and skill concerned with the nature, functioning and interpretation of legislation ('statute law').

- The intended readership of this book is either law orientated or fact and party orientated.

- Law as integrity asks judges to assume that the law is structured by a coherent set of principles about justice and fairness and procedural due process, and requires them to enforce these (Dworkin).

- This book is both descriptive and prescriptive.

- Legislation is what the legislator says it is; the legal meaning of legislation is what the court says it is.

- Successful handling or management of legislation by the practitioner requires mastery of certain essential concepts, some of which are as follows.

- The basic unit of legislation is the enactment, consisting of a distinct proposition of law.

- An enactment must be given an informed construction, that is one which takes account of its context, its legislative history, and any court rulings on it.

- Where they differ, what matters is the legal rather than the literal meaning of an enactment.

- The legal meaning of an enactment is the one that is taken to correspond to the original legislator's intention.

- It is the exclusive function of the courts authoritatively to declare the legal meaning of an enactment.

- In practical terms, the legal meaning is the one most likely to be adopted by the highest court if the point comes before it.

- To be acted on, a doubt as to the legal meaning must be real, that is substantial and not merely conjectural or fanciful.

- The phenomenon of differential readings may lead to different judicial minds reaching different conclusions on the legal meaning.

- There may be difficulty over the position of a person who has acted on a court decision as to legal meaning where a later court overrules the decision; but the problem must be decided by reference to common law principles of legal policy.

- Ignorance or mistake as to the legal meaning, whether by the subject or a legal adviser, is not accepted as an excuse for non-compliance.

- The usual effect of an enactment is that, when the facts of a case fall within an indicated area called the factual outline, specified consequences called the legal thrust ensue.

- The statutory factual outline may be modified by the court of construction if that is necessary to implement the legislator's intention.

- Elements in the legal thrust of an enactment may be left unexpressed by the drafter.

- Unexpressed elements are to be treated as imported because of a general presumption, based on the nature of legislation, that, unless the contrary intention appears, an enactment by implication imports any principle or rule of law (whether statutory or non-statutory) which is relevant to its operation. This may be referred to as an 'implied ancillary rule'.

- Upon this principle, unless the Act creating an offence indicates to the contrary, proof by the prosecution of a guilty mind or *mens rea* is needed to establish the commission of a statutory offence.

- Implied ancillary rules do not stand still. Because there has been a general shift from objectivism to subjectivism in the criminal law, belief in absolving facts no longer needs to be reasonable provided it is genuine.

Chapter 2: Basic concepts II: opposing constructions; literal, purposive and developmental interpretations

- Where there is an existing court decision on the legal meaning of an enactment this does not necessarily represent the law, since the decision may later be held incorrect.

- The importance of the enactment as the unit of inquiry rests on the fact that it is usually the operation of an enactment that gives rise to crucial *issues* of fact or law.

- An issue of fact may be whether a party committed a certain act. Before it can be determined whether that question is material, it must first be ascertained whether a fact of that kind is required by the relevant factual outline laid down by the enactment.

- Before the issue of fact can arise of whether or not a party did a relevant act, it may be necessary to settle an issue of law, namely which of the opposing constructions put forward by the rival parties is correct?

- It can sometimes be said of the opposing constructions that one presents a wider and the other a narrower legal meaning.

- Although the rival advocates put forward opposing constructions, the court may reject both and substitute its own. Or it may hold that there is no real doubt as to the legal meaning.

- One type of case where, although there may be real doubt over the meaning of an enactment, opposing constructions do not arise is where the enactment requires the exercise of judgment or confers a discretion. Here more than one correct answer may be possible, though it is not right to say that the enactment is therefore ambiguous.

- The formulating and resolution of opposing constructions of an enactment, and the exercise of judgment or discretion, are aspects of the central function of a legal practitioner. This is to go through the mental process of reaching a legal conclusion by applying the relevant law to the relevant facts, which is a continuous two-way operation.

- Is the interpreter's task (*a*) to arrive at a literal meaning and apply that every time (literal construction), or (*b*) sometimes to go further and apply a purposive but strained meaning (purposive construction), or (c) occasionally to depart altogether from the text, using it merely as a starting point for developing the underlying juridical idea (developmental construction)?

Chapter 3: *Grammatical and strained meanings*

- Does the drafter intend the user always to adopt a literal interpretation, or where necessary use a purposive but strained interpretation, or even on occasion arrive at a developmental interpretation?

- The starting point must always be the ordinary linguistic meaning of the words used, that is their grammatical meaning apart from legal considerations.

- The grammatical meaning of an enactment is the meaning it bears when construed according to the rules and usages of grammar, syntax and punctuation, and the purely linguistic canons of construction. It includes implications.

- The grammatical meaning may be clear, ambiguous or obscure. It is clear when, apart from legal considerations, there is no real doubt about it. It is ambiguous when grammatically capable of more than one meaning. It is obscure when the language is disorganized, garbled or otherwise semantically confused or opaque.

- An enactment may be clear, ambiguous or obscure in relation to all possible facts (absolute clarity, ambiguity or obscurity), or certain facts only (relative clarity, ambiguity or obscurity).

- Where it is obscure, one first needs to determine what was the intended grammatical meaning. The version thus arrived at ('the corrected version'), is then to be dealt with as if it had been the actual wording.

- Where the grammatical meaning is clear, that is the literal meaning. Where it is ambiguous, any of the grammatical meanings may be called the literal meaning. Where it is obscure, the meaning of the corrected version, or, where that is ambiguous, any of its meanings, is the literal meaning.

- To give an enactment a literal construction is to apply the literal meaning or, in the case of ambiguity, one of the literal meanings.

- The so-called literal rule of construction requires that an enactment always be given a literal construction. This dissolves nowadays into a rule that the text is the primary indication of legislative intention, but that the enactment is to be given a literal meaning only where this is not outweighed by more powerful factors.

- One of these arises where to apply a literal construction would not further the purpose of the legislator. A construction which promotes the remedy Parliament has provided to cure a particular mischief is now known as a purposive construction. This term is usually confined to cases where the literal meaning is departed from. This is also called a strained construction.

- A strained meaning is any meaning other than the literal meaning. Sometimes the arguments against a literal construction are so compelling that even though the words are not, within the rules of language, capable of another meaning they must be given one.

- Developmental construction requires the court occasionally to depart altogether from the text, using it merely as a starting point for developing the underlying juridical idea.

- Nowadays, the drafter never intends the literal rule to be adopted.

- In the case of a common law enactment unaffected by European considerations, or delegated legislation made thereunder, the drafter now intends the interpreter to apply the common law or Global method and where necessary adopt a purposive-and-strained construction.

- In the case of legislation where the European approach applies, the drafter intends the interpreter when necessary to adopt a Developmental construction using the text merely as a starting point

Chapter 4: Consequential and rectifying constructions

- There are four main reasons for a strained construction: (1) where the consequences of a literal construction are so undesirable that Parliament cannot have intended them, (2) an error in the text, (3) a repugnance between the words of the enactment and those of another enactment, and (4) passage of time since the enactment was originally drafted.

- It is presumed to be the legislator's intention that when

considering, in relation to the facts of the instant case, which of the possible readings of the enactment corresponds to its legal meaning, the court should assess the likely consequences of adopting each construction not only for the parties in the instant case but also (if similar facts should arise in future) for the law generally.

- Consequences should be considered not only where a strained construction may be necessary but also where the grammatical meaning is ambiguous.

- If on balance the consequences of a particular construction are more likely to be *adverse* than *beneficent* this tells against that construction. The prospect of a strongly adverse consequence in itself *raises* doubt.

- Where the literal application of an enactment would yield adverse results this indicates that the court should *curtail* its application, a procedure known as strict construction. Where the application yields a beneficent result the opposite applies, a procedure known as liberal construction.

- It is presumed that the legislator intends the court to apply a construction, called a rectifying construction, which puts right any error in the drafting of the enactment.

- Intended words may be omitted, or unintended words included, or the words may be confused. The Queen's printer will correct minor typographical errors.

- Rectification of a more substantial kind may be required where the error is latent rather than apparent. The drafter may have misconceived the legislative project, or based the text on a mistake of fact, or mistaken the applicable law.

- Where the literal meaning goes narrower than the object of the legislator (*casus omissus*), the court may need to apply a rectifying construction widening that meaning. A distinction can be drawn between 'interpretative gap-filling', which is legitimate, and 'substantive gap-filling', which is not.

- The opposite of a *casus omissus* is a *casus male inclusus*, where the wording of the enactment goes wider than is necessary to remedy the mischief aimed at. Here the court may apply a narrow or strict construction.

Chapter 5: Contradictory enactments and updating construction

- The third of the four main reasons for a strained construction is where there is a repugnance between the words of the enactment in question and those of another enactment, whether in the same or another Act.

- When two relevant texts contradict each other, both cannot be given a literal application without contravening the logical principle of contradiction or *principium contradictionis*.

- Where, on the facts of the instant case, the literal meaning of the enactment under inquiry is inconsistent with the literal meaning of one or more other enactments in the same Act, the combined meaning of the enactments is to be arrived at.

- An Act is to be read as a whole, so that an enactment within it is not treated as standing alone but is interpreted in its context as part of the Act.

- Construction as a whole means three principles should be applied: (1) every word in the Act should be given a meaning, (2) the same word should be given the same meaning, and (3) different words should be given different meanings.

- If no other method of reconciliation seems possible, the court may under the rule in *Wood v Riley* adopt the principle that the enactment nearest the end of the Act prevails.

- Where the literal meaning of a general enactment covers a situation for which specific provision is made elsewhere in the Act, it is presumed that the situation was intended to be dealt with by the specific provision. This is expressed in the maxim *generalibus specialia derogant* (special provisions override general ones).

- If a later enactment makes contrary provision to an earlier, Parliament (though it has not expressly said so) is taken to intend the earlier to be repealed so far as needed to remove the conflict. A similar doctrine applies to amendment.

- The last of the four reasons for departing from the literal meaning and adopting a strained construction is the need to apply an updating construction.

- Usually an Act is intended to develop in meaning with developing circumstances (an ongoing Act).

- A fixed-time Act has a once and for all effect. A common case is where the Act is of the nature of a contract, an obvious instance being the private Act.

- It is presumed that Parliament intends the court to apply to an ongoing Act (which is to be treated as always speaking) a construction which continuously updates the language of the Act.

- Different types of change can call for an updating construction: changes in the mischief, changes in relevant law, changes in social conditions, developments in technology and medical science, and changes in the meaning of words.

Chapter 6: Drafting techniques and the Interpretation Act

- Drafting techniques have a profound influence on the way law operates, or should operate.

- Different types of Act are drafted in different ways. One type is the consolidation Act, which confines within one new Act provisions from various existing Acts that are *in pari materia*.

- There is one prime distinction to be drawn in relation to consolidation Acts, which is between straight consolidation and consolidation with amendments. There is presumed to be no change of meaning in the former.

- Drafting technique is particularly important in relation to statutory definitions. These are required for various purposes, the most obvious of which is to clarify the intended legal meaning of a term being used.

- The Interpretation Act 1978, which lays down many statutory definitions of general application, states that they apply 'unless the contrary intention appears'. Similar statements usually appear in Acts providing *ad hoc* definitions. Whether the defining enactment says so or not, a statutory definition does not apply if the contrary intention appears from the place in which the defined term is used.

- In addition to clarifying definitions there are at least five other types of statutory definition, as follows.

- A *labelling definition* uses a term as a label denoting a complex concept that can then be referred to merely by the label, instead of the drafter having to keep repeating the full description.

- A *referential definition* attracts a meaning already established in law, whether by statute or otherwise.

- An *exclusionary definition* deprives the term of a meaning it would or might otherwise be taken to have.

- An *enlarging definition* is designed to make clear that the term includes a meaning that otherwise would or might be taken as outside it.

- A *comprehensive definition* sets out to provide a full statement of everything that is to be taken as included in the term.

- A definition may be qualified by what is known as *the potency of the term defined.* This indicates that whatever meaning may be expressly attached to a term, its dictionary meaning is likely to exercise some influence over the way the definition will be understood by the court.

- Wherever possible the good drafter engages in what might be called *weightless drafting.* This shortens and simplifies wording where there is no weight on its exact meaning (on this see also chapter 8).

Chapter 7: Transitional provisions and the Cohen question

- A legislative drafter must possess and use imagination. By visualizing what a scheme will mean in terms of real life, the drafter may effect improvements and avoid defects.

- Unless the contrary intention appears, an enactment is presumed not to be intended to have a retrospective operation. The basis of this principle is the need for fairness.

- Where an Act contains substantive, amending or repealing enactments, it commonly also includes transitional provisions. These regulate the coming into operation of those enactments and modify their effect during the period of transition.

- Where the drafter forgets to include transitional provisions expressly, the court must draw such inferences as, in the light of the interpretative criteria, it considers Parliament to have intended regarding transitional arrangements.

- The interpreter must realize, and bear constantly in mind, that what appears to be the plain meaning of a substantive enactment is often modified by transitional provisions located elsewhere in the Act or implied.

- A vexed question concerning the drafting of legislation is: for what type of reader is the text intended?

- The 'Cohen question' is: what would an ordinary person think the enactment in question meant? The following factors indicate this is only rarely the right question.

- What appears clear to the lay person may not be certain in meaning to the courts or resistant to legal challenge.

- Legislative language needs to conform to the language of the existing law.

- Obscurity in legislation is often caused not by unnecessary complication of language but by complication (whether unnecessary or not) of thought.

- A Bill has to run the gauntlet of parliamentary debate and amendment in both Houses of Parliament.

- The conclusion is that, whether we like it or not, law like medicine is an expertise. That is why we have a legal profession.

- So most laws are really meant to be read exclusively by legal experts, who nevertheless have a duty to ensure that the lay public have the best explanations possible.

Chapter 8: Words in pairs

- Pairs of words used in statutes may have opposite meanings (antonyms), identical meanings (synonyms), shared meanings (overlapping terms), conjoined meanings (hendiadys) or different meanings.

- *Examples of antonyms* 'natural or unnatural', 'British or non-British'.

- *Examples of synonyms* 'fit and proper', 'unsafe or unsatisfactory', 'just and equitable', 'true and fair'.

- *Examples of overlapping terms* 'harsh and unconscionable', 'show and explain', 'sports and pastimes', 'exercise or recreation', 'repair or maintenance', 'building or structure', 'goods or materials', 'building or engineering work'.

- *Examples of hendiadys* 'law and heraldry', 'co-operate and assist'.

- *Examples of different meanings* 'criticism or review', 'recognition and enforcement', 'town or village'.

- Where there are overlapping terms or hendiadys the meaning is conjoint, the signification of each term merging with, and partaking of, that of the other.

- A pair of words may be linked conjunctively (requiring both terms to be satisfied) or disjunctively (requiring only one of the terms to be satisfied).

- It is not the case that where the link is 'and' the terms are conjunctive and where it is 'or' the terms are disjunctive. The terms 'and' and 'or' are often indistinguishable in English usage.

- A further example of weightless drafting (described in chapter 6) is the use of a pair of terms where a doubtful case must fall within one or other of the terms but it does not matter which because the legal effect of the enactment is the same either way.

Chapter 9: Rules of interpretation

- The basic rule of statutory interpretation is that enactments shall be construed according to the numerous general guides laid down for that purpose by law; and that where these conflict the problem shall be resolved by weighing and balancing the interpretative factors concerned.

- The guides to legislative intention, otherwise known as interpretative criteria, are: (1) common law and statutory *rules*; (2) *principles* derived from legal policy; (3) *presumptions* based on the nature of legislation; and (4) general linguistic *canons* applicable to any piece of English prose.

- Rules of statutory construction can be divided into those laid down at common law and those laid down by statute.

- Rules laid down at common law include: (1) the rule that regard must be had to the juridical nature of an enactment; (2) the plain meaning rule; and (3) the commonsense construction rule.

- Statutory rules are principally laid down by the Interpretation Act. Main rules so laid down include definitions of 'person' and 'land', and provisions as to gender, number, time, and powers and duties.

Chapter 10: Legal policy

- A *principle* of statutory interpretation embodies the policy of the law, which is in turn based on public policy.

- So far as concerns statutory interpretation by the courts, the content of public policy (and therefore of legal policy) is what judges think and say it is. However in this the court is guided by relevant legislation.

- No Act can convey expressly the fullness of its intended legal effect, so Parliament assumes that interpreters will draw necessary inferences.

- General principles of law and public policy underlie and support the rules laid down by the whole body of legislation. If it were not so the rules would be merely arbitrary.

- Legal policy consists of the collection of principles the judges consider the law has a general duty to uphold, such as: that law should serve the public interest, that it should be fair and just, that it should be certain and predictable, that it should be self-consistent and not subject to casual change, and that it should not operate retrospectively where this would be unfair.

- Neither principles of law nor those of wider public policy are static. On some aspects legal policy may change drastically over a period.

- The court ought not to enunciate a new head of policy in an area where Parliament has demonstrated its willingness to intervene when considered necessary.

- Because it takes Parliament as intending that general principles of legal policy should apply unless the contrary intention appears, the common law has developed specific principles of statutory interpretation by reference to those general principles.

- Even an interpretative criterion which appears to be limited to the construction of Acts may be found on analysis to have a wider base.

- In a particular case different elements of legal policy, for example the safeguarding of personal liberty and the need for state security, may conflict.

- It is a principle of legal policy that municipal law should conform to public international law. This has been given statutory effect in relation to the European Convention on Human Rights by the Human Rights Act 1998 s. 3(1).

- Many of the principles embedded in that Convention correspond to, and are indeed derived from, those of British legal policy.

- The passing of the Human Rights Act 1998 means that many principles of legal policy which hitherto had been embedded in common law will henceforth be given statutory force. They will also continue to be directly enforceable at Strasbourg under the regime established by the Convention.

Chapter 11: Interpretative presumptions

- An interpretative *presumption* is laid down at common law, that is by the judges. It affords guidance, arising out of the essential nature of legislation, as to the legislator's prima facie intention regarding the legal meaning of an enactment.

- It is presumed that in construing an enactment its text, in its setting within the Act or other instrument containing it, is to be regarded as the pre-eminent indication of the legislator's intention.

- It is then presumed that the literal meaning of the text is to be followed (unless that is outweighed by other factors).

- The 'literal meaning' corresponds to the grammatical meaning where this is straightforward. If however the grammatical meaning, when applied to the facts of the instant case, is ambiguous then any of the possible grammatical meanings may be taken as the literal meaning. If the grammatical meaning is semantically obscure, then the clear grammatical meaning likely to have been intended (or any of them in the case of ambiguity) is taken as the literal meaning.

- A well-known presumption arises under the rule in *Heydon's Case*. This gave rise to what is sometimes known as the mischief rule; and later to what is today perhaps the most important presumption of all, that a purposive construction is to be given.

- There is a presumption that a *consequential* construction is to be given.

- There is a presumption that a *rectifying* construction is to be given where necessary.

- It is presumed that Parliament does not intend 'absurd' consequences to flow from the application of its Act.

- This tends to avoidance by the interpreter of six types of undesirable consequence: an unworkable or impracticable result, an inconvenient result, an anomalous or illogical result, a futile or pointless result, an artificial result, and a disproportionate counter-mischief.

Chapter 12: Linguistic canons and interpretative technique

- A linguistic canon of construction reflects the nature or use of language generally, and does not depend on the legislative character of the enactment in question or its quality as a legal pronouncement.

- The first linguistic canon is that an Act or other legislative instrument is to be read as a whole.

- Different words in a consolidation Act may be given the same meaning because derived from different Acts.

- It may happen that no sensible meaning can be given to some word or phrase. It must then be disregarded.

- The concept that an Act is to be read as a whole is also applied to a group of Acts if they are *in pari materia*.

- A number of linguistic canons are best known in their Latin form. One of these is *noscitur a sociis*, meaning 'it is recognized by its associates'.

- The Latin phrase *ejusdem generis* (of the same kind or nature), has been attached to a principle of construction whereby wide words associated in the text with more limited words are taken to be restricted by implication to matters of the same limited character.

- The rank principle lays down that where a string of items of a certain level is followed by residuary words, it is presumed that the residuary words are not intended to include items of a different rank.

- The *reddendo singula singulis* principle (render each to each) concerns the use of words distributively. Where a complex sentence has more than one subject, and more than one object, it may be the right construction to render each to each, by applying each object to its appropriate subject. A similar principle applies to verbs and their subjects, and to other parts of speech.

- The maxim *expressum facit cessare tacitum* embodies the principle that no inference is proper if it goes against the express words Parliament has used.

- The last of these Latin maxims, *expressio unius est exclusio alterius* (to express one thing is to exclude another) is an aspect of the principle *expressum facit cessare tacitum*.

- The interpretative criteria are general in nature. What is required in an actual case is a method of applying the relevant interpretative criterion or criteria to the specific enactment in question and the specific facts of the case.

- The first step is to identify, in relation to the enactment, the factual outline and the legal thrust. The usual legal effect of an enactment is that, when the facts of a case fall within an indicated area called the factual outline, specified consequences called the legal thrust ensue.

- The next step is to identify the relevant interpretative *factors*. The term 'interpretative factor', in relation to an enactment, is used to denote a specific legal consideration which: (1) derives from the way a general interpretative criterion applies to the text of the enactment and the facts of the instant case, and (2) serves as a guide to the construction of the enactment in its application to those facts.

- Where the interpretative factors do not all point one way, it is necessary for the interpreter to assess the respective weights of the relevant factors and determine which of the opposing constructions they indicate *on balance*. This is the final step.

Chapter 13: The nature of judgment

- An enactment is not to be dismissed as ambiguous just because its perfectly normal wording calls for the exercise of judgment or discretion.

- Broadly, judgment is objective while discretion is subjective.

- Arriving at a judgment, or exercising a discretion, can be accomplished only by taking a decision; so the legal rules of decision-taking apply.

- Discretion is free, except for limitations placed upon it (expressly or impliedly) by the defining formula. Judgment is necessarily confined, because its sole purpose is to arrive at a conclusion of fact or law which accurately reflects reality.

- The decision-taker may first need to exercise judgment in determining whether required conditions are satisfied; and then, if they are, may be called on to judge whether or not to exercise a discretion, and then to decide in what way.

- The effecting of judgment, or judgment-forming, means one must relate the particular facts to the abstract concept in question, often expressed as a broad term.

- A broad term may be a verb, adverb, adjective or substantive.

- A broad term may be mobile or static, whether in time or place (or both).

- A broad term may be a processed term (where its legal meaning has been previously determined by a court) or an unprocessed term (where it has not).

- Although where judgment is required there is notionally one right answer, in practice there is what has been called 'the area of judgment'.

- A court or other adjudicating authority arriving at a judgment needs to have regard to the phenomenon of differential readings, where different minds conscientiously arrive at different assessments.

Chapter 14: The nature of discretion

- Discretion, as opposed to judgment, is usually to be applied where it is expressly left to the functionary to make a determination at any point within a given range. It is also possible for a discretion to relate only to two possible alternatives.

- The most obvious way for an enactment to confer a discretion is by the use of the term 'may'.

- The laying down of guidelines is often, though not always, the sign of a discretion.

- In so far as a court purports to ascertain and declare an uncertain or disputed legal rule and apply it in the instant case, the decision by which it does this is properly called an exercise of judgment. If however the court purports to go beyond this and *alter* the relevant law, it is exercising a discretion.

Chapter 15: *Human rights and the European Union*

• The Human Rights Acts 1998 has revolutionized the unwritten British constitution. Under it we now have in effect a written constitution under which unelected judges second guess what Parliament decides. This is set alongside the situation under the European Communities Act 1972 by which the Court of Justice of the European Communities (CJEC) enjoys an even stronger position in relation to Acts of Parliament.

• Within the United Kingdom, a European Community law may have direct effect or be transposed into specifically British legislation.

• There are various methods of transposition: a member state may incorporate the provisions of the Community law into an existing legislative code, adopt a separate law or refer in a separate law to provisions of the general civil law. The first of these three methods is known as 'copyout'.

• Where a required transposition has not been effected by the state the position regarding remedies is subject to the rule in European jurisprudence that a breach has vertical effect (that is between states or between the state and a subject) but not horizontal effect (that is between subjects).

• In construing Community law operating by any method in the United Kingdom, the system of interpretation to be used by our courts is that practised by the CJEC, namely the Developmental method.

• It is called the Developmental method because in advancing the 'spirit' of the law in question the CJEC is always ready to depart from the text, if it deems this necessary. Another difference is that the Developmental method pays far less regard to precedent than the common law or Global method does.

• The compatible construction rule laid down by the Human Rights Act 1998 s. 3(1) says that so far as 'possible' United

Kingdom legislation (whenever enacted) must be read and given effect in a way which is compatible with the Convention rights.

- In determining the ambit of a Convention right a court must take into account relevant decisions etc. of the European Court of Human Rights and the European Commission of Human Rights, bearing in mind the margin of appreciation afforded to individual states.

- An additional criterion, which may be called the fundamental rights criterion, is also imported by the compatible construction rule.

- What the compatible construction rule means is that the general guides to statutory interpretation now include the strong principle that it is highly desirable that legislation should be taken to conform to the Convention. The rule should be applied using the Developmental method.

- The fact that this powerful new criterion has been added to the existing guides to statutory interpretation reopens all precedents in relation to pre-1998 Act legislation.

Chapter 16: Jurisprudential basis of the common law or Global method

- There is a growing need to seek out and grasp the jurisprudential basis of the common law or Global method of statutory interpretation, based as it is on common law principles prevailing through most of the English-speaking world.

- This need is strengthened by the fact that it is now understood that the whole basis of our law is interpretative.

- Some politico-philosophical colouring for analysis of the common law or Global method can be based on Ronald Dworkin's seminal book *Law's Empire*.

- In Dworkin's view law as integrity is 'a distinct political virtue'.

- Law as integrity supposes that people are entitled to a coherent and principled extension of past political decisions even when judges profoundly disagree about what this means. In other words integrity takes rights seriously.

- The claims of law as integrity can be divided into two more practical principles, the principle of integrity in legislation (which asks those who create law by legislation to keep that law coherent in principle) and the principle of integrity in adjudication (which asks those responsible for deciding on the legal meaning of legislation to see and enforce it as coherent in that way)

- No aspect of law as integrity has been so misunderstood as its refusal to accept the popular view that there are no uniquely right answers in hard cases at law.

- Dworkin's thesis can be criticized as linking law as integrity to standards which are too vague and leave too much to the vagaries of individual judges. It ignores the importance of legal policy.

- Linked to this criticism is one of Dworkin's apparent view that there are no objective rules of statutory interpretation. 'A judge must ultimately rely on his own opinions in developing and applying a theory about how to read a statute.' This is heresy.

- Dworkin's theory also needs modification in its reliance on 'our' community. The simple idea that a body of law serves one culture and one community no longer applies in the multicultural, pluralistic Britain of the twenty-first century. So a particular item of our law now needs to be interpreted according to the demographic group in which it holds sway, whether the European Union, the nations who have ratified the European Convention on Human Rights, the United Kingdom, or a devolved area inside the United Kingdom.

- There is what David Robertson calls a 'level of analysis problem'. The concise analysis, relying on a few well-known rules such as the mischief rule, prevails at the level of overt and public judicial argument. The detailed analysis deals with the hugely complex and detailed mass of rules and techniques underlying this.

- The two levels should correspond, but it is doubtful if they do.

Chapter 17: The common law system in America

- The common law world has an agreed system of statutory interpretation applicable to all legislation. However in the United States, a prominent common law country, there are some who think constitutional enactments should be construed differently from the rest.

- Some English judges are now drifting in that direction, even without the aid of a written constitution.

- Judges, being human, will usurp power if there is nothing effective in the constitution to stop them.

- A written constitution is incomplete unless it contains instructions on how it is intended by the framers to be interpreted and applied.

- So a constitution should specify how it is to be interpreted. This rarely if ever happens, because framers of constitutions are usually inexperienced in what they are about.

- Many lawyers in the common law world have not woken up to the fact that legislation has assumed the dominant role.

- Professor Mary Ann Glendon said that though more than a century has passed since legislative enactments displaced case law as the starting point for legal reasoning, United States lawyers still operate with craft habits of the former age.

- So in the United States today there is disagreement between the proponents of textualism and those who believe in the living constitution.

- The textualist Justice Scalia denies judges authority to pursue broader purposes or write new laws.

- Justice Scalia stresses that textualism does not mean blind adherence to a so-called literal rule of interpretation. He believes proper statutory interpretation has been undermined by the resort to legislative history.

- On the other hand Professor Gordon S. Wood says Justice Scalia's insistence on textualism is not commensurate with the severity of the problem.

- Justice Scalia's doctrine of textualism triumphed when he persuaded the US Supreme Court to follow the letter of the law in the disputed presidential election of 2000.

Chapter 18: The techniques of law management

- Officials and lawyers need to be taught and use certain techniques of dealing with legislation, which can be called 'law

handling' or 'law management'. To command them is the surest
way to thread the legislative maze.

- Ability effectively to *manage* the relevant law is central to any
  lawyer's or law student's functioning. It is a complex intellectual skill, to which neither academia nor the profession has so
  far paid full attention.

- A central area where intellectual manipulation of materials is
  required concerns the application of a legal rule to a particular
  set of facts, which may be called basic lawyering.

- Law management techniques are needed for both solving and
  avoiding problems, since each depends on exposing the legal
  thrust applicable to the factual situation.

- Law management can be defined as the general skill, applied in
  the context of particular facts (whether actual or hypothetical)
  and supplemented where necessary by detailed knowledge of
  the particular area of law in question in a case, of identifying
  the legal issues involved, formulating the relevant legal rule(s)
  and, by intellectual manipulation of the materials (witness statements, case reports, legislative enactments etc.), reaching the
  legal resultant (or arguable legal resultant) of applying the
  rule(s) to the facts. All this needs to be accompanied by the
  working out and formulation of explanations and arguments.

- In arriving at the legal result of applying the rule to the facts a
  lawyer has to unlock and release some part of the intellectual
  endeavour originally put into the composing of the judgment or
  enactment in question.

- An important element in law management techniques is the
  ability to assess the nature and extent of doubt concerning the
  legal meaning of a relevant enactment.

- The critical approach to the reading of decided cases, where the
  arguments presented by the advocates and in the judgments are
  tested and assessed, may be called the appellant's approach,
  because the 'law manager' is placed in the position of a possible
  appellant from the decision.

- There is a technique of isolating the part of the Act which is
  relevant in the case, known as an 'enactment'. This is the unit of
  inquiry upon which the decision will turn. There is a practical
  technique (known as selective comminution) for isolating this

without violating Parliament's actual language. There is a further technique (interstitial articulation) for expanding the official words of an enactment with detail either drawn from reported cases on the enactment or put forward by the advocate in advancing argument. Where there is dispute about the legal meaning of the enactment, there is a technique of putting forward the opposing constructions of the enactment, and the arguments for and against each construction.

* Isolated elements of law management are already taught under such names as problem solving, the doctrine of precedent, statutory interpretation and legal method. This fragments what is essentially one skill.

* The chapter ends by suggesting details of a syllabus for teaching the techniques of law management.

Books, articles, etc. referred to

Books

Allen, Sir Carleton Kemp, *Law in the Making*, 4th edn. 1946 (Oxford: Clarendon Press).

Atiyah, P. S. and Summers, R. S., *Form and Substance in Anglo-American Law*, 1987 (Oxford: Clarendon Press).

Baker, J. H., *An Introduction to English Legal History*, 3rd edn. 1990 (London: Butterworths).

Bell, John and Engle, Sir George (eds.), Cross, Sir Rupert, *Statutory Interpretation*, 3rd edn. 1995 (London: Butterworths).

Bennion, F. A. R., *Constitutional Law of Ghana*, 1962 (London: Butterworths).

—— *Statute Law*, 2nd edn. 1983 (London: Longman).

—— *Statute Law*, 3rd edn. 1990 (London: Longman).

—— *Statutory Interpretation*, 3rd edn. 1997, supp. 1999 (London: Butterworths).

Birks, P. B. H. (ed.), *Examining the Law Syllabus: Beyond the Core*, 1993 (Oxford: Oxford University Press).

—— (ed.), *Reviewing Legal Education* 1994 (Oxford: Oxford University Press).

Blackstone, Sir William, *The Commentaries on the Laws of England*, Adapted to the present state of the law by Robert Malcolm Kerr, 4th edn. 1876 (London: John Murray).

Blom-Cooper, Sir Louis, *The Birmingham Six and other cases*, 1997 (London: Duckworth).

Chalmers, Sir MacKenzie, *Sale of Goods*, 12th edn. 1945 (London: Butterworths).

Clark, Andrew (ed.), *The English Register of Godstow Nunnery, near Oxford*, 1905 (London: Kegan Paul, Trench, Trübner).

Craies, W. F., *A Treatise on Statute Law*, 7th edn. 1971 (London: Sweet & Maxwell).

Cross, Sir Rupert, *Precedent in English Law*, 3rd edn. 1977 (London: Butterworths).

—— *Statutory Interpretation*, 1st edn. 1976 (London: Butterworths).

Devlin, Patrick, *The Enforcement of Morals*, 1965 (Oxford: Oxford University Press).
—— *The Judge*, 1979 (Oxford: Oxford University Press).
Dicey, A. V. and Morris, J. H., *The Conflict of Laws*, 12th edn. 1993 (London: Sweet & Maxwell).
Dickerson, Reed, *Materials on Legal Drafting*, 1st edn. 1986 (Boston: Little Brown).
Driedger, Elmer, *The Construction of Statutes*, 1st edn. 1974 (Toronto: Butterworths).
Dworkin, R., *Law's Empire*, 1st edn. 1986 (Oxford: Hart Publishing 1998).
—— (ed.), *The Philosophy of Law*, 1977 (Oxford: Oxford University Press).
Gold, N., Mackie, K., and Twining, W., *Learning Lawyers' Skills*, 1989 (London: Butterworths).
Griffith, J. A. G., *The Politics of the Judiciary*, 5th edn. 1997 (London: Fontana).
Harris, D. J., O'Boyle, M., and Warbrick, C., *Law of the European Convention on Human Rights*, 1995 (London: Butterworths).
Hine, Reginald, *Confessions of an Un-Common Attorney*, 1946 (London: Dent).
Ilbert, Sir Courtenay, *Legislative Methods and Forms*, 1901 (Oxford: Oxford University Press).
Jenkins, D., *Eight Centuries of Reports*, 1734 (London: In the Savoy).
Judicial Studies Board, *Crown Court Bench Book: Specimen Directions*, 1999 (London: Judicial Studies Board).
—— *Guidelines for the Assessment of General Damages in Personal Injury Cases*, 4th edn. 1998 (London: Blackstone).
MacCormick, N., *Legal Reasoning and Legal Theory*, 1st edn. 1978 (Oxford: Clarendon Press).
—— and Summers, R. S., *Interpreting Statutes: A Comparative Study*, 1st edn. 1991 (Aldershot: Dartmouth).
Marmor, Andrei (ed.), *Law and Interpretation: Essays in Legal Philosophy*, 1995 (Oxford: Oxford University Press).
Maxwell on the Interpretation of Statutes, 12th edn. 1969 (Bombay: N. M. Tripathi).
Megarry, Sir Robert, *Miscellany-at-Law*, 1955 (London: Stevens).
Mikva, Abner J. and Lane, Eric, *An Introduction to Statutory*

Interpretation and the Legislative Process, 1st edn. 1997 (New York N.Y: Aspen Law & Business).

More, Sir Thomas, *A fruteful and Pleasaunt Worke of the best State of a Publyque Weale, and of the newe Yle called Utopia,* 1551 (London: Abraham Nell).

Munro, Colin R., *Studies in Constitutional Law,* 2nd edn. 1999 (London: Butterworths).

Oxford English Dictionary, 2nd edn. 1992 (Oxford: Oxford University Press).

Pearce, D. C. and Geddes, R. S., *Statutory Interpretation in Australia,* 4th edn. 1996 (Sydney: Butterworths).

Pope, Alexander, *Essays on Criticism* (London: 1709).

Rastall, W., *Les Termes de la Ley,* 1624 (London: Stationers' Company).

Robertson, David, *Legal Reasoning and Legal Theory,* 1st edn. 1998 (Oxford: Clarendon Press).

Robinson, R., *Definition,* 1950 (Oxford: Clarendon Press).

Salway, Peter, *Roman Britain,* 1st edn. 1981 (Oxford: Clarendon Press).

Scalia, Antonin, *A Matter of Interpretation: Federal Courts and the Law,* 1997 (Princeton: Princeton University Press.

Stubbs, William, *Select Charters,* 9th edn. 1913 (Oxford: Clarendon Press).

Sullivan, A. M. QC, *The Last Serjeant,* 1952 (London: Macdonald).

Thring, Lord, *Practical Legislation,* 1902 (London: John Murray).

Twining, W. and Miers, David, *How To Do Things With Rules,* 4th edn. 1999 (London: Butterworths).

Whately, R., *Logic* (London, 1827).

Articles, etc.

Amos, Sir Maurice Sheldon, 'The Interpretation of Statutes' (1934) 5 CLJ 163.

Barnes, Jeffrey W., 'Statutory Interpretation, Law Reform and Sampford's Theory of the Disorder of Law' Pt II (1995) *Federal Law Review* (Australia) 77.

Beatson, Jack, 'Has the common law a future?' 6th Report of the Select Committee on the European Communities, *Unfair Contract Terms,* H.L. Paper 28, January 1992, p. 96.

Bennion, F. A. R., 'A naked usurpation?' 149 NLJ (1999) 421.

—— 'Distinguishing judgment and discretion' [2000] PL 368.

—— 'How they all got it wrong in *Pepper v. Hart*' (1995) *British Tax Review* 325.

—— 'Jaguars and Donkeys: distinguishing judgment and discretion' 31 University of West Los Angeles Law Review (2000) 1.

—— 'Last orders at *La Pentola*' 148 NLJ (1998) 953, 986.

—— 'Legislative technique' 129 NLJ (1979) 748.

—— 'What interpretation is "possible" under section 3(1) of the Human Rights Act 1998?' [2000] PL 77.

Birks, Peter, 'The academic and the practitioner' 18 *Legal Studies,* 1998 (London: Butterworths) 397.

Campbell, Lisbeth, 'Drafting Styles: Fuzzy or Fussy?' *E Law— Murdoch University Electronic Journal of Law,* Vol. 3, No. 2 (July 1996).

Edwards, Susan, 'Beyond belief - the case of Zoora Shah' 148 NLJ (1998) 667.

Finlay, Thomas A., 'Community Legislation: How Big a Change for the National Judge?' [1996] *Stat. L.R.* 79.

Gold, N., 'The Professional Legal Training Program: Towards Training for Competence' 41 *The Advocate* (Canada) (1983) 247.

Irvine of Lairg LC, Lord, 'The Development of Human Rights in Britain under an Incorporated Convention on Human Rights' [1998] PL 221.

Klug, Francesca, 'The Human Rights Act 1998, *Pepper v. Hart* and All That' [1999] PL 246.

Llewellyn, Karl N. *et al.*, 'The Place of Skills in Legal Education', Report of Committee on Curriculum, Association of American Law Schools (Chairman, Karl N. Llewellyn) 45 *Columbia Law Rev.* (1945) 345.

McGlynn, Clare, 'Will women judges make a difference?' 148 NLJ (1998) 813.

Making the Law, The report of the Hansard Society Commission on the Legislative Process, issued on 2 February 1993 (London: The Hansard Society for Parliamentary Government).

Marshall, Geoffrey, 'Interpreting interpretation in the Human Rights Bill' [1998] PL 167.

—— 'Two kinds of compatibility: more about section 3 of the Human Rights Act 1998' [1999] PL 377.

O'Doherty, Stephen, 'Rape and indecent assault—changing perceptions' 162 JP (1998) 676.

O'Reilly, James, 'Coping with Community Legislation—A Practitioner's Reaction' [1996] *Stat. L.R.* 15.

Pannick, David, 'Principles of Interpretation of Convention rights under the Human Rights Act and the discretionary area of judgment' [1998] PL 545.

Posner, Richard A., 'Statutory Interpretation—in the Classroom and in the Courtroom' 50 *University of Chicago Law Review* (1983) 800.

Pound, Roscoe, 'The Path of the Law' 10 *Harvard Law Review* (1897) 457.

Ramsey, Lynn E., 'The Copy Out technique: More of a Cop Out than a Solution?' [1996] *Stat. L.R.* 218.

Richards, Sir Stephen Price, 'Public powers: preventing misuse' *JSB Journal*, Issue Nine 2000 7.

Samuels, Alec, 'Incorporating, Translating or Implementing European Union Law into UK Law' [1998] *Stat. L.R.* 80.

Sedley, Sir Stephen, Review of David Robertson, *Legal Reasoning and Legal Theory* 58 *Cambridge Law Journal* (1999) 627.

Twining, W., 'Legal Skills and Legal Education' 22 *Journal of the Association of Law Teachers* (1988) 4.

Wainwright, Richard, 'Techniques of Drafting European Community Legislation' [1996] *Stat. L.R.* 7.

Index

absurdity
  anomaly 104
  artificiality 105
  futility 105
  impracticality 104
  inconvenience 104
  meaning of 103–5
  presumption against 103–5
  and see counter-mischief, avoidance
    of
Act of Parliament
  early 32
  fixedtime 57–8
  ongoing 57–8
  private 55, 57–8
  retrospective, *see* retrospectivity
  transitional provisions of, *see*
    transitional provisions
  types of 61
action, cause of, *see* cause of action
administrative law, *see* decision-taking
  rules; judicial review
administrators 9, 30–1
adviser, legal, *see* advocate
advocate 10–11, 186–7, 193
  age 111–12
  and see central function of legal
    practitioner
Allen, Sir Carleton 14, 29–30
ambiguity (grammatical) 40–1
amendment to Act, implied 56
America, *see* United States
Amos, Sir Maurice 50n
ancillary rules of law, implied application
  of, *see* interpretative criteria
anomaly, *see* absurdity
artificiality, *see* absurdity
Atiyah, P. S. 191
audience, legislative, *see* user of
  legislation

Balcombe LJ 138
Barber principle 24–5
Barnes, Jeffrey W. 84–5
benefit from own wrong 97, 172
Bennion, Francis
  Statute Law 16n, 75n, 196n
  Statutory Interpretation 2, 11,
    15–16, 69–70, 175, 179–80

Bentham, Jeremy 16
Bill, Parliamentary 75
  and see drafter; drafting technique
Bingham of Cornhill, Lord 130, 132,
  141–2, 155–6
Birks, Peter 6–7, 166
Blackburn, Lord 31, 109
Blackstone, Sir William 14, 18
Brett LJ, *see* Esher, Viscount
Bridge of Harwich, Lord 71, 127, 134
broad terms 119–31, 150
BrowneWilkinson, Lord 67, 102
Buckley LJ 73
Buckmaster, Lord 121
Buxton LJ 177
by-laws 23

Campbell, Lisbeth 155
canon law, *see* ecclesiastical law
canons of construction, linguistic, *see*
  interpretative canons, linguistic
casus male inclusus, see rectifying
  construction
casus omissus, see rectifying
  construction
cause of action 27
Cave, Viscount 19
central function of legal practitioner
  36–7, 203
certainty (of law), *see* legal policy
Chalmers, Sir Mackenzie 87
charters 31
children 77, 88–90
  and see foetus
Christianity 95
civil law, the 6, 7, 151
  and see European law
Clauson J 105
Clinton, President 61, 62
Clyde, Lord 154–5
codification 194–5
Cohen question, the 72–3
Coke, Sir Edward 33, 55
Coleridge, Lord 128
commencement of Act, *see*
  retrospectivity; transitional
  provisions
commination , *see* selective
  commination

common law
  codification of, *see* codification
  common law statutes 1, 5, 8
  interpretation, *see* Global (or
    common law) method of
    statutory interpretation
  nature of 166, 179–80
  and see ancillary rules of law,
    implied application of; civil law,
    the; common law world, the;
    custom; European law
common law world, the 1, 3, 177, 201
  and see common law
Common Law World Review 1
commonsense construction rule 87–8
  and see absurdity; ambiguity
    (grammatical)
Commons, House of 149
  and see Parliament
consequential construction 45–7
  and see absurdity; strict and liberal
    construction
consolidation Act 48–9, 61, 109
  and see plain meaning rule
constitution, interpreting, *see* statutory
    interpretation
constitutional rights, *see* human rights
construction as a whole 54–5,
    107–9
  and see *noscitur a sociis*
construction as one 109
  and see incorporation by reference
context, *see* construction as a whole;
    noscitur a sociis
contradiction, principle of, *see* logic
contradictory enactments, *see*
    repugnancy
Cotton LJ 84
Counsel, *see* advocate
counter-mischief, avoidance of 105
court, *see* judges; statutory
    interpretation
Court of Justice of the European
    Communities (CJEC)
  Barber principle (retrospectivity of
    judgments) 24–5
  expansive aims of 155–6
  interpretation by, *see*
    Developmental construction
  nature of 152–8
criminal law, see *mens rea*
criteria, interpretative, *see*
    interpretative criteria

Cross, Sir Rupert 83–4, 87, 132–3
custom 29–32

decision-taking rules
  fairness, *see* fairness
  legal policy, influence of, *see* legal
    policy
  natural justice, *see* fairness
  nature of 116–17
deeming 105
definitions, statutory
  clarifying definitions 62–3
  comprehensive definitions 66
  contrary intention 63
  enlarging definitions 65–6
  exclusionary definitions 65
  Interpretation Act 1978, in, *see*
    Interpretation Act 1978
  labelling definitions 64
  nature of 62–7
  potency of the term defined 66–7
  referential definitions 64–5
  and see pairs of words
Denning, Lord 31n, 43, 51, 99, 144,
    155
Developmental method of statutory
    interpretation 4, 44, 153–8
  and see purposive construction
Devlin, Lord 78, 96
devolution 6–8
Dickerson, Reed 40n
differential readings 19–20, 133–5
different words
  construed in different ways 109
  construed in same way 109
Diplock, Lord 27, 28n, 73, 95, 131, 154
discretion
  guidelines as to exercise of 140–2
  judgment, distinguished from
    115–17, 142–4, 215–17
  nature of 35–7, 115–17, 137–47,
    216–7
disorganised composition, *see*
    obscurity, semantic
Donaldson, Lord 98, 140
doubt as to legal meaning
  causes of 36–7
  must be 'real' 19–20, 162
  resolution of 191–2
  and see broad terms; differential
    readings; discretion; doubtful
    penalisation, principle against;
    judgment, exercise of; words

doubtful penalisation, principle against
97–8, 114
Douglas J (U.S.) 147
drafter, legislative 9, 39, 44, 67n,
69–70, 74–6, 109
drafting error 47–52
drafting technique 9, 61, 74–6, 189n,
190–1, 208
and see broad terms; definitions,
statutory; hendiadys;
retrospectivity; weightless
drafting
Dworkin, Ronald 13–14, 98, 117,
118, 165–75

ecclesiastical law 31
Edwards, Susan 15
ejusdem generis principle 110
enactment
legal meaning of, *see* legal meaning
legal thrust of 17, 25–7, 33–4, 113,
117
mischief of, *see* mischief
nature of 16–17, 196
opposing constructions of, *see*
opposing constructions
purpose of, *see* purposive
construction
unit of inquiry, as 33, 196, 203
error, *see* drafting error; legal meaning;
mistake
Esher, Viscount (Brett LJ) 48, 57
European Convention on Human
Rights 6, 8, 99–100, 143,
149–52, 156
and see doubtful penalisation,
principle against; Human Rights
Act 1998
European Court, *see* Court of Justice of
the European Communities
(CJEC)
European law
common law, relation to 7, 165
direct effect of 152–8
effect on British law of 6, 8, 44,
152–8
interpretation of, *see* Developmental
method of statutory
interpretation; purposive
status of 152–8
transposing of 152–3
and see civil law, the; margin of
appreciation

Evans-Lombe J 153–4
Eveleigh J 126
Evershed, Lord 73
exclusionary rule, the, *see* legislative
history
explanatory memorandum, *see* Bill,
Parliamentary
ex post facto law, *see* retrospectivity
expressio unius principle 112
expressum facit cessare tacitum
111–12

factors, interpretative, *see* interpretative
factors
factual outline, the 17, 25–7, 33–4,
113, 117, 193
fairness 27, 168
and see justice
fiction, *see* absurdity; deeming
foetus 90
Forbes J 18, 50
four corners doctrine 75
fundamental rights criterion 161
and see principle of legality
futility, *see* absurdity

garbled text, *see* rectifying construction
Geddes, R. S. 80n
gender 90–1
generalibus specialia derogant 55–6
Gibbon, Edward 2
Gibson, Peter J. 47
Glendon, Mary Ann 180
Global (or common law) method of
statutory interpretation
jurisprudential basis of 165–75,
218–19
nature of 3–4, 173–5
use of 44
and see statutory interpretation
Goddard, Lord 87, 115n
Goff of Chieveley, Lord 145
Gold, N. 184–5
golden rule, so-called 2, 12, 83–4,
165
Goode, Sir Roy 187–8, 190
grammatical meaning, *see* ambiguity
(grammatical); implication; legal
meaning; literal meaning;
ordinary meaning; plain
meaning rule
Griffith, J. A. G. 15n
Griffiths, Lord 124, 132

legal policy (*cont.*):
  security of the state 98
  and see benefit from own wrong;
    retrospectivity
legal practitioner, *see* advocate; central
    function of legal practitioner
legal thrust of enactment, *see*
    enactment
legislation
  British 8
  meaning 7
  user of, *see* user of legislation
legislators, *see* judges; Parliament;
    politicians
legislative history 181–2
  and see Pepper v Hart, rule in;
    Posner, Richard A.
legislative intention, *see* intention,
    legislative
lex provinciae 29
liberal construction, *see* strict and
    liberal construction
linguistic canons, *see* interpretative
    canons, linguistic
literal construction
  'literal rule', so-called 2, 12, 41, 45,
    83–4, 102–3, 165
  nature of 41
  presumption favouring 102
  and see textualism
literal meaning
  judicial massaging of 14
  nature of 40–1, 101–2
  weight to be attached to 102
  and see ambiguity (grammatical);
    implication; legal meaning;
    literal construction; ordinary
    meaning; plain meaning rule
Llewellyn, Karl 186–7
Lloyd, Lord 133
logic
  contradiction, principle of 54
  judgment and 119
Lushington, Dr 105

MacCormick, Neil 133
McGlynn, Clare 15
magistrates 10
Mansfield, Lord 109
margin of appreciation 143–4, 158
Marmor, Andrei 165–6
Marre Report (1988) 186–7
Marshall, Geoffrey 158, 160, 163

masculine and feminine, *see* gender
meaningless terms 108
mens rea 27–8
Miers, David, see *How To Do Things
    With Rules* by Twining and
    Miers
Millett LJ 51
Milton, John 3
mischief of an enactment 42
  and see counter-mischief; *Heydon's
    Case*, rule in; 'mischief rule', so-
    called
'mischief rule', so-called 2, 12, 83–4,
    165
  and see *Heydon's Case*, rule in
mistake
  Act, in 47–52
  law, of 47–52, 144–5; and see *per
    incuriam* decisions
  and see drafting error; printing
    corrections; rectifying
    construction
More, Sir Thomas 74
Munro, Colin R. 164n
Mustill, Lord 46, 131

natural justice, *see* fairness
Neill of Bladon, Lord 155n, 156
Nicholls of Birkenhead, Lord 19,
    55
noscitur a sociis principle 81–2, 110,
    130
  and see *ejusdem generis* principle;
    rank principle
Nourse J 47–8
number 91–2

obscurity, semantic 40–1
  and see rectifying construction
omission of words, *see* rectifying
    construction
opposing constructions
  ambiguity and, *see* ambiguity
    (grammatical)
  examples of 35
  nature of 34–7, 196
  and see interpretative factors
overlapping meaning 81, 108

pairs of words 77–82
Paris, Matthew 31
Parke, Baron 45
Parker, Lord 60, 108